WINGS OF VALOUR

WINGS OF VALOUR

TRUE STORIES OF THE INDIAN AIR FORCE'S DARING OPERATIONS

SWAPNIL PANDEY

HarperCollins *Publishers* India

First published in India by HarperCollins *Publishers* 2025
HarperCollins *Publishers* India, Cyber City,
Building 10-A, Gurugram, Haryana – 122002, India
www.harpercollins.co.in

2 4 6 8 10 9 7 5 3 1

Copyright © Swapnil Pandey 2025

P-ISBN: 978-93-6989-173-3
E-ISBN: 978-93-6989-725-4

The views and opinions expressed in this book are the author's own
and the facts are as reported by her, and the publishers are not in any
way liable for the same.

Swapnil Pandey asserts the moral right
to be identified as the author of this work.

All rights reserved. No part of this publication may be reproduced,
stored in a retrieval system, or transmitted, in any form or by any means,
electronic, mechanical, photocopying, recording or otherwise,
without the prior permission of the publishers.

Without limiting the exclusive rights of any author, contributor or the
publisher of this publication, any unauthorized use of this publication to
train generative artificial intelligence (AI) technologies is expressly prohibited.
HarperCollins also exercise their rights under Article 4(3) of the Digital Single
Market Directive 2019/790 and expressly reserve this publication from the text
and data-mining exception.

Typeset in 11.5 pt/15.2 Adobe Garamond Pro
by HarperCollins *Publishers* India Pvt. Ltd

Printed and bound at
Saurabh Printers Pvt.Ltd

This book is produced from independently certified FSC® paper to ensure
responsible forest management.

HarperCollins *Publishers*, Macken House, 39/40 Mayor Street Upper,
Dublin 1, D01 C9W8, Ireland

Dedication

नभः स्पृशं दीप्तम्

To all the Indian Air Force personnel and their families.
This book is a tribute to your brave fraternity of men and women.
A gift you can share with your children, friends and loved ones—
to remind them that legacies are not only built through sweat and toil
but through sacrifices made in the face of adversity
and the selfless determination to fight against all odds.

Donning the IAF uniform is the highest honor, one that no wealth can buy.

I hope, through this book the next generation of knights will
understand the weight of valour they must carry,
and the legacy of the shoes they must fill.

With deepest respect and gratitude,

Jai Hind!

★ ★ ★ ★

FOREWORD

1. As we reflect on the history of Indian Air Force, we are reminded of its unwavering commitment to defend nation's blue skies while upholding the highest standards of excellence. In every operation undertaken by IAF, its core values of mission, integrity and excellence have been consistently exemplified. From the early days of independence to the present day, our air warriors have consistently demonstrated courage and valour in the face of adversity. Their stories are a powerful reminder of the human spirit that drives individuals to put their nation before themselves.

2. Beyond its primary role, IAF has been a beacon of hope during humanitarian assistance both within India and abroad. The IAF's role in disaster relief, search and rescue operations and medical evacuations has saved countless lives and brought comfort to those in need. This book is a testament to the bravery, sacrifice and selfless service of the air warriors.

3. The author has undertaken a remarkable task in researching and chronicling the history of the IAF and the acts of valour displayed by its brave air warriors. This book has adopted a unique approach for narration of the heroic acts by capturing the human side of each hero by presenting their stories through the eyes of friends, family members and comrades who knew them best. While doing so, Ms. Swapnil Pandey has successfully captured the essence of what drives individuals to make the ultimate sacrifice, providing a deeper understanding of the motivations, values, and beliefs that underpin their actions.

4. This book is a tribute not only to the IAF heroes but also to their families, who have been the pillars of strength. I commend the author for her meticulous research, dedication, and passion in telling the stories of these brave air warriors. I am confident that this book will resonate with its readers, inspiring future generations to follow in the footsteps of these heroes.

Jai Hind!

(AP Singh)
Air Chief Marshal
Chief of the Air Staff

A Note to Readers

by Mrs Sarita Singh, President,
AIR FORCE FAMILIES WELFARE ASSOCIATION

I SPENT MY childhood in the quiet township of Bassi Pathana, Punjab—a place where time moved at its own unhurried pace. As the youngest of three daughters, with a younger brother following after me, I grew up in a traditional Punjabi household where family bonds held more value than any material possession. Ours was a world of simplicity and structure—school to home and back again, with little room for distractions. No movies, no unnecessary outings, just the sheltered existence.

Shy and reserved, I moved through life unnoticed, content within the cocoon of my small-town upbringing. No one—not even I—could have imagined that this simple, timid girl would one day take charge of her own destiny, lead her family and stand tall with her husband in all appointments doing her part of duty.

My marriage was arranged, as was tradition. We had never met before the engagement—a leap of faith, a gamble that, as life would prove, turned into a beautiful journey. The first time our eyes met was on our engagement day; the second, on our wedding.

Between those two milestones lay six months of courtship, during which we connected through letters. He was in Chennai, I was in Punjab. Separated by distance, yet connected by ink and paper. In those letters, we unraveled the little details of our lives—our likes and dislikes, favorite colors, dreams, and quirks. And woven into those words was my first introduction to the world of the Indian Air Force, a world I would soon become a part of in ways I had never imagined.

I had no idea what life had in store for me. Becoming an Air Force wife was unlike anything I had ever known, a journey far removed from the sheltered existence I had led until then. My first taste of this new life came immediately after my wedding when I left with my husband to his place of posting.

Until the age of twenty-two, my world had been confined to my place in Punjab. I had never stepped beyond its familiar lanes, never boarded a train, never known the uncertainty of travel. But within fifteen days of marriage, adventure came unannounced. It arrived in the form of a few train journeys and a missed train at Kolkata railway station—a moment that, in hindsight, makes me smile, but at the time, felt overwhelming.

We were on our way to Bidar, with multiple train connections along the route. Somewhere in the chaos of shifting platforms, we missed one at Kolkata. There I was, sitting on the platform, surrounded by ten to twelve pieces of luggage while my husband ran around to find a place in the next possible option.

I sat there for hours—six or seven at least—watching the endless rush of people, the hum of conversations in unfamiliar accents filling the air. For someone who had never traveled alone, never navigated the unpredictability of the outside world, this was a test of patience and trust. A fleeting, ridiculous thought crossed my mind: What if he never comes back? What if he has abandoned me and fled?

But he returned, just as determined as ever, only to deliver more news—we had no reservation on the next train. With all our luggage in tow, we boarded anyway, finding a cramped spot near the train's toilet. Eventually, we reached another station, Kalaikunda, where a course mate came to meet us, his eyes widening in disbelief at the sight of the 'new bride' arriving in such a state. He advised us to travel the next day with a confirmed reservation that he was confident of and invited us to spend the night at his place. The next morning, we travelled to Hyderabad, our last halt before reaching our final destination. Of course, the confidence of getting reservation was misplaced. We finally landed up travelling by sleeper class with luggage well beyond permissible limits and landed up paying all the money in the wallet in paying the fine. And we reached Bidar, our destination, an end to an adventurous journey.

Looking back, that chaotic journey was my first real initiation into the unpredictable, adventurous life of an Air Force wife—a life where plans could change in an instant, where resilience mattered more than comfort, and where every challenge eventually turned into a story worth telling.

I also remember my first house, which I could call my home—a modest space, yet one brimming with possibilities. We built our home from scratch, piece by piece, collecting small but essential things—utensils, cleaning supplies, the simplest of household necessities. I still remember our very first trip to the market on his bike, returning with a broom, a mop, and a bucket, only to clean the house together. Today, I can say that as a new Air Force wife, those little things wove the fabric of our new life together, turning a house into a home.

It was in Bidar that my life as a woman married to a man in blue truly began. My husband was a social soul, the kind who made friends effortlessly and cherished the camaraderie of his fellow officers. Despite his demanding schedule, he loved having his comrades over, filling our home with laughter and stories of the skies. As an instructor, his duty was relentless, with days and nights spent flying. When he had night-flying missions, he would return home at dawn, exhausted from hours in the air.

To ensure he got the rest he needed, I transformed our home into a sanctuary of silence. Thick curtains, blankets over the windows, and strict instructions to the maids and milkman—no doorbells, no disturbances so that his sleep does not get disturbed before he wakes up and prepares for his night duties. It was a small gesture but one that made all the difference. In those initial days, our bond deepened. We weren't just husband and wife, we became each other's greatest source of strength. We relied on each other for advice, trusted each other, and above all, became the best of friends.

Even today, when young couples ask for advice, I tell them this: be a friend to your spouse first. Trust him, rely on him, and confide in him before anyone else. Build a home where warmth, laughter, and understanding thrive because, in the end, that is what truly matters.

Looking back now, I can't help but smile. For a shy girl from a small town, oblivious to the whirlwind that life as an Air Force wife would bring, I have turned into who I am today. I didn't know then that this journey would not only toughen me up and make me independent but also deepen my faith—in God, in destiny, and in the goodness of people.

I vividly remember the time I was pregnant with our first child in Bangalore. My husband was undergoing test pilot training, a rigorous program that kept him busy throughout the day. I had to spend the whole day alone in our small suburban house, surrounded by vast empty spaces and distant neighbors. In those days, Bangalore was not the bustling city it is today—houses were sparse, infrastructure minimal, and facilities scarce.

There was no question of moving back to my family, nor could anyone come to stay with me for months. Medical facilities were few and far between. Understanding my situation, AP found the only shopkeeper in the vicinity with a telephone and asked him for a favor—if an emergency arose, he was to call his office immediately and arrange for an ambulance. That tiny shop, standing alone in the quiet neighborhood, became my lifeline. But by God's grace, everything went smoothly, and we were blessed with a son. Four years later we welcomed our daughter. At that moment, life felt truly complete. Being with a loving husband, raising our children, and embracing this unpredictable yet beautiful journey—there was nothing more I could ask for.

Many have asked if I ever felt afraid, knowing the risks that came with being a pilot's wife. My answer has always been the same: 'No.' Faith has been my anchor, the quiet voice assuring me that whatever came our way would be for the best. I placed my life in God's hands completely. So why worry at all? This belief carried us through life—a philosophy my husband and I held onto, side by side, through every challenge, every joy, and every leap of faith.

As the wife of an Indian Air Force officer, the roar of fighter jets didn't just become a familiar sound—it became the rhythm of my life. I learned the unspoken rules of this world: to be fiercely independent yet always available, to celebrate every homecoming while preparing for the next farewell, and to build a home out of whatever was given, no matter how temporary. Above all, I learned that a military wife has no option but to be brave.

One such test of resilience came during our time in Hasimara. His second tenure there in the squadron, and as the senior-most lady of the squadron, I shouldered responsibilities I had never imagined. The squadron was deployed on detachment, leaving the families behind. Our accommodation was in the mess about seven kilometres from the Air Force Station's residential quarters—a considerable distance, especially in an era without mobile phones, online grocery deliveries, or instant emergency services. With AP going away on an operational deployment, I was going to be alone with our two children—a four-year-old son and a three-month-old daughter. Managing everything without him for so many days was daunting.

The night before he left we were attending a squadron dinner, where a newlywed officer's wife noticed my predicament and kindly offered, 'Why don't you stay with me? My husband is also going.' Grateful for the companionship, I accepted without hesitation.

Three days later, tragedy struck. News arrived from the operational area—there had been an air crash. The officer, whose wife had so generously opened her home to me, had made the supreme sacrifice. As the senior-most lady in the squadron, duty called. I set aside my own emotions, entrusted my children to another officer's wife, and stepped in to support the grieving widow. Her relatives arrived soon after, but theirs had been a love marriage, and old family rifts resurfaced in the face of loss. Amidst the grief, I found myself navigating not just her sorrow but the tensions that emerged. My responsibility was to console her, to ensure she was not left alone, to be her pillar of strength when her world had suddenly crumbled. At the same time I was to comfort the parents who had lost their young son.

That day, I truly understood what it meant to be part of the Air Force fraternity. In times of loss, uncertainty, and fear, we weren't just friends—we were family. We held each other up when the weight of this life became too heavy to bear alone.

People often see the glamour of Air Force life—beautiful houses, the elegant mess functions, the crisp uniforms. What they don't see is the sacrifice, the quiet resilience, the emotional strength it demands. Our men serve the nation in uniform, but we serve in our own way—by standing strong beside them, ensuring they can focus on their duty without a single worry about the home they leave behind.

As my husband rose to senior positions, my involvement with the Air Force Families Welfare Association (AFFWA) deepened. Founded on 28 October 1970, AFFWA was envisioned as a platform to empower Air Force wives, foster camaraderie, and build a strong support system for families. While officers worked together in their squadrons, AFWWA provided an opportunity for ladies to bond together and empower themselves—giving us the confidence, a sense of purpose, and a space to grow together.

In 2022, the name of AFWWA (Air force wives welfare association) was changed to AFFWA (Air force families welfare association) to expand the scope of its benefits and welfare programs. With an increasing number of women officers, the organization has expanded its reach beyond just wives to encompass all Air Force families. This also allowed us to extend welfare initiatives to the children of women officers married to civilians, ensuring they receive the same care and assistance. This shift mirrors the progressive and inclusive ethos of the IAF, reflecting the spirit of resilience and unity that binds us all.

Among the many causes close to my heart, supporting children with special needs holds a special place. Parents of such children often live with the silent fear—what will happen to them when we are gone? As President AFFWA, I felt a deep responsibility to do more. We initiated vocational training programs, equipping these children with skills for independent lives. Collaborations with various NGOs and corporate organizations opened doors for employment, and the joy was unparalleled when recently one of our special children secured a job at Microsoft hospitality wing. Their warm smiles, their excitement when they present me with handmade cards or hug me—these moments reaffirm my belief in the power of compassion and collective effort.

AFFWA also endeavors to uplift underprivileged children beyond the IAF, contributing to the betterment of society as a whole. Through various programs, we support children from families of laborers and those living below the poverty line. We provide them education. While transforming every life may not be possible, empowering even a few children through education is a step toward a brighter future.

Another cause that deeply resonates with me is our work for Veer Naris—the young women who have lost their husbands in service to the nation. Their quiet courage and dignity are humbling and have taught me so much about strength. The IAF has tried to build a strong support system for them, offering emotional solace, employment opportunities, scholarships, grants, and assistance for their children's education. Many airmen's wives come from modest educational backgrounds, and we work to provide them with stable employment within AFFWA's ventures, ensuring financial independence while keeping them connected to the air force family.

None of these initiatives are the work of a single person. Every AFFWA President before me has given her best to the organization, striving to create a positive impact. The credit belongs just as much to every 'sangini' and every staff member who has been an integral part of this journey. Together, we have strengthened the creed of the air warrior's wives—in our little capacity.

When I met Swapnil Pandey, she told me about her quest to bring forth stories of valour from the Indian Air Force, and how a book on the IAF would be incomplete without honoring the silent strength of Air Force wives, I couldn't agree more. It was a privilege to write this piece about us—the women who stand resolutely behind Indian Air Force personnel, embodying courage, resilience, and unwavering support.

I hope that as people read this book and cherish its stories of valor, they also recognize the quiet yet profound sacrifices made by the IAF wives. The strength, grace, and fortitude of military wives deserve to be celebrated. I extend my heartfelt wishes to Swapnil for this remarkable endeavour.

Mrs Sarita Singh
President
Air Force Families Welfare Association

Author's Note

AFTER TEN TRANSFORMATIVE years of writing, my journey has become one of evolving purpose and growing responsibility. From the early days of honing my craft to the moment when my fourth book, *Balidan: The Stories of India's Greatest Para Special Forces Operatives*, was declared one of the national bestselling books of 2023 within a month of its publication. I have always believed that my writing should serve a higher cause. And that stories have the power to inspire.

I have always been driven by a desire to uncover and share the unsung stories that deserve recognition before they fade into obscurity. Each book I write is a new journey of personal growth and discovery, and it is the challenge of bringing a new narrative to life that excites me.

I was searching for that next compelling theme when, during a literature event, a young teenager's question stirred something profound within me: why had I not written about the other services of the Indian military, like the Air Force or Navy? And thus began my journey to tell the glorious, untold stories of the Indian Air Force.

They say that if you truly desire something, the universe conspires to make it happen. My opportunity came when I had the privilege of meeting the then of the Air Staff, Air Chief Marshal Vivek Ram Chaudhari. In my nervous excitement, I expressed my desire to write about the women officers of the Indian Air Force. You will no doubt agree that these young women, in their blue uniforms and Ray-Ban sunglasses, embody the image of a modern and dynamic Air Force. His response was thoughtful: 'An officer is simply an officer, regardless of gender. However, we can support you in covering the Indian Air Force as a collective force—where personnel have bled, sacrificed and faced unimaginable odds for the nation.'

Thus began my journey to create an entire book on and about the Indian Air Force. The book highlights 'the men behind machines' and is a first hand account based on interviews and personal testimonies shared by personnel directly involved in or witness to the events described. While every effort has been made to present these stories with accuracy and authenticity, some details may reflect the subjective experience, perceptions and memories of the narrators, which had been further scrutinised by Indian Air Force.

Gathering information that has traditionally never been archived is an arduous task. It involves identifying, locating, contacting and interviewing people scattered across the nation, or even the world. Then comes the equally daunting task of verification and cross-verification. This painstaking process was made possible with the support of Directorate of Operations (Media & Public Relations), Air Headquarters, which opened its doors unreservedly and provided invaluable assistance.

The mission was to create a book that captures the essence of the modern Indian Air Force. It began with officials sending me rare and exquisite books from their libraries across the nation. Initially, it was overwhelming: How does one write about an entire force with such diversity and a rich history spanning decades? The challenge was not in deciding which missions to include, but which to leave out. So many operations deserved inclusion, but due to page limits—and a bit of fate—they had to be left behind. Nonetheless, we tried our best to include at least one story from each stream—fighter, transport, helicopter and even the elite Special Forces of the IAF, the Garud, who surprisingly have never been part of any book based on the Indian Air Force even after them being in active duty since 2004. Together, they embody the spirit of the wings that unite the Indian Air Force as a formidable collective force.

Writing, as they say, is a spiritual journey—as I delved into the lives of Air Force personnel, uncovering stories of valour and sacrifice, I came to realize that their courage is omnipresent, enduring against all odds and seemingly impossible circumstances.

The pilots of Cheetahs, Chetaks and Cheetals fly over the risky terrain of Siachen, where the fear of being struck by an enemy missile is as real as the challenges posed by the extreme weather. Yet, ask the pilots of these single-engine helicopters, and they will tell you that flying over Siachen remains one of the most profound experiences of their careers.

Then there are the crews of Mi-8 and Mi-17 helicopters, who have countless tales of hope and bravery navigating the perilous Himalayas and the rugged northeastern terrain. Similarly, the crews of transport aircraft like the Chinook, C-17 Globemasters and C-130J Super Hercules are redefining India's aviation landscape, breaking barriers and accomplishing feats once thought impossible.

Over the course of eight months, I kept travelling from one Air Force base to another, where I met personnel across various stations. I was deeply humbled by the stories shared by hundreds of personnel and their families. At one Air Force station, I stood on the tarmac beside the mighty C-130J Super Hercules, listening to pilots recount daring night landings while at a squadron housing the colossal C-17 Globemaster, I learnt about their extraordinary global missions. And beneath the towering Chinooks and the powerful Mi-17 helicopters, I felt an awe that resonated in my soul.

I also had the privilege of sharing meals in the exclusive squadron cafeteria with pilots of lethal fighter jets—looking dashing in their green overalls and G-suits—as they grabbed a quick bite before their sorties.

Conversations with the pioneering pilots and commanding officers of aircraft like Tejas, Rafale, Apache and Prachand were equally exhilarating. It wasn't just about the aircraft—I also learnt a great deal about the spirit of our Air Force, only to bring that experience to you. My visit to the Garud units was equally moving. Meeting some of their finest.

But my defining moment came when, just before the book was about to go to printing, Operation Sindoor happened. A book on the Indian Air Force's valour looked incomplete without a mention of it, and it was then that the Indian Air Force very kindly allowed me a peek into this landmark operation. I had the rare honour of meeting the then Director General, Air Operations, and now Deputy Chief of the Air Staff, Air Marshal Awadhesh Kumar Bharti, AVSM, VM, whose iconic line, 'Our job is to hit the target, not to count the body bags,' has reverberated across the world. Needless to say I was in complete awe. Another surreal moment was when I had the privilege of meeting Air Vice Marshal Joseph Suares, YSM, VM (G) whose vision and guidance helped shape these stories.

Listening to these exceptional men and women expanded my perspective on life. Their resilience made me realize how trivial many of my own concerns are. The challenges they face, while flying massive aircraft with unwavering smiles, put everything in perspective. Every conversation—from talks with Officers to casual chats with airmen—played a vital role in shaping this book.

I would also like to mention the distinct honour and rare privilege of meeting the present Chief of the Air Staff, Air Chief Marshal Amar Preet Singh, and Mrs Sarita Singh, whose insights further enriched the scope of this book.

My deepest hope is that I have done justice to these extraordianry stories. For the brave men who sacrificed their lives, I have relied on the accounts of their commanding officers and comrades who were on the ground with them—these accounts bring deep authenticity to the stories.

These stories also underwent rigorous scrutiny by the Directorate of Operations (Media & Public Relations) at Air HQ, as well as by the individuals featured. They were further refined by the exceptional editors at HarperCollins. To paraphrase the common saying, it truly takes a village to write a book. I have taken utmost care to verify facts and have approached these accounts with integrity and respect but if any errors are present, they are unintentional and solely my responsibility.

My hope is that you recognize the intent behind this work and the effort invested in immortalizing the unsung bravery within the Indian Air Force over a period of two years after months of painstaking research and dedication. Through these stories, I aim to inspire India's youth to consider a future in the Air Force and foster a deep sense of gratitude for the force where, too often, the machines overshadow the 'soldiers in blue' who ignite life in those beautiful systems.

With this humble endeavour, I seek to bring these heroes into the light. Let the stories begin.

Contents

History of the Indian Air Force — xxv

Prologue: Operation Sindoor — 1

Humanitarian Assistance and Disaster Relief — 26

1. Operation Kaveri; Wadi Seidna: An Audacious Rescue Mission in Sudan — 30

2. Deoghar Cable Car Rescue: A Legendary Ropeway Rescue Mission — 82

The Garud: Indian Air Force's Elite Special Forces — 128

3. Corporal Gursevek Singh, SC (Posthumous): The Immortal of the Pathankot Attack — 133

4. Sergeant Milind Kishor Khairnar, SC (Posthumous) and Corporal Nilesh Kumar Nayan, SC (Posthumous): The Heroic Supreme Sacrifice — 164

5. Corporal Jyoti Prakash Nirala, AC (Posthumous): The Valiant Ashoka Chakra Awardee — 189

Operation Safed Sagar: A Milestone in Military Aviation 217

6. Flight Lieutenant Kambhampati Nachiketa: The Kargil
  Prisoner of War who Challenged Death Thrice 222

Indian Peace Keeping Operations 260

7. Operation Pawan; Jaffna University Helidrop:
  Against All Odds 266

8. The Might of the Indian Air Force 295

Acknowledgements 329

History of the Indian Air Force

THE INDIAN AIR Force holds third position in the global air powers ranking 2025 according to the World Directory of Modern Military Aircraft, but it had its humble beginnings as a fledgling unit comprising just four aircraft. Officially established on 8 October 1932, the Air Force of India was born through a historic proclamation in the Gazette of India:

> *'No 564: In pursuance of sub-section (2) of section 1 of the Indian Air Force Act, 1932 (XIV of 1932), the Governor General in Council is pleased to appoint 8th October 1932 as the date from which the said act shall come into force.'*
>
> *'No 565: The Governor General in Council is pleased, with effect from the 8th October 1932, to establish the Indian Air Force.'*

This small yet determined force began its journey with Westland Wapiti IIA biplanes, six trained officers and nineteen Hawai Sepoys.[1] Despite its modest size, the IAF proved its mettle early, fighting alongside the Allied Forces during World War II. Its role in the European, South Asian and Burmese theatres earned it global recognition, and, on 12 March 1945, the IAF was awarded the title 'Royal' in honour of its valour and contributions.

---

1 Hawai Sepoys were the historical equivalent of today's airmen in the Indian Air Force.

When India gained independence on 15 August 1947, the Air Force too achieved freedom from British control. Air Marshal Sir Thomas Elmhirst sent out a landmark signal to every station, declaring that the IAF was now an independent entity, owing its allegiance to independent India—with Sardar Baldev Singh as the first Defence Minister, and Pandit Jawaharlal Nehru as the country's first prime minister. The following day, the IAF proudly flew its Spitfires, Tempests and Harvards over the Red Fort, marking the dawn of a new era.

While the history and evolution of the Indian Air Force is a vast topic, I have tried to compile a few streaks as simply as possible for the basic understanding of an average reader. After Independence, the nation immediately had to deal with Pakistani raiders attempting to take over Jammu and Kashmir. While we all acknowledge the brave fights the Indian Army had put up to safeguard the area, the contribution of Air Force had been disregarded. Just to highlight RIAF's role a bit in the defence of Kashmir, mentioning how when the raiders were at the gates of Kashmir in October 1947, the No. 12 squadrons along with civilian Dakotas had kept the air bridge open and landed troops under enemy fire in Srinagar.[2] The close air support to the Army in Jammu and Kashmir by Spitfires from the Advanced Flying School at Ambala and Tempests from No. 7, 8 and 10 squadrons of the RIAF is also worth mentioning.

There had been many incidents of Tempests, Spitfires and Harvards of RIAF firing at raiders, bombing and strafing targets. One such incident worth mentioning is the bitter battle near Srinagar airfield between Kumaonis and 700 raiders on 3 November where seven air strikes were launched, and were successful in inflicting a large number of casualties and destroying the raiders' lorries. The

---

2 Puspindar Singh, *Himalayan Eagles: History of the Indian Air Force*, Vol. 2, Chapter 16, 'In Defense of Kashmir', Society of Aerospace Studies, March 2007.

No. 1 operational group RIAF under Air Commodore Mehar Singh DSO which controlled all frontline fighters, communication and reconnaissance, air operations, and ancillary organizations, was responsible for all the air operation in Jammu and Kashmir. 'Baba' Mehar Singh, aka Air Commodore Mehar Singh, DSO, AOC No. 1 (Operations) group played important role during those days, and not just commanded the complete authority of the men under him but also continued to set an example in almost everything he did. The books I read on Indian Air Force history also mention Air Chief Marshal Dilbagh Singh then a Fg Offr who was 'Mentioned in Despatches' for his role in the Kashmir operations. There are many more names of air warriors I wish I could have mentioned but let's just stick to the role of the RIAF in airlifting thousands of troops, and thousand tonnes of supplies, ammunition, medical kits using a few RIAF Dakotas along with civilian planes it is worth mentioning here that the courage of the civilian air crew was no less than that displayed by the faujis. Many reconnaissance and patrolling duties were also carried out by RIAF fighters. Despite inclement weather and enemy fire, the RIAF did whatever was possible to help hard pressed garrisons.[3]

Then there is an incredible story of an air brigade of Poonch —refugees affected by the brutal communal riots during Partition in Poonch, under the leadership of Brigadier Pritam Singh of the Indian Army, had constructed an improvised airstrip to facilitate the regular flow of supplies not just for the Poonch brigade but also for around 10,000 locals and 35,000 refugees within a week.[4] On the same airstrip, on 8 December 1947, Air Vice Marshal Subroto Mukerjee and Air Commodore Mehar Singh made the first landing for dropping vital supplies. Over the next six days, the IAF flew 73 sorties, delivering 210 tons of supplies, and continued

---

3   Puspindar Singh, *Himalayan Eagles*, 'In Defence of Kashmir', p 20.
4   Puspindar Singh, *Himalayan Eagles*, 'In Defence of Kashmir', p 30.

these missions until the ceasefire of 1 January 1950.[5] Meanwhile, the tales of Tempests and Harvards based in Jammu flying offensive reconnaissance over Poonch helped raise the morale of the garrison. The air brigade was maintained till the declaration of ceasefire on 1 January 1950.

As India declared itself a republic in January 1950, the Royal Indian Air Force officially shed the 'Royal' prefix, becoming the Indian Air Force.[6] This act was deeply symbolic of the IAF's unyielding commitment to the nation, pledging its unwavering service to India and its people. On 1 April 1954, IAF celebrated its twenty-first anniversary with a memorable fire power demonstration at Tilpat Range with around 100 aircraft taking part before the citizens of Delhi and neighbouring towns. It was an iconic day in every sense because it was on this day that the President of India presented the colours to the IAF in an impressive ceremonial parade as a mark of recognition of the services that the IAF had rendered to the country. That was also the day Air Marshal Subroto Mukerjee took over as the first Indian Chief of Air Staff of the IAF, marking the complete 'Indianization' of IAF since all the RAF officers who were seconded to the IAF had now left the country, handing over their changes to Indian officers.[7] Air Marshal Subroto Mukerjee is called the 'Father of the Indian Air Force'.

During the 1951-52 period, the government alerted the armed forces about imminent hostilities with Pakistan, and the Indian Air Force had to urgently raise a number of emergency units. In 1952, the government accepted the recommendation of a high powered

---

5 So that others may live : Indian Airforce in the service of nation published in June 2011 by Indian Air force with Air Mshl NAK Browne as chief patron / chapter the poonch air brigade
6 Ibid/ chapter The republic and its air force
7 Puspindar Singh, *Himalayan Eagles*, 'Consolidation and Expansion', p 51.

Armed Forces Reorganization Committee that the Air Force should be expanded to a fifteen squadron force by March 1957. This was to consist of eight fighter bomber squadrons, one night fighter squadron, one photo reconnaissance squadron, two light bomber squadrons, one maritime reconnaissance squadron, two transport squadrons, ancillary and supporting formations plus training units[8]. In its early years, the IAF steadily expanded its operations by introducing heavier transport aircraft, like the Caribou and the C-117 Fairchild Packet. These aircraft greatly improved the IAF's ability to carry personnel, supplies and equipment over long distances, even to the remotest regions. The addition of helicopters further extended its reach, connecting areas that were previously inaccessible, thus increasing its responsibilities. The considerable expansion of fighter squadrons are also worth mentioning; however, the details of this would be beyond the format and scope of the book.

Today, the IAF is undergoing a significant transformation, evolving from a tactical force to one with strategic reach and advanced capabilities. With cutting-edge technology, it now employs space-based assets such as satellites and drones to improve its efficiency. The operational effectiveness of the Indian Air Force and its Integrated Air Command and Control Systems had been a matter of national pride during Operation Sindoor in 2025. The IAF also plays a role in the Integrated Space Cell, working closely with the Department of Space and the Indian Space Research Organisation (ISRO) to secure India's interests in space. At the time of editing this book, news portals are filled with Group Captain Shubhanshu Shukla, an Indian Air Force test pilot and ISRO astronaut, and his upcoming flight to the International Space Station as part of the Axiom 4 mission—thus becoming India's second national astronaut and Air Force pilot to go to space since 1984.

---

8 Puspindar Singh, *Himalayan Eagles*, 'Consolidation and Expansion', p 46.

While the primary task of the IAF remains the defence of Indian airspace, its role has expanded to encompass a wide range of missions. From military operations to humanitarian efforts, the IAF has repeatedly demonstrated its versatility. Time and again, it is called upon to assist civil authorities during natural disasters and humanitarian crises, offering aid and relief to those in need. This dual role of both defender and benefactor showcases the IAF's commitment not only to national security but also to the well-being of its people.

Currently, the IAF is the fourth-largest air force in the world in terms of quantity of aircraft, but it holds the third position in the global ranking of armed air services of the world in terms of modernization, logistic support, attack and defense capabilities, special missions, dedicated bomber force, CAS, training and some other factors. It operates with seven Air Commands—five operational, one training and one maintenance—each overseeing numerous stations and units spread across the country. These commands are equipped with some of the most advanced aircraft and systems, giving the IAF the ability to respond swiftly and effectively to any threat or mission.

However, the IAF's most valuable asset—past, present and future—remains its personnel: The countless men and women who don the blue uniform. They serve with immense pride and dedication, ensuring that the nation sleeps peacefully, knowing its skies are in capable hands.

It is because of these men and women that the legacy of service, sacrifice and honour remains unwavering.[9]

---

9 Additional reference materials include official Indian Air Force archives, research papers accessed through IAF libraries, and works including: *Himalayan Eagles: The History of the Indian Air Force*, by Pushpinder Singh; *The Duels of the Himalayan Eagle: The First Indo-Pak Air War*, by Air Marshal Bharat Kumar; Various Indian Air Force coffee table books, and content from the official Indian Air Force website and Indian Air Force doctrine.

Prolouge

Operation Sindoor

IT BEGAN LIKE any other night. But by dawn, the rules of engagement between India and Pakistan had changed forever.

7 May 2025, somewhere in a highly guarded control room, India's top military minds watched a set of blinking dots on their screens—each one representing a nest of terror. Nine such dots. Nine facilities across Pakistan and Pakistan-occupied Kashmir—each one deeply tied to the pain and rage etched into India's memory.

And then came the command. A quiet order. Calm. Precise. Devastating.

Operation Sindoor was in motion.

For the next twenty to twenty-five minutes, the Indian Air Force deployed a lethal mix of platforms including Rafale, Sukhoi (Su-30MKI) Mirage 2000 fighters, various drones and missiles. These precision-guided munitions, launched from multiple aircraft, hit their targets with pinpoint accuracy—without a single jet crossing Indian airspace. Simultaneously, the Indian Army unleashed its 155 mm artillery guns, alongside unmanned combat aerial vehicles and loitering munitions—deadly suicide drones—to pulverize key terror bases. While the Indian Navy was prowling the North Arabian Sea, like a pack of wolves, ready to punish any indiscretion by the Pakistanis, there were reports of live firing and naval combat drills over the sea, a signal to Pakistan that the Indian Navy was also prepared.

Later Hon'ble Raksha Mantri Sri Rajnath Singh said, 'Our mighty Carrier Battle Group, albeit silent, ensured that the Pakistani Navy did not venture out or else it would have faced the consequences.'

What shocked the enemy was that Indian missiles struck with precision, specific points of terror infrastructure, some of them 300 km deep inside Pakistan, at a time when their forces were already on high alert—a clear display of India's reach and readiness.

This was no reckless aggression but a measured, meticulously planned strike by the Indian Armed Forces, while staying well within our own borders. The targets were hit from afar—an offensive action with precision, which stunned the world and rattled Pakistan even more. These weren't just ordinary camps. They were high-value terror fortresses, protected and glorified by Pakistan's military establishment.

It was revealed clearly that the Indian Armed Forces had sent a clear and deliberate message—which was just a glimpse of what they were capable of. The objective was singular: to hit hard and deliver a crushing blow to terror infrastructure.

Indian authorities had made a conscious decision not to target any military or civilian establishments in its strike, despite having the capability to do so. The weapons, the delivery systems—everything was carefully selected from an arsenal that included options capable of area bombing and mass destruction. But restraint was chosen. This wasn't about inflicting maximum damage—it was about sending a clear message, wherein, the strikes were precise on verified terror hubs.

In a simultaneous attack the targets within Pakistan to be reduced to rubble were:

Markaz Subhan Allah in Bahawalpur—JeM's pride, their headquarters. A sprawling compound 100 km from the international border, not just the residence of Masood Azhar, but the snakes' nest from where the Pulwama suicide bombing had been conceived—Azhar's venomous speeches against India had echoed through its walls. Hundreds of terrorists had trained there in arms, explosives, and had been indoctrinated with hatred. That night, several of Azhar's relatives—long protected by the Pakistani deep state—were among the dead. Where, the very next day after the IAF strike, the top brass of Pakistani Armed Forces stood in grief and laid wreaths on the coffins of the slain terrorists. For once, the line between 'non-state actors' and state actors had burned away in the fire India sent from its skies. It showed the whole world the vicious nexus between the Pakistani military establishment and terrorist organizations.

The Indian Armed Forces also unleashed its fury on the Mehmoona Joya terrorist facility near Sialkot—Only 12 km from the international boundary was Hizbul Mujahideen territory. The attack on the Air Base at Pathankot was planned and carried out from this terrorist camp. For years, it operated with impunity under the protection and patronage of the Pakistani military.

Sarjal, Tehra Kalan just 6 km from International Borders, was crucial to cross-border tunnel operations, drone launches, and smuggling of arms into Indian territory and was used by the JeM as forward launch pads to infiltrate Jammu and Kashmir. It also serves as a communications hub from where handlers used to keep in touch with terrorists operating in J&K, but on that night, they were hit with pinpoint accuracy.

The headquarters of Lashkar-e-Taiba at Muridke were also targeted. This was just 25 km from the Indian border—and for years, had thrived under Pakistan's protection. The same compound where the 26/11 Mumbai massacre had been planned. The same campus where Ajmal Kasab and his fellow terrorists were trained.

Where David Headley and Tahawwur Rana were regular guests. For the construction of which, Osama bin Laden himself had donated money.

Targets based in Pakistan Occupied Kashmir were also hit. Barnala Camp, Bhimber in Pakistani occupied Kashmir, just 9 km from the Line of Control, and a regular staging ground for LeT terrorists was also annihilated. This camp had seen more footfall than any mosque or school in the area and used to funnel weapons into Rajouri, Poonch, and Reasi. It had served as a direct threat to the locals of Jammu. The Indian Military made sure it would never do so again.

Gulpur camp and Abbas camp in Kotli—home to two separate facilities, both major terrorist powerhouses were also pulverised. One trained LeT suicide bombers, the other served as the nerve centre for Hizbul's Border Action Teams, snipers, and high-altitude guerrilla squads. These were elite terror outfits, specifically trained to operate in the Indian territory. Their instructors were mostly retired Pakistani soldiers, their targets were Indian soldiers. Their buildings no longer exist.

The Shawai Nallah Camp, Muzaffarabad—a brutal terror academy where Ajmal Kasab had once trained—was destroyed in a single, staggering blow. The adjacent Markaz Syedna Bilal, known for its joint operations between JeM and the Pakistani Army's Special Services Group, also met the same fate. It had trained hundreds to sneak into Indian soil, kill civilians, plant IEDs, blow up schools and buses—and die doing it. They mindlessly called it Jihad, or holy war, which they proudly glorified from within these very premises oblivious to the fate that 7 May 2025 would bring them. Sheltered in their safe heaven, they were oblivious to the fate that this day had in store for them, and that it would… bring them pain and suffering more horrific then their worst nightmares.

This was not an isolated reaction. This was answering decades of provocation.

This was retribution for Pulwama, for 26/11, for Pathankot, for Uri, and the decades of bloodshed in Kashmir and most recently Pahalgam—where on 22 April 2025, terrorists had opened fire on unarmed tourists, selectively targeting them for their faith. Women widowed. Sindoor wiped off their foreheads.

The message they left behind: 'Go tell Modi.'

They thought India would hesitate. That it would fall back on 'strategic restraint' like in the past. Instead, enemies woke up to Operation Sindoor.

Pakistan had anticipated an Indian reaction and had accordingly fortified their defences and had deployed surface-to-air missiles, re-armed posts, braced for cross-border commando strikes, but India didn't take the expected path. This wasn't Kargil-style mountain warfare, nor a Balakot-style aerial punch.

This was a new war strategy. No soldier crossed the LoC, yet every target burned.

Surveillance drones had hovered for weeks. Signals were intercepted. Patterns tracked. Timings were chosen and then, nine terror epicentres were struck simultaneously—with surgical precision that sent shudders through Pakistan's top brass. Not one target was missed. Within twenty to twenty-five minutes, mayhem reigned across nine terror hubs out of which five were in Pakistan occupied Kashmir and four in the powerful Pakistani province of Punjab.

It was the beginning of a new dawn—a moment when India roared back with unapologetic clarity. With Operation Sindoor, the government under Prime Minister Narendra Damodardas Modi decisively broke away from decades of restraint. The message was unambiguous: any Pakistani transgression would now be met with punitive force. The era of mere condemnation was over. India had redrawn the line—boldly and irreversibly.

Pakistan, henceforth, would pay very dearly for any misadventure it dared to undertake.

Indian Defence Minister Sri Rajnath Singh , addressing Indian Army soldiers at Badami Bagh Cantonment, Srinagar, just days after the strike, captured this shift in a thunderous declaration 'Prime Minister has re-defined India's policy against terrorism,'

He declared. 'From now onwards, any attack on Indian soil will be considered an act of war.'

Air Marshal Awadhesh Kumar Bharti AVSM VM, then Director General of Air Operations, shared with me, 'They targeted civilians,' he said, his voice firm. 'Tourists, families, people who had gone to enjoy a peaceful break. And they were shot at point-blank range. I'd call that inhuman. As a nation, we want peace. We want to live and let live. But when you're provoked repeatedly, there comes a point when you must react and we did. We targeted their terror bases, their training centres, their hideouts. We didn't target civilians—we targeted terror".

He was right. India had struck terror infrastructure deep into the heart of Pakistan—but it wasn't just the militants who were rattled. It was the Pakistani state that scrambled. In the hours following India's audacious 7 May airstrikes, Pakistan's military machinery whirred to life in a frenzy. Assets were mobilized, defences activated, and its Air Force placed on high alert.

And then, the skies roared.

According to some estimates, nearly 125 fighter jets from both nations swarmed the skies in a high-stakes aerial confrontation. Indian and Pakistani aircraft locked radars and exchanged long-range missile fire in a ferocious aerial combat that raged for over an hour. Amid various conflicting claims of downed aircraft, came a now-iconic response from the then Director General of Air Operations (DGAO) in Delhi (Later in a press conference on 11 May 25) 'We are in a combat scenario. Losses are a part of combat. The question you must ask is—have we achieved our objective? And the answer is a thumping yes. The results are for the whole world to see.'

The sheer magnitude of India's precision strikes on terror hubs had sent Pakistan into shock. But their shock quickly turned into senseless comments and wild rage. Across Islamabad's corridors of military and government power they declared the Indian action an 'act of war'.

That same day, Pakistani Prime Minister Shehbaz Sharif took to X, issuing a statement 'Pakistan reserves the absolute right to respond decisively to this unprovoked Indian act. A resolute response is already under way … the enemy will never be allowed to achieve its malicious aim.'

He apparently 'granted' the Chief of Army Staff of Pakistan, Syed Asim Munir Ahmed Shah, full freedom and authority to take any action deemed fit.

Right since 24 April 2025, Pakistan had been violating the ceasefire agreement daily by initiating small arms fire and indiscriminate shilling along the LOC in an attempt to provoke Indian Armed forces or help infiltration by terrorists.

However, after the Indian strike on 7 May, Pakistan initially, further intensified the artillery shelling and small arms fire at sensitive points across the Indian side of Jammu and Kashmir from Kupwara, Baramulla, Uri to Poonch, Rajouri, and Akhnoor. The border villages and towns bore the brunt. Artillery shells rained down, killing many civilians and damaging homes, schools even religious places of different faiths. Meanwhile, Pakistan claimed that Indian shelling had damaged its Neelum–Jhelum Hydropower Plant.

That night, Pakistan also launched a barrage of drones and missile attacks across India's northern and western front—targeting not just military installations, but densely populated regions Jammu, Kashmir, Punjab, Rajasthan, and even Gujarat came under fire. Their target was unmistakable: fifteen frontline Indian military bases, including Awantipura, Srinagar, Jammu, Pathankot, Amritsar, Jalandhar, Bathinda, Adampur, Ludhiana, Chandigarh, Nal, Phalodi, Utarlai, and Bhuj.

Pakistan named its counter-operation 'Bunyan al Marsus'[1], which translates to 'a solid wall of lead.' India was not just prepared, but in absolute charge, thwarting very Pakistani attempt of targeting Indian civil and military installations. The enemy was desperate; their empty threats of a nuclear response and other military threats were being exposed. Every drone, every missile, met a wall of impregnable defence and a strategy developed over decades of lessons learnt and assets acquired.

India's integrated Counter-Unmanned Aircraft System (CUAS) and multi-layered air defences grids kicked in with ruthless efficiency. One by one, the incoming threats were neutralized mid-air.

Though there was another battle going on beyond skies, land and water. While Indian missiles thundered through the skies on 7 May, another war was brewing—one which wasn't fought with jets or artillery, but in the chaotic, borderless world of the internet. The digital frontier had opened.

Shortly after Islamabad lifted its fifteen-month ban on X, the social media platform lit up. Though the official handle of the Pakistani military remained eerily dormant, its digital proxies sprang to life. Deepfakes, misinformation, and coordinated psychological warfare began flooding timelines. Among those was a doctored video of India's External Affairs Minister, Dr S. Jaishankar, designed to sow confusion and distrust, which was swiftly identified and debunked by India's Press Information Bureau.

But the message was clear—this war wouldn't be fought on one front alone. Every form of media had been weaponized.

Indian Armed forces were well prepared. Following the Balakot airstrikes, while India had spoken limitedly on the strike and the

---

1 According to Al Jazeera report the operation name was picked from an Arabic phrase in Quran (Surah As-Saff, 61:4) that describes soldiers fighting in close formation as if they were a 'solid wall'.

terror attack which had led to the Indian strike, Pakistani propaganda had run amok, creating a false narrative of denial and deceit that found traction in global media. Six years later, India wasn't about to allow Pakistan to succeed in its disinformation wargames.

This time, the response was not only sharp—it was strategic. The information campaign ran in parallel with kinetic operations. There was clear coordination at the highest levels, and narratives were being shaped with surgical precision. After the Pahalgam attack, the Indian side didn't just release statements—they told the truth with impact. The perpetrators were exposed across digital platforms, and India's messaging cut through noise and propaganda.

The first official response came not from a single podium, but through a powerful trio—Colonel Sofiya Qureshi of the Indian Army, Wing Commander Vyomika Singh of the Indian Air Force, and Foreign Secretary Shri Vikram Misri. Their calm, measured tone and sharp articulation made headlines. But it was also the composition of the team that turned heads—two women in uniform standing alongside a senior diplomat. This was noticed, interpreted and acknowledged as, inclusivity, resolve, unity and strength, not just to Pakistan, but a statement to the world.

When I asked the Wg Cdr Vyomika Singh about it later, she responded with quiet dignity, 'I was just doing the duty assigned to me'.

A senior officer echoed the sentiment with clarity, 'She is part of our team—it's her role. We assigned it to her based on professional capability. We had many excellent officers—men and women—equally capable. There was no agenda. No tokenism. We functioned as one unit, one force. Be it launching missiles, flying sorties, managing air traffic, coordinating logistics, or the Garud Special Forces—it was a seamless operation. Every individual gave their all, and we are proud of that.'

The IAF had its own battlefield to manage. 'Our biggest challenge was countering misinformation swiftly and accurately.' We wanted to put out facts—not chest-thumping, not bravado—just simple, credible updates, in a controlled, responsible manner. You would have heard the rumours that were peddled online by the other side, involving a woman pilot being captured. But we refused to be provoked. They can say what they want to. That's not how a professional force behaves.

This was not just a new style of warfare—it was a new era. Where retribution wasn't just about hitting back. It was about telling your story with facts and proof. In the skies, on the ground, and across every screen.

By the morning of 8 May, it was clear—India wasn't just responding, it was reshaping the battlefield while also changing the precedence for India's response to terror. In a cold, calculated response to the senseless Pakistani escalation and attempts to terrorize the general populace of India, Indian forces struck deep—not only tactically, but symbolically. An air defence system near Lahore, one of Pakistan's most significant urban centres, were obliterated. The message was unmistakable: nowhere was safe—not even Lahore. As tensions mounted, Pakistan upped the ante. On 8 and 9 May, its military violated Indian airspace multiple times across the western border and intensified heavy-calibre shelling along the LoC. The conflict, which had already lit up the skies, now fully embraced the new age of warfare.

Various reports across Indian and Pakistani news portals stated that Pakistan deployed between 400 to 500 drones—many Turkish-made models—intruding across thirty-six locations from Leh to Sir Creek. Among them, one armed UAV made a brazen attempt to target the Bathinda military station—but it never made it. Indian Air Defences intercepted and neutralized it before impact.

Along the LoC, Pakistan rained artillery and drone strikes on Tangdhar, Uri, Poonch, Mendhar, Rajouri, Akhnoor, and Udhampur, resulting in some casualties and injuries on the Indian side. But India was far from helpless. Utilizing an arsenal of cutting-edge unmanned systems, India not only defended its territory but struck back with deadly precision. Many Pakistani drones were brought down using a mix of kinetic and non-kinetic means.

Pakistani provocation and escalation continued, with short-range surface-to-surface missiles targeting Udhampur and Pathankot airbases as well. That was when India unleashed one of its most formidable shields—the S-400 Triumf missile defence system. This Russian-made beast was in its element, its first operation for India, intercepting multiple aerial threats with efficiency. Capable of detecting threats up to 600 km away and engaging 36 targets simultaneously at altitudes up to 30 km, the S-400 performed like the nation's favourite guardian.

India's own Akash surface-to-air missile system, developed by DRDO, played a vital role. Integrated into the multi-layered air defence network and working in tandem with the Integrated Air Command and Control System (IACCS), Akash batteries responded rapidly—neutralizing waves of incoming drones and missiles, defending vital infrastructure and cities. Even legacy systems like Pechora performed well, intercepting enemy threats with precision.

The war witnessed many other types of missiles, drones, air defence systems and aircraft in action. Indigenous LCA Tejas also was a part of live operations for the first time since its induction in the Indian Air force, operating along with Rafales, Sukhoi, MiGs and Mirages. I would also like to mention the IAF's elite special force Garud, who displayed great valour. There were reports of them shooting aerial platforms using their sniper rifles along with other heroics which we can hope will be revealed in the future.

As the sun set on 9 May, Pakistan launched a third wave of its assault. This time, twenty-six locations were in its crosshairs—including military bases, civilian centres and even religious sites. Drones, heavy artillery and tactical missiles blanketed the western front.

Yet, along the Indian boundaries, something remarkable unfolded—Indian citizens, unfazed by the chaos above, stood firm. Videos emerged of locals filming intense aerial combat in the skies, turning fear into fierce pride. Instagram reels captured aerial platforms streaking across the heavens, as if the war had become a spectacle of national defiance. The Indian Armed Forces had not just defended the nation but also won the unshakable confidence of the nation.

But Pakistan wasn't done yet. In a dramatic escalation, as many international and national news portals suggest, it fired its indigenously developed Fatah-II guided artillery rocket, aiming straight at New Delhi. The missile never reached—it was intercepted mid-air over Sirsa. In response, India didn't just deny damage; it released high-resolution images of its untouched airbases to demolish Pakistan's claims. And then, it struck back. At dawn on 10 May, the Indian Air Force unleashed the BrahMos-A—and air-launched cruise missiles streaked the skies. Their targets were strategic: Pakistan Air Force (PAF) bases. The first impacts were confirmed at Chaklala[2] near Rawalpindi and Sargodha in the Punjab province—key aviation and logistics hubs.

But India had not done just that.

Confirmed by an Indian government press release within hours, eleven military installations were hit: Nur Khan, Rafiqui, Muridke, Sukkur, Sialkot, Pasrur, Chunian, Sargodha, Skardu, Bholari, and Jacobabad. These weren't just airbases—they were command centres, radar sites, weapons depots, and logistical arteries. Satellite images before and after the strikes told a grim tale—entire structures reduced to rubble, their strategic capacities vaporized.

When I met Air Marshal Awadesh Kumar Bharati and ask him about it, his voice was firm as he recounted the precision and restraint

---

2 Also know as Nur Khan Airbase.

with which India had struck. 'We did exceedingly well. Took out their radars. Neutralized key missile systems. That first wave was decisive—but calculated. They came at us with drones and missiles—this was their military acting, not proxies. Only then did we respond, and even then, our strikes were measured. Our message was clear: if you side with terrorists, if you dare strike our bases or civilians, we will reach you—no matter where you hide.'

He paused—just long enough for the silence to underline what came next, 'We hit deep. We hit hard. And we kept enemy heads down.'

He wasn't exaggerating. India had, over consecutive days, demonstrated its remarkable ability to launch pinpoint standoff strikes deep inside Pakistani territory. Wave after wave of precision, long-range attacks shattered the myth of invulnerability long harboured by Pakistan. Though some of India's attempts may have been challenged by Pakistani air defences, the broader truth had been laid bare: that Pakistan has a serious vulnerability to Indian air attacks, and this became known not only to India but the whole world as well.

This wasn't just another border skirmish. It was a shift in the balance of deterrence. No wonder world superpowers are rattled.

For decades, Pakistan had wielded its nuclear arsenal as a shield behind which it sponsored terror, believing it would keep India's response in check. Not this time. In 2025, for the first time in history, a country had successfully launched airstrikes on the military installations of a nuclear-armed adversary—at a time, place, and intensity of its own choosing. India had redefined the rules of engagement. And the world had taken notice.

As an Indian, this fact alone stirs deep pride in my heart.

Later, an image released by the Indian government made its own statement—a half-burnt portrait of Pakistani President Asif Ali Zardari lay amidst the charred remains of Rahimyar Khan Air Base.

'This,' the Indian government said in its release, 'is symbolic of the devastation Pakistan has brought upon itself—the shattered image of a nation exposed for what it is.'[3]

Prime Minister Modi also took a dig at it. Addressing his first public rally after Operation Sindoor in Rajasthan's Bikaner, he said, *'When I came from Delhi to here, I landed in Bikaner's Nal Airport. Pakistan has also tried to make this a target but they failed to damage this airbase. There is a Rahim Yar Khan airbase situated on the other side of the border. It is in ICU. Don't know when it will open? India's forces have destroyed this air base.'*

That scorched, tattered portrait—perhaps torn from a command wall by the force of the strike—captured what no briefing ever could: the collapse of a myth. The unravelling of Pakistan's pride, built on its belief in a 'war by a thousand cuts'.

India didn't just strike back. It rewrote the doctrine.

What further turned Pakistan into a subject of international mockery were reports by *Reuters*, stating that Pakistan had appealed to its international partners—including the World Bank—for additional loans, citing 'heavy losses inflicted by the enemy' following Indian military strikes. Though the loans were approved despite India's objections, the incident exposed the fragile state of Pakistan's military and government. Instead of resolving internal economic crises and governance issues, Pakistan remained obsessed with launching attacks on India through terror networks and proxy wars—only to be defeated every single time by India. In all the wars initiated by Pakistan's military, the country's de-facto ruler, India had emerged victorious.

---

3   https://economictimes.indiatimes.com/news/defence/a-hidden-symbol-at-a-pakistani-air-base-speaks-of-its-shattered-pride/articleshow/121112915.cms?from=mdr// A hidden symbol at a Pakistani air base speaks of its shattered pride//EconomicsTimes,May 13, 2025

What made Operation Sindoor truly remarkable was the seamless display of the Indian Armed Forces' newly adopted doctrine of jointness. The nation witnessed a tangible spirit of synergy among the army, navy, and air force, exemplified through the Integrated Air Command and Control System (IACCS)—an automated infrastructure developed by the Indian Air Force. IACCS integrates real-time data streams from radars, fighter jets, unmanned systems, and surveillance platforms to create a live, comprehensive airspace picture. It fuses intelligence, surveillance, weapon systems, and decision-making tools across the IAF, Army, Navy, and other allied units.

Even the prime minister lauded India's air defence during his surprise visit to Punjab's Adampur Airbase on 13 May 2025, after the ceasefire—an airbase that Pakistan had falsely claimed to have destroyed. Photographs of the prime minister shouting patriotic slogans alongside the air warriors of Adampur—with a MiG-29 jet and an intact S-400 air defence system in the background—debunked Pakistan's propaganda.

He famously declared, 'I extend heartfelt appreciation to the leadership of all air bases and every air warrior of the Indian Air Force. You have done a fantastic job. I'm proud that our forces took great care not to harm civilian aircraft. Behind the rapid and effective retaliation was a digital backbone—IACCS. This network-enabled command structure helped coordinate India's multi-tiered air defence in real time, thwarting aerial threats while safeguarding civilian and strategic targets.'

In four relentless days during Operation Sindoor, India rained precision fire across Pakistan's key military installations, terror camps, airbases and shooting down everything Pakistan threw at India. The photographs post the operation show airbases, runways, selected structures and hangars accurately hit. The message was unmistakable—India could strike at will, not just across the border, but deep into the nerve centre of Pakistan's government and military command.

And it didn't stop there.

Looming silently off the coast was the Indian Navy, its warships enforcing a de facto blockade of Karachi Port—the economic lifeline of Pakistan. Ready for escalation, ready for war. The message the naval fleet sent was loud and clear: if Pakistan dared to press further, it would be a war they could not afford and would not survive.

The devastation rattled Islamabad. According to multiple reports, it was after the devastating airstrikes that the Pakistani prime minister and army chief reached out to the United States—pleading for help.

The media mockingly summed it up with a phrase that echoed across headlines: 'They cried uncle.'

Back in Delhi, there was intense global pressure on Prime Minister Narendra Modi to de-escalate. But he stood his ground. According to *India Today* (26 May 2025), the honourable prime minister, communicated to the US in no uncertain terms:

'India's response will be far more forceful, strong, and devastating.'

In his televised address to the nation, the prime minister went a step further 'India will not tolerate nuclear blackmail. If provoked, we will strike decisively—and we will not differentiate between the hand that pulls the trigger and the one that loads the gun.'

India—a rising superpower—never sought a full-scale war. But if forced, it would fight to finish it.

Even as ceasefire negotiations were underway, the chaos was compounded by an unexpected disruption—a tweet from U.S. President Donald Trump. Before either India or Pakistan had formally announced the ceasefire, Trump posted on X, boasting that the U.S. had averted a nuclear war. Worse still, he linked the situation to the 'Kashmir issue'—a claim that sent shockwaves through the South Block. India's response was swift and uncompromising. New Delhi dismissed any reference to Kashmir as irrelevant, making it abundantly clear: this was not about territory—this was about terrorism. Operation Sindoor had demonstrated that India would not be drawn into false equivalencies. The only root cause of the conflict was state-sponsored terror.

The Indian prime minister didn't mince his words: *'There will be no more talks on the status of the Valley post the abrogation of Article 370. Our position is clear—terror and talks, terror and trade, cannot go together.'*

The real story of how the war ended quietly emerged days later. According to government sources, it was after Pakistan's airbases were crippled that they pleaded for U.S. intervention. The Americans had already been in touch with both sides, sensing the situation was inching toward the red line. But what forced Washington's hand was a classified alert concerning Pakistan's strategic assets.

On 10 May, in a call that would signal the beginning of the end, Pakistan's Director General of Military Operations, Maj Gen Kashif Abdullah, reached out to his Indian counterpart, Lt Gen Rajiv Ghai. 'We want a ceasefire,' he said.

The Indian DGMO relayed the request to his superiors, and on confirmation, he called back. 'India agrees.'

Thus ended the eighty-eight-hour war—a war born of terror, shaped by fire, and ended not with negotiations or diplomacy, but with overwhelming force and clear deterrence.

The 18 May, 2025 print version of *India Today* had quoted a senior Indian official: 'Pakistan didn't want a ceasefire because someone spoke good English. They wanted it because something hit their bases, hard, from the sky.'

Among the many non-military measures taken by the Indian government in the wake of the Pahalgam terror attacks, one stood out for its historic weight and symbolic impact—the suspension of the sixty-five-year-old Indus Waters Treaty. A treaty that had withstood the shockwaves of four wars was now hanging by a thread.

The waters of the Indus River system are Pakistan's lifeline—especially for the provinces of Punjab and Sindh. These rivers are more than geographical features; they are seen as Pakistan's jugular vein. Though the suspension did not physically block the flow of water overnight, it sent a different kind of shockwave—a psychological one. The very threat of India reviewing the treaty rattled Islamabad.

'Water and blood cannot flow together,' Prime Minister Modi declared—a chilling metaphor that echoed across international corridors.

The message was clear: unless Pakistan turned off the tap on terror, India would keep the pressure mounting. The suspension was more than a policy move—it was a strategic signal that India was ready to challenge even long-standing diplomatic arrangements if national security demanded it.

In the same breath, the prime minister of India also rejected U.S. President Donald Trump's offer to mediate on the Kashmir issue. 'I want to tell the global community,' he said firmly, 'our stated policy is—if there are talks with Pakistan, they will only be about terrorism. And they will only be about Pakistan-occupied Kashmir.'

These weren't just words. They marked a seismic shift in India's diplomatic stance—a clarity forged in the fires of repeated betrayal.

The same prime minister who now stood like a rock against Pakistan was once the statesman who had extended a hand of friendship. In 2015, he made a surprise visit to Lahore to meet then-Pakistani Prime Minister Nawaz Sharif—a gesture of goodwill that stunned the world. But just days later, India was hit by the Pathankot airbase attack.

History, it seemed, was repeating itself. Back in February 1999, Prime Minister Atal Bihari Vajpayee had boarded a bus to Lahore—a historic peace overture that was met with the cold betrayal of the Kargil War.

Time and again, Indian leaders had chosen forgiveness, generosity and diplomacy. Time and again, Pakistan's military establishment had responded with gunfire and bloodshed. It became increasingly clear: the military in Pakistan had no real interest in peace. Its grip over the nation depended on sustaining enmity with India—an enmity that justified its power, its control, and its very existence.

India, under Prime Minister Modi, had now drawn the line— diplomacy would no longer be a one-way street.

The same fiery sentiment echoed through the ranks of India's senior military leadership during a press conference that followed days after the ceasefire. The atmosphere in the room was electric— heavy with pride, intensity, and purpose. On the large screen behind the officers, a video rolled with images of India's retaliatory might unfolding to the thundering cadence of the Shiv Tandav Stotra. Accompanying it were powerful verses from Ramcharit Manas.

The symbolism was unmistakable—this was not just a show of strength; it was a declaration of ethos of a civilization that worships peace but does not hesitate to wield thunder when provoked. When the officers were later asked about the choice of verses and the tone of the message, Air Marshal A.K. Bharti stepped forward. Calm, composed, and resolute, he chose not to offer analysis, but something far more profound.

He recited a chaupai from the Ramcharitmanas that, in a single stroke, distilled India's posture, '*Main bas aapko Ramcharitmanas ki kuchh panktiyan yaad dilaoonga, aap samajh jaayenge ... Binay na manat jaladhi jad, gaye teen din beet. Bole Ram sakop tab, bhay bin hoi na preet. Toh samajhdar ke liye ishaara hi kaafi hai.*" (*I will only remind you of a few lines from the Ramcharitmanas, and you'll understand. For the wise, a hint is enough.*)

For those unfamiliar, the verse tells of Lord Ram warning the ocean—having pleaded peacefully for three days, he declares that love or civility means little unless backed by the fear of consequence.

'*Bhay bin hoi na preet*' means, without the fear of reprisal, there can be no true respect, no lasting peace.

That one verse—a bridge between scripture and strategy—said it all.

Later, I had the profound honour of meeting Air Marshal A.K. Bharti—a figure of composed authority and sharp strategic insight. Despite the weight of national responsibilities and an unrelenting schedule, he graciously offered his invaluable time for this book. In an age overwhelmed by fleeting tweets and headline-driven noise, where depth is too often traded for immediacy, this book is a lasting chronicle meant to echo far beyond the scroll of screens, reaching into towns and villages with a clear message: the unwavering might, discipline, and readiness of the Indian Air Force.

I asked him whether the Indian armed forces faced any challenges during Operation Sindoor, and what lessons were drawn from the conflict, his response was immediate and unwavering—marked by his trademark clarity and conviction.

'There were no challenges,' he said firmly. 'We train every single day with the same aggression and intensity we bring to a real war. For us, readiness is not a moment—it is a way of life. Wars can break out any time. If you observed closely, our retaliation after the Pahalgam attack came swiftly—within days. That only means our plans and doctrines were already in place. We don't wait for war to prepare. We escalate when the trigger comes.'

He paused, the steel in his gaze softening just a notch. Then came the punch of insight—calm but fierce.

'As for lessons,' he continued, 'Operation Sindoor only reinforced what we already knew—that we can strike deep. That we can deliver our weapons precisely, surgically, right into the enemy's heartland. But yes, it also taught us a great deal about the adversary. You see, you only truly understand your enemy when you confront him face to face. And now that we have, we know them better. That knowledge—that intimacy with their methods—will serve us well in the days ahead.'

I pressed further, asking if, conversely, the enemy might have also learned about India's capabilities—our tactics, our equipment, our evolving doctrine. He smiled—the knowing smile of a man who'd already considered the question a hundred times,

'Well,' he said with quiet confidence, 'we constantly change our tactics. That's the nature of modern warfare—adaptation, improvisation, evolution. No matter how many ways Pakistan may attempt to challenge us—through proxies, through propaganda, through provocations—we always have the means to respond. Whether it's a tactic, a weapon, or a doctrine, we possess the precision and force to deliver the reply we choose, at the time of our choosing. That's what it means to be a professional military. We don't stay still. We introspect, we innovate, we improve. Our objectives are crystal clear. And we are always ready."

Air Marshal Bharti also spoke passionately about the spirit of jointmanship displayed by all three services during Operation Sindoor. However, since the focus of my book *Wings of Valour* remained solely on the Indian Air Force, I requested his insights on what the future holds for the IAF as a force.

Without hesitation, he replied.

'The Indian Air Force is inherently technology-intensive. Unlike the army and navy, which are confined to the limits of a medium and related environmental constraints, air power must be prepared to fight across land, sea, and the skies. That makes us an omnipresent, pervasive force. To be relevant and effective in the conflicts of tomorrow, we must maintain a cutting-edge advantage—always.'

He paused for a moment before continuing with resolute conviction. 'Even during peacetime—during natural disasters or global crises—the Indian Air Force is almost always the first responder. We are a force that reacts with speed, stabilizes situations, and adapts rapidly, whether it's war or peace. We carry the maximum ordnance, strike with precision, and possess the capability to hit deep into enemy territory—swiftly and decisively. When the nation needs rapid action, the IAF delivers. Targets deep within hostile zones, substantial impact in minimum time. That's where we come in. We are not bound by geography. We are built for reach, power, and precision.'

I also asked him about his roots during the interaction he replied with quiet pride and humility.

'I am an Indian first. Yes, I take pride in my native place, as anyone would. But the ethos of the armed forces has never been about regional identities. Every soldier belongs to a state, yes, but that is all there is to it. What matters is how meaningfully your efforts serve the country."

Finally, I was curious about how he was handling the sudden fame that came after he became a household name post Operation Sindoor.

He smiled, and with utmost modesty said, "Someone had to do it. My seniors gave me the task, so I did it. It's only my good fortune that I wake up every morning and get to do what I love—serve the Indian Air Force. Honestly, coming from a military background, I've always had limited interaction outside that world. So, I don't follow much of what's being said, and that helps me stay focused on what truly matters: the mission."

That conversation left a deep, lasting impression on me. My respect for the Indian Armed forces—already immense—only deepened further. There is something exceptional about the senior leadership of our armed forces. Time and again, in moments of crisis and conflict, they have led the nation with unwavering courage—often at great personal cost.

These leaders are truly a class apart, driven by one uncompromising belief: the nation comes first.

During Operation Sindoor all opposition parties stood shoulder-to-shoulder with the government, reflecting a rare show of national solidarity in a moment of gravest need and later an all-party delegation was sent to visit key partner nations, including members of the UN security council, to carry forth India's message to the world.

In a region stained by decades of hostility and war, Operation Sindoor marked a watershed moment for India. It was not merely an effective military riposte—it represented a strategic leap forward on multiple fronts.

For the first time, India executed a sustained series of precision strikes deep into Pakistan without crossing international borders or violating enemy airspace—a defining shift in the doctrine of engagement. The bold and calibrated attack on military infrastructure in Pakistan, sent a clear signal: the era of restraint had come to an end.

Yet, what made Operation Sindoor historic was not just what was done—but how it was done.

Each strike was delivered with devastating precision, at the time and place of India's choosing, annihilating the myth of the enemy's nuclear deterrence in one swift, coldly calculated message. It was a psychological blow as much as a physical one—a reminder that India's hand, though restrained by choice, was capable of overwhelming force. Another hallmark of the operation was the deployment of drones in roles that went far beyond surveillance or payload delivery. For the first time, these unmanned platforms played a central role in real-time target acquisition, battle-space awareness, and coordinated strike orchestration—setting a new precedent for future warfare.

But perhaps the most defining feature of Operation Sindoor was the sheer harmony with which India's military, diplomatic corps, and strategic agencies functioned. The synergy between the armed forces, intelligence units, foreign service, and political leadership reflected a matured national warfighting doctrine, a textbook execution of standoff warfare.

In many ways, this was India's first real step into the future of combat: wars driven not just by boots and bullets, but by brains, bandwidth, and jointness.

It's hard to predict what the future holds. Is Pakistan shaken? Yes, perhaps for a while. But has it truly learned its lesson? That remains doubtful. After all, this is a nation teetering on the edge of economic collapse, marred by internal instability, and historically gripped by the shadow of military coups. If it failed to introspect even after the catastrophic defeat of 1971, expecting strategic maturity now may be too generous a hope.

To my fellow compatriots, I say this: we, as citizens, can indeed breathe a little easier knowing that one of the world's most formidable militaries guards our borders—we need not to worry and continue building our nation constructively as one people, one nation.

By the time this book was sent to press, Air Chief Marshal Amar Preet Singh revealed, in an event in Bengaluru, the taking down of five Pakistani fighter aircraft and one large aircraft. He also mentioned hitting hangars at the Pakistani airfield.

He said (sic), 'we have five confirmed kills and one large aircraft, which could be either an ELINT aircraft or AEW&C aircraft which has taken at a distance of about 300 kilometers. This is actually the largest ever recorded surface-to-air kill that we can talk about.'

He also talked about a F-16 hangar in Shahbaz Jacobabad airfield getting damaged. He said, 'We were able to get at least two command and control centres like Muridke and Chaklala. At least six radars …we have an indication of at least one AEW&C in that AEW&C hangar and a few F-16s which were under maintenance there.'

He also chuckled (sic) 'No Pakistani aircraft could come near the boundaries of Akash. Sargodha … We have grown up in Air Force, dreaming about days like this. Someday we 'll get a chance to go there. So it just happens that I got my chance just before I retired .. .So we took on a airfield there.'

In his keynote address he also praised the Chief of Defence Staff Lt Gen Anil Chauhan for his role in bringing all the forces together, the efforts of National Security Advisor Sh Ajit Doval and clear political will.

As of now, Operation Sindoor remains classified, its full scope known only to the government and military leadership. This book brings together only what has been made available in the public domain and aprooved off. Yet, I sincerely hope that one day, the curtain will lift, even slightly, allowing us a glimpse into the lives of the pilots, ground crew, technicians, and battlefield commanders who stood tall when the stakes were at their highest—when enemies were at the gates.

A senior official from the IAF once told me, 'There are countless stories of human grit, resilience, and the will to defy all odds during Operation Sindoor. In time, those stories will surface.' That thought alone fills me with hope, because it is these very stories of courage and character that inspire future generations to rise, to endure, and to overcome.

After all, what is the world, if not a story?

So, turn the page and let the stories of resilience, sacrifice, and unshakable spirit unfold before you. Stories that honour the glorious legacy of the magnificent service we proudly call the Indian Air Force.

Humanitarian Assistance and Disaster Relief

THE INDIAN GOVERNMENT describes Humanitarian Assistance and Disaster Relief (HADR) as efforts to help people affected by disasters such as cyclones, floods, earthquakes, droughts and wars. Air power is important in these missions because it is fast, flexible and can reach remote areas quickly. The Indian Air Force leads these efforts, employing its aircraft, and leveraging its airlift and operational capabilities both within India and in neighbouring countries.

Since Independence, the IAF has been involved in numerous disaster relief missions, becoming a trusted force in times of crisis. Emergency teams are stationed at major bases such as Hindon, Palam, Bengaluru, Guwahati and Chandigarh, ready to provide medical aid through Rapid Aero Medical Teams (RAMT).[1]

---

1 Air Marshal Anil Chopra (Retd), 'Role of the IAF in Nation Building', SP's Aviation, Issue 8, 2024, https://www.sps-aviation.com/story/?id=3572&h=Role-of-the-IAF-in-Nation-Building#:~:text=IAF%20has%20its%20own%20emergency.

A key aspect of the IAF's humanitarian work is helping Indian citizens abroad. With millions of Indians living overseas, the IAF has developed expertise in evacuating people from danger zones. It has helped evacuate Indians, and even foreign nationals, from conflict areas such as South Sudan, Yemen, Ukraine, Israel and Afghanistan. These efforts have earned India respect and goodwill worldwide.

The IAF has enhanced its HADR capabilities by building a robust transport fleet that includes aircraft like the C-17 Globemaster III, Ilyushin IL-76, C-130J Super Hercules, An-32 and C-295. This is supported by a diverse helicopter fleet, including the heavy-lift Chinook, various versions of the Mi-8/Mi-17 medium-utility helicopters, the ALH, and the Chetak, Cheetah and Cheetal light helicopters. Together, these assets enable the IAF to uphold its legacy as a first responder in times of crisis.

Here is a list of some of the recent HADR operations conducted by the IAF abroad under the directives of Government of India:[2]

1. Operation Rahat (2015)

Location: Yemen

Description: Amidst Yemen's intensifying civil conflict, India evacuated over 4,000 Indians and foreign nationals from Aden, providing safe passage out of the war-torn region.

---

2 Ministry of External Affairs, Lok Sabha, Unstarred Question No. 1258, Answered on 9 February 2024, Available at: https://www.mea.gov.in/lok-sabha.htm?dtl/37593/QUESTION+NO1258+EVACUATION+OF+INDIANS#:~:text=Operation%20Ajay%3A%20So%20far%2C%20a,at%20Government%20of%20India's%20cost. (The data given as available on Ministry of External affairs and other government websites)

2. Vande Bharat Mission (2020)
Location: Various countries
Description: Launched to repatriate stranded Indians during the COVID-19 pandemic, this mission facilitated the evacuation of 3.2 crore people from twenty-four countries by the end of December 2020.

3. Operation Devi Shakti (2021)
Location: Afghanistan
Description: Following the Taliban's takeover, India evacuated 669 people—including Afghan nationals—ensuring their safe return during the volatile transition period.

4. Operation Ganga (2022)
Location: Ukraine
Description: In response to the Russia–Ukraine war, India safely evacuated 18,282 nationals, mainly students, via neighbouring countries with the support of IAF and commercial flights.

5. Operation Kaveri (2023)
Location: Sudan
Description: During the Sudan conflict, India evacuated over 4,097 people—including 136 foreign nationals—through IAF sorties, Navy ships and commercial flights.

6. Operation Ajay (2023)
Location: Israel
Description: Following the Israel-Hamas conflict, India launched this operation to safely return Indian nationals, OCI cardholders and Nepalese nationals from Israel.

Beyond the widely recognized HADR operations, the IAF has a profound, often undocumented, legacy of rescue missions, both within India and abroad. We must take great comfort and pride in knowing that, whether facing floods, landslides, earthquakes, enemy attacks or any other disaster, the IAF will always be there.

While it's impossible to document every HADR mission undertaken by the IAF, I've chosen to highlight two incredible operations: Operation Kaveri's Wadi Seidna mission and the Deoghar Cable Car rescue. These stories not only showcase the meticulous planning and immense effort behind such missions but also underline the significant risks undertaken by the brave Air Force personnel eventually revealing what it truly takes to fly into a disaster zone or a conflict-ridden area, and return safely.

1

Operation Kaveri; Wadi Seidna: The Audacious Rescue Mission in Sudan

Wadi Seidna Airbase
22 kilometres north of Khartoum
Sudan
27 April 2023

THE NIGHT DESCENDED into pitch darkness, clouds veiling the sky and shrouding the stars. Only sporadic flashes of light from mobile phones and torches pierced through, casting brief, eerie glows. Tension and fear hung heavy in the air, mingling with the cacophony of desperate voices.

Hundreds had gathered in an open field near the Wadi Seidna Airbase, clinging to the dwindling hope of evacuation. The scene was a stark tableau of despair. For days, they had witnessed unspeakable horrors—bodies strewn about, twisted in grotesque angles, a testament to the brutality unleashed. The ground was stained with blood, the air thick with the acrid stench of smoke and decay, tangible reminders of the havoc wrought upon this scarred landscape.

The conflict—yet another grim chapter in Sudan's turbulent history—pitted the Sudanese military against its paramilitary force, the Rapid Support Forces (RSF), also known as the Janjaweed. Rooted in political power struggles, ethnic tensions and resource disputes, the fighting had turned Khartoum, the capital city of Sudan, into a battlefield.

Wadi Seidna, a desolate airfield 22 kilometres away from the capital, became a refuge during a brief seventy-two-hour ceasefire announced by the Sudanese government. This fragile window allowed foreign countries an opportunity to evacuate their citizens, turning the once-isolated Wadi Seidna[1] into a chaotic hub for rescue efforts—especially for those unable to reach Port Sudan from Khartoum.[2]

Amid the throngs of desperate souls were 118 Indian nationals, clinging to hope in the midst of this hell. Women wept uncontrollably, clutching their children tightly, their tears catching the dim light, glistening like tiny beacons of despair. The elderly, frail and exhausted, huddled together for support, their eyes scanning the crowd for any sign of salvation. Amidst this chaos stood Sudanese military personnel—an ominous force.

Few nations had the aircraft or the resolve to carry out a rescue mission in the darkness of an already volatile Sudan. India was among the few that could.

---

1 Many people from various countries, unable to travel the 816 km from the capital city of Khartoum to Port Sudan, had taken refuge at Wadi Seidna—an old airbase located just twenty-two kilometres from Khartoum—hoping to be evacuated, even though their own nations were not running rescue sorties because during the ceasefire, a few countries were conducting evacuation operations from this site, India being one among them.
2 Port Sudan, a port city on the Red Sea in eastern Sudan, was the main hub for evacuations by different nations, including India. Meanwhile, Khartoum—the capital—remained the epicentre of the civil war.

The crowd of desperate people from different nations continued to grow.

The Sudanese soldiers, rigid and unyielding, did what they could to control the masses. They barked orders in harsh tones, their voices adding to the pandemonium. Anyone who dared approach the barricades was met with the brutal force of rifle butts, the sharp crack of metal against flesh echoing through the night. Cries of pain and fear intermingled, creating a symphony of chaos. Children screamed, their high-pitched wails piercing the air. Some clung to their mothers, their tiny fingers digging into fabric. The ground was littered with discarded belongings—bags, shoes and personal items—hastily abandoned in the scramble for safety. People jostled against each other, their movements frantic and uncoordinated, driven by the primal instinct to survive.

In this hellish scene, the distant sound of an approaching aircraft provided a glimmer of hope. The roar of engines grew louder, cutting through the chaos.

It was a Lockheed Martin C-130J Super Hercules of the Indian Air Force.

It arrived as a beacon of hope in the midst of turmoil. In the cockpit, the tension was palpable as the pilots pushed the limits of tactical flying, attempting a daring landing in complete darkness, battling turbulence and bad weather. Meanwhile, the Garud Special Forces on board prepared for the unknown threats ahead.

None of them knew what awaited them on the ground—whether enemies lurked in the darkness, ready to fire upon the aircraft, jeopardizing not only the safety of the aircrew but also the aircraft itself. Yet, each one of them was willing to risk it all for their brothers, for the mission, for India. Families were awaiting the safe return of their fathers, mothers, sons, daughters and loved ones.

That was the mission: Operation Kaveri, launched to bring stranded Indian nationals home from Sudan.

The daring rescue at the Wadi Seidna Airbase was part of this operation, during which 118 Indian nationals and three Sudanese citizens were safely evacuated—part of a total of 4,097 Indians rescued (including 136 foreign nationals).

The Wadi Seidna mission stands as one of the Indian Air Force's most daring rescues, etched forever in the nation's legacy.

Khartoum
15 April 2023

Ghan Sham, an Indian citizen, was selling oil with his brother in the central market area of Khartoum when, suddenly, he heard gunshots. Before he could understand what was happening, he saw people shouting and running in his direction. Someone yelled, 'Take cover! Take cover! Danger!' Driven by the primal urge for survival, he ducked behind a pillar, his brother alongside him.

Ghan Sham and his brother belonged to the Hakka Pakki tribe[3] from Karnataka and had been staying in Khartoum for the past five months to sell their herbal oil. As they took cover, they could clearly hear the rattling of bullets and the blasts of grenades. Their hearts pounded as a Sudanese soldier approached with his gun pointed at them.

In desperation, Ghan Sham shouted, 'Indian! Indian!'

---

3 'Explained: Who are the Hakka Pakki tribe stranded in Sudan?' *Deccan Herald*, 23 April 2023, Available at: https://www.deccanherald.com/india/karnataka/explained-who-are-the-hakka-pakki-tribe-stranded-in-sudan-1212222.html#:~:text=But%20who%20are%20the%20Hakki,of%20bird%20catchers%20and%20hunters.

Their identity seemed to have a magical effect on the soldier, who then escorted them safely to a nearby hotel and advised them to remain inside, warning them that it was no longer safe to venture out.

They were not the only ones caught in the chaos. The grim situation had engulfed the city, home to over 6 million people, including thousands of foreign nationals from around the world, many from India among them. In addition to the 1,500-strong Indian diaspora in Sudan—which dates back 150 years[4]—Indian nationals frequently visited the Sudan for work, family visits or tourism. At the time, an estimated 4,000 were in the country, all of them suddenly facing grave danger when the Battle of Khartoum began on 15 April 2023, plunging the nation into conflict.[5]

The violence erupted after days of mounting tension reached a breaking point. Members of the Rapid Support Force (RSF)[6] were redeployed across the country—a move perceived by the Sudanese armed forces as a direct threat.

In response, the army took decisive action, and soon the entire city of Khartoum was engulfed in heavy artillery fire. Military jets roared overhead, while armoured vehicles rumbled through the streets.[7]

The once-bustling city was transformed into a war zone. Relentless firefights and grenade blasts claimed hundreds of lives, many of them

---

4 Embassy of India, Khartoum, SUDAN, 'Indian Diaspora in Sudan', Available at: https://eoikhartoum.gov.in/indian-diaspora-in-sudan.php#:~:text=The%20settled%20Indian%20community%20in,Aden%20in%20the%20early%201860s.

5 After the crisis and ensuing violence in Sudan, the Indian diaspora in the country dropped to just around 100 people.

6 The Rapid Support Force is Sudan's paramilitary organization, which was fighting against the Sudanese Armed Forces.

7 As the conflict was between Sudan's own paramilitary and military forces, the nation was in the midst of a civil war.

civilians. The battle for control of key installations—including the capital's airport—was fierce and unfolded in densely populated urban areas, making civilians unwitting victims. Civilian airplanes were set ablaze, and air force strikes targeted RSF bases, which had been strategically moved to residential neighbourhoods, resulting in even more civilian casualties. Those who could, locked their doors, turned off their lights and huddled indoors. Many others, caught in transit, found themselves trapped as bridges and roads were barricaded and schools went into lockdown.

Fear and panic swept through the population. It was a tragic irony that those charged with their protection were now the source of their greatest danger. The streets of Khartoum, once lively and vibrant, became scenes of chaos and devastation.

Ghan Sham shared with me how the militia fired live ammunition at the house next door, forcing him and his brother to cower in fear. The intense conflict persisted for days, leaving entire neighbourhoods in Khartoum destroyed and abandoned, as over a million residents fled.

This April conflict was the latest episode in the ongoing tensions that following the 2019 ousting of long-serving President Omar al-Bashir.[8] A deepening rift between the country's military and paramilitary forces had left Sudan without a functioning government since October 2021, when the military dismissed Prime Minister Abdalla Hamdok's transitional government and declared a state of emergency—a move decried by political forces as a 'coup'.

---

8   Rachel Savage, 'Sudan's civil war: how did it begin, what is the human cost, and what is happening now?', *The Guardian*, 22 March 2024, https://www.theguardian.com/global-development/2024/mar/22/what-caused-the-civil-war-in-sudan-and-how-has-it-become-one-of-the-worlds-worst-humanitarian-crises.

The sudden eruption of violence during the onging civil war posed a grave threat to the safety of foreigners stranded in Sudan, including Indian nationals.

The Prime Minister of India, Sri Narendra Damodardas Modi contacted the minister of external affairs, Dr Subrahmanyam Jaishankar, to confirm that a crisis management plan was in place and to ensure that Indian ambassadors were reaching out to the concerned nations. The prime minister also inquired whether the Indian Air Force and Indian Navy had been placed on standby.

Just days earlier, at an event, Dr Jaishankar had highlighted India's proactive foreign policy in evacuating nationals during global crises, reaffirming the government's commitment to standing by its citizens.

He famously said: 'When you leave the borders of India and go out into the world, go with full confidence that the Indian government is standing with you. A country that abandons its people will never earn respect.'[9]

While travelling during the crisis, Dr Jaishankar met with United Nations Secretary-General António Guterres in New York to seek the United Nations' assistance in ensuring the well-being and evacuation of nearly 4,000 Indian citizens stranded in Sudan.[10]

Upon his return to India, he joined National Security Advisor Sri Ajit Doval, KC and other senior officials in a high-level meeting chaired by the prime minister. There, the prime minister instructed

---

9 ANI, 'When you leave borders, go with full confidence, govt is standing with you: Jaishankar assures safe return home for Indians worldwide, *Economic Times*, 3 April 2024, https://economictimes.indiatimes.com/news/india/when-you-leave-the-borders-go-with-full-confidence-indian-government-is-standing-with-you-s-jaishankar-assures-safe-return-home-for-indians-worldwide/articleshow/108979371.cms?utm_source=contentofinterest&utm_medium=text&utm_campaign=cppst

10 https://thewire.in/diplomacy/sudan-on-transit-visit-through-new-york-jaishankar-meets-un-secretary-general

officials to prepare contingency plans for the evacuation, given the rapidly deteriorating security situation.

This directive mobilized the entire governmental machinery. India began coordinating closely with partner countries to ensure the safe evacuation of its citizens.

Meanwhile, the MEA reached out to the Indian community in Khartoum, through both formal and informal channels, issuing several advisories. A 24/7 dedicated control room was established to provide information and assistance to Indians stranded in Sudan. Despite the volatile situation, MEA personnel—both in India and abroad—worked tirelessly to make this possible.

MEA spokesperson Sri Arindam Bagchi later revealed that they had received over 100 calls within the first twenty-four hours. While challenging, this effort was instrumental in preparing a verified list of Indian citizens requiring evacuation from the conflict-torn country, amid the millions affected by the crisis.[11]

Initially, at the request of the Indian government, a few friendly nations evacuated several hundred Indians. However, this was not enough, as thousands more remained stranded in the country amidst rapidly changing and volatile conditions.

India eventually deployed its own assets,[12] positioning them at Port Sudan—approximately 850 kilometres from Khartoum, the epicentre of the conflict—and began its rescue operations.

Port Sudan, equipped with both an airport and a port, emerged as the most viable evacuation hub for rescuing stranded Indians. The Saryu-class Indian Navy vessel, *INS Sumedha*, brought 278 people in

---

11 ANI, 'India in continuous touch with Indians in Sudan, says S Jaishankar', *Business Standard*, 21 April 2023, https://www.business-standard.com/india-news/india-in-continuous-touch-with-indians-in-sudan-says-s-jaishankar-123042100047_1.html.

12 These assets were Indian Navy ships and Indian Air Force aircraft.

its first batch, transporting them from Port Sudan to Jeddah.[13] From there, the massive C-17 Globemasters and some commercial flights flew evacuees back to India in non-stop long-haul flights—sortie after sortie.

The Indian Navy's warship *INS Teg*—the fourth Talwar-class frigate[14]—also joined the operation to bolster the ongoing evacuation efforts. However, even this was not enough. Many individuals stranded in Khartoum, unable to reach Port Sudan, were in grave danger and needed immediate extraction.

Here, the Indian Air Force was called in.

In a high-level meeting, then Chief of the Air Staff (CAS), ACM[15] Vivek Ram Chaudhari, along with AM[16] Amar Preet Singh, the then Vice Chief of the Air Staff (VCAS), reviewed the Government of India's directive to evacuate Indian citizens stranded in Sudan. As head of Air Force operations, the VCAS swiftly activated all necessary verticals, coordinating intelligence, logistics and operational strategies. Reporting directly to the CAS, who liaised with the

---

13 https://www.aninews.in/news/world/asia/operation-kaveri-first-batch-of-278-stranded-indians-reaches-jeddah-second-leaves-port-sudan20230426020253/'Operation Kaveri': First batch of 278 stranded Indians reaches Jeddah, second leaves Port Sudan/ 26 april 2023 / aninews
14 A type of warship. The role of a modern frigate ship is to protect other ships of the fleet, merchant marine ships, amphibious expeditionary forces and so on from threats emanating from the sea, specially from submarines. It is thus accordingly fitted with a variety of sensors and weapons.
15 Air Chief Marshal
16 Air Marshal; equivalent to Lieutenant General in the Army, and Vice Admiral in the Navy.

Ministry of Defence. The senior hierarchy and structure ensured seamless execution.

'The situation in Sudan was uniquely challenging,' recounted Air Vice Marshal S. Srinivasan, then Assistant Chief of Air Staff Operations (Transport and Helicopter) and nodal officer for the Indian Air Force's HADR operations.

'I've led evacuations in Yemen, Iraq, Afghanistan and Ukraine, but Sudan's crisis brought unprecedented uncertainty. Few nations dared attempt an evacuation due to limited resources or lack of will. It was the resolve of the Indian government and the Indian Air Force that made Operation Kaveri possible. The risks of aircraft being targeted were high, the ground situation was dire, and communication channels were scarce. Even before the prime minister's meeting, we had contingency plans ready, anticipating the IAF would be called upon.'

The CAS had, in fact, submitted a tentative action plan to the Ministry of Defence, which was subsequently shared with the MEA ahead of the prime minister's high-level meeting. This groundwork helped the prime minister to make an informed decision about deploying Indian aircraft, despite the risks to both personnel and assets.

Then, after the prime minister's green signal to evacuate every Indian willing to leave Sudan, the CAS convened a high-level meeting at Air Headquarters. Senior officers were briefed on the mandate, and two C-130J Super Hercules aircraft were also deployed to commence the mission. The resolute decisions taken by the highest levels of the Indian Air Force leadership resonated like a clarion call, and the plans were communicated to the Indian government.

On 24 April 2023, the Minister of External Affairs Dr S. Jaishankar announced the launch of Operation Kaveri and tweeted:

Operation Kaveri gets underway to bring back our citizens stranded in Sudan. About 500 Indians have reached Port Sudan. More on their way. Our ships and aircraft are set to bring them back home. Committed to assisting all our brethren in Sudan.[17]

In addition to deploying its transport aircraft fleet, the IAF appointed AVM S. Srinivasan as the nodal officer for the operation. Simultaneously, the Director Garud was tasked with assigning elite Garud Special Forces to accompany each aircraft launched during the mission. The Garud—known for their lethality and expertise—are never deployed lightly. Their presence is reserved for situations where the threat is high, and this mission was no exception.

Closely monitoring the unfolding crisis in Sudan, the Director was deeply moved by harrowing visuals of families fleeing violence and facing genocide. As a father of three daughters and a devoted husband, he felt a deep empathy for those stranded, desperate to reunite them with their loved ones.

The senior leadership at Air HQ faced the formidable challenge of aligning every detail before the aircraft could take off. The mission required flying over several countries before reaching Sudan, and each overflight required prior clearance—a complex process managed by the MEA in coordination with its embassies in the respective regions. Time constraints further complicated matters, as all clearances had to be obtained before the scheduled departure.

---

[17] https://economictimes.indiatimes.com/nri/latest-updates/india-launches-operation-kaveri-to-evacuate-its-nationals-from-sudan/articleshow/99733068.cms?from=mdr/ Apr 25, 2023,/ India launches Operation Kaveri to evacuate its nationals from Sudan

Furthermore, many of the soldiers did not have passports—these were prepared in just a few hours. Putting everything together within a very short timeframe, while ensuring that the soldiers on the ground could focus on their tasks, was a true test of senior leadership. And, the MEA, IAF and various concerned bureaucrats delivered precisely what was asked of them.

Meanwhile, the crew was briefed and began preparing for take-off. Everyone was racing against the clock, knowing they had little time, as the situation in Sudan was rapidly deteriorating, putting the lives of stranded Indians at even greater risk.

As soon as the approvals came through, AVM Srinivasan recalled how various documents along with the Government of India's authorizations, were physically handed to the crew moments before departure.

> He remarked, 'For three days, we didn't return home, and slept in our chairs. But what stood out was the cohesion and coordination among various defence departments, bureaucracies and ministries working tirelessly around the clock to make this happen.'

The volatile situation in Sudan posed significant risks to aircraft and personnel, but the Indian Air Force did not hesitate.

This wasn't the first time they had been called into action on short notice. Their evacuation operations in Nepal, Yemen, Gaza, Sudan and Afghanistan, and numerous other such crisis zones, had already demonstrated the IAF's unwavering commitment to serve the nation—well beyond the call of duty.

Indian Air Force Station, Hindon
Uttar Pradesh
April 2023

Amid the unfolding Sudan crisis, clarity remained elusive as new information flooded in by the second, forcing authorities to revise plans constantly.

> One of the pilots involved in the mission recounted: 'During the Sudan rescue, uncertainties were rife. We didn't know the condition of the Khartoum runway—smooth or damaged—weather conditions, external threat assessment, airfield condition, ATC conduct, etc. Initially, there was talk of landing at Khartoum airport [as] the majority of Indians [were] stranded there in the capital city, but the ground situation was a blank. Could they fire at us? Launch a missile upon touchdown? Our reaction time in emergencies is critical, so we plan every step from flying the aircraft, to landing to even our back-up plans beforehand to gain us quick reaction time, but with the unfolding chaos in Sudan there was no clarity about anything.'

The Garud faced the same challenges. Normally, they arm themselves based on ground reports to protect the aircraft, crew and evacuees. However, the situation in Sudan was unfolding with relentless unpredictability. Reports streamed in of grenade blasts, militias seizing military installations, and haunting images of burning aircraft and buildings engulfed in thick, grey smoke. Civilians were seen carrying MANPADS (man-portable air-defence systems),[18]

---

[18] A man-portable air-defence system is a lightweight, shoulder-launched weapon designed to protect soldiers on the battlefield from attacking aircraft. In the volatile situation in Sudan, where national forces were

rocket launchers and firearms, desperately seeking escape routes amidst the chaos.

When your job is to safeguard lives and avert a national crisis, unknown variables like these are daunting—even for professional soldiers trained to handle contingencies. Meticulous planning, well-chosen equipment and exceptional human skill are the cornerstones of mission success.

Here, the Indian Air Force was tasked with venturing into a war-torn foreign country amid reports of mass genocide and the displacement of millions. Their mission was to locate thousands of Indian nationals scattered among millions of desperate civilians and bring them home safely, all while ensuring the safety of their aircraft and crew in an extremely volatile country.

The tension was palpable, but the resolve of these brave souls was unwavering.

Every airfield in Sudan had been shut down, so the Indian Air Force, working closely with the MEA, mapped the closest and safest routes to Sudan. The initial plan was to assess the situation and then fly to Khartoum, the capital, to evacuate the Indians. Each aircraft was accompanied by detachments of Garud Special Forces. The Commanding Officer of the No. 81 Squadron, the 'Sky Lords', Group Captain Sameep Nijhawan,[19] was tasked with deploying massive C-17 Globemasters for the critical mission.

---

firing at each other, many Sudanese civilians carried weapons and equipment to protect themselves or to exploit the chaos by attacking and looting others, including foreign nationals. These weapons posed a grave threat to any aircraft attempting to land.

19 Group Captain Sameep Nijhawan received a Mention in Despatches for gallantry during Operation Kaveri.

One of the urgent calls from Air HQ was received by a young Garud CO, Squadron Leader Pritam Singh Jaitawat,[20] who commanded the lethal 612 Garud flight.[21] He was training with the US Air Force's Special Forces at Panagarh when he received the call from the Director Garud,[22] instructing him to immediately join his flight at Hindon Airbase.

The thirty-one-year-old CO from Rajasthan, set out by road from Kalaikunda to Kolkata Airport at 2300 hours and took a flight the next morning, reaching Hindon by 0900 hours. Upon his arrival at Hindon, the overall Garud Mission Component Coordinator—CO of another Garud Flight with the call sign 'Jaggi', who was senior to Jaitawat—briefed him on the mission objective.

Meanwhile, on the pilot's side, one of the calls was received by Wing Commander[23] Rajneesh Chandra Uniyal,[24] a transport pilot specializing in flying the C-130J Super Hercules.

Coincidentally, he too was training with the US Air Force during the bilateral air exercise at Panagarh. Wing Commander Uniyal quickly wrapped up and boarded a service aircraft, arriving at Hindon by 0200 hours. There, his Flight Commander informed him to be ready for departure at any time after the morning briefing.

The situation in Sudan was deteriorating rapidly.

---

20 The rank of Squadron Leader in the Indian Air Force is equivalent to the rank of Major in the Army and Lieutenant Commander in the Navy.
21 Garud units are called Garud flights.
22 The Head of the Directorate of Garud is an administrative officer holding the rank of Group Captain. He is also referred to as 'Group Captain Garud' or 'D Guard'. He serves as the highest representative of the Garud Special Forces at Air Headquarters.
23 Equivalent to a Lieutenant Colonel in the Army and a Commander in the Navy
24 Wing Commander Uniyal later received a Mention in Despatches for his contributions to Operation Kaveri.

One Indian national had already been killed in the skirmishes, and thousands were posting videos of themselves hiding without food for days, pleading for immediate evacuation by the Indian government.

During the early morning briefing, all crew components gathered in the mission planning room of No. 77 Squadron (Veiled Vipers). This included pilots, combat systems operators, loadmasters, the flight commander and the CO, Group Captain Ravi Nanda—earlier awarded with a Vayu Sena medal while rescuing Indians from Afghanistan in August 2021 as part of Operation Devi Shakti. He was a highly qualified and exceptional Commanding Officer.

A meticulous crew planning session ensued.

Wing Commander Rajneesh Chandra Uniyal shared:

The situation in Sudan was fluid and changing rapidly. As a result, it was difficult to predict how many aircraft or how many missions would have to be executed. So, we decided to have double sets of aircrew on each aircraft. There was a high probability of flying the aircraft 24/7, so reserve crew members were selected to replace the fatigued crew. The CO handpicked each one of us based on our expertise in special operations. Since we had no time to plan meticulously, we could only rely on our training and past experience. There were pilots who had flown during Operation Devi Shakti in Afghanistan, Operation Raahat in Yemen, and many other such foreign operations.

He paused before stating further, 'there were too many unknowns, so the CO ensured maximum crew deployment. Even with our best planning, each pilot had to fly straight for many hours under distressful conditions, and flying with a fatigued mind is not advised.'

He concluded with a smile:

'You see, the aircraft has no limitations, but humans do.'

The morning briefing ended with urgent orders to leave immediately.

All crew members rushed to change into their flying uniforms, preparing for a risky mission. Wing Commander Uniyal quickly took out his mobile phone and typed a brief message to his wife. He informed her that he might be away on a long mission and would return after several weeks.

However, he deliberately withheld the fact that he was being deployed to war-torn Sudan. The horrifying visuals on television were reason enough to spare her added anxiety. He knew it was not easy being a pilot's wife, living on the edge every time he took his aircraft high into the sky. The news that he was now flying amidst missiles and airstrikes would only deepen her distress.

He put the phone away. *Later, once I return, I'll tell her everything*, he thought, rushing to the aircrew gear room, which was already buzzing with activity.

Within moments, he had donned his flying overalls, zipped up his boots and was ready to go.

His squadron patches flashed in all their glory: The one on the right reading 'Kargil Knights', marking his squadron's exceptional night landing in Kargil; another featuring a vicious-looking snake with the motto 'Strike to Kill', representing the squadron of the Veiled Vipers. The full Air Force wings above it signified he was a flying pilot. On his right arm, a patch bearing 'IAF SPECIAL OPS' alongside the silhouette of a C-130J Super Hercules reflected his participation in risky special operations with the Super Hercules.[25]

---

25 Aviators are renowned for the distinctive Velcro badges and patches on their uniforms, indicating their squadrons, expertise and various achievements. These patches serve as their identification tags.

With his 'flying bag' containing all essential documents, he moved towards the tarmac along with the rest of the crew. The vast concrete expanse, surrounded by lush greenery, gleamed in the morning light—a sight that never failed to stir his soul. The mighty C-130Js were lined up, one after the other, as Mi-17 helicopters flew overhead and ground staff in fluorescent vests bustled about in a flurry of activity.

He admired his first love, the mighty C-130J Super Hercules, the Special Operations aircraft he was about to board.

A source of national pride, the C-130J Super Hercules—crafted by the American aerospace company Lockheed Martin—epitomized cutting-edge aviation technology, solidifying its status as a cornerstone of military capability.[26]

Boarding of the C-130J had begun.

Pilots, clad in their crisp flight suits adorned with squadron insignias, strode purposefully towards the waiting aircraft. Each step resonated with a quiet confidence, a testament to their training and readiness.

Garud Special Forces operatives, their uniforms a blend of camouflage and tactical gear, moved with calculated efficiency, their eyes scanning the horizon with unwavering focus. Around them, ground crews completed final checks under the watchful gaze of senior officers, ensuring every detail was meticulously attended to. Amid the hum of engines warming up and the sharp tang of aviation fuel in the air, the C-130Js stood as silent sentinels of national resolve.

The loading ramps closed with a decisive thud, and the pilots requested permission to taxi from air traffic control (ATC) at Hindon Airbase.

---

26 Find more about the C-130J aircraft in the last chapter of this book, 'The Might of the Indian Air Force'.

'India Foxtrot Charlie 4019 to ATC.'

'ATC to India Foxtrot Charlie 4019—go ahead.'

'India Foxtrot Charlie 4019 requesting taxi.[27] POB 40.[28]'

The pilots taxied out for some distance, ensuring they were clear of other aircraft, then contacted ATC for the final take-off.

'ATC. India Foxtrot Charlie 4019 is ready for take-off.'

'India Foxtrot Charlie 4019. You are clear for take-off,' came the final approval by ATC.

All checks complete, the pilot applied full power, released the brakes, and the aircraft began accelerating down the runway. As it reached the necessary speed, the pilots pulled back on the flight controls, and the aircraft lifted gracefully into the air.

International Airport
Close to Sudan
24 April 2023

As the Indian Air Force C-130J Super Hercules touched down at the foreign airbase,[29] the setting sun bathed the Red Sea in a golden glow. The aircraft taxied smoothly, engines humming softly, guided by ground crews in fluorescent vests to a designated parking spot. In the

---

27 'Taxi' refers to the movement of an aircraft on the ground under its own power. This process is usually directed by air traffic control (ATC) to ensure safety and proper coordination on the airfield.
28 The number of persons on board (POB) is forty.
29 The name of the airport cannot be published as the author was unable to connect with the concerned authorities of the particular foreign nation. However, details are available through open-source information.

cockpit, the pilots observed the bustling airport with a mix of relief and anticipation. Airport staff approached the craft for refuelling and logistical support. The air was heavy with the smell of jet fuel and the salty tang of the sea breeze—a reminder of the long journey still ahead. The immigration process was set to begin soon.

This landing marked a pivotal moment, a brief pause before their humanitarian mission continued towards Port Sudan amidst the nation's turmoil.

In the airport lounge, the aircrew met Indian Embassy officials. The embassy team quickly provided detailed updates to the group captains[30] about the ground situation, evacuation progress and certain protocols the crew needed to follow while operating on foreign soil.

Colonel Gurtej Singh Grewal, SC (now Brigadier),[31] the then Defence Attaché in that foreign nation, recalled, 'The situation was grim. We first received alarming reports on 15 April, when a commercial aircraft was shot down by small arms fire at Khartoum Airport. We immediately began closely monitoring the situation, gathering as much intelligence as possible to relay back to India.

However, within the next four or five days, the situation escalated rapidly. The Qatar Embassy was ransacked, an Egyptian diplomat was killed, and heavy fighting broke out near the Indian Embassy, close to Khartoum Airport. Such attacks on embassies were

---

30 A Group Captain is equivalent to a full Colonel in the Army. In this context, it refers to the Captains of both C-130J aircraft.
31 Col Gurtez Singh Grewal : https://www.aninews.in/news/world/middle-east/all-of-you-will-reach-home-safely-assures-indias-defence-attache-to-sudan-returnees-in-viral-video20230427040237/ All of you will reach home safely, assures India's Defence Attache to Sudan returnees in viral video/ANI

unprecedented. It was then decided to evacuate the entire Indian Embassy in Sudan.

He further shared that by then, the Ministry of External Affairs had set up a command centre in India, and Indian Navy ships and aircraft were deployed.

Reflecting on the difficulties, he said:

There was no clarity about the situation, no reliable information, and very little network coverage. When the first nations evacuated their citizens, we learnt from their reports about the nine-hour journey they undertook to reach Port Sudan from Khartoum, the numerous checkpoints they crossed, and the threats they faced. Many were shot at, and some were looted. The biggest challenge we faced was the lack of ground reports about the Port Sudan airport, where our aircraft were due to land.

He then recalled how, as soon as the Indian Navy ships arrived, he was sent to Port Sudan to assess the situation at the airport and determine whether it was feasible for Indian aircraft to land and streamline evacuation efforts amidst the volatile conditions in Sudan.

He further shared:

'It was when the C-130J aircraft were deployed on the mission on 24 April 2023 that the evacuation process was escalated.'

A seasoned army officer, Colonel Grewal was the one to receive the crew of the C-130J Super Hercules and give them a detailed briefing on the situation in Sudan. Meanwhile, MEA personnel at the embassy sent crucial information back to India. This interaction shaped the planning process, relying heavily on various civil and armed forces components.

The MEA team facilitated the Indian air crew's immigration formalities and secured suitable accommodation for their operations.

A joint planning cell (JPC) was established, comprising IAF personnel, the MEA team and local embassy staff. Embassy officials gathered local intelligence, set mission objectives, assisted with ground movements and created an operational corridor. MEA and IAF personnel worked tirelessly on their tactical computers, managing their respective assignments.

Meanwhile, the Intelligence Network Tasking Cell gathered and processed information, liaising with various embassies for daily and next-day tasking. Each team meticulously prepared data, compiling checklists of requirements and resources. For additional data gathering, the JPC also relied on open-source information—scouring platforms like X (formerly Twitter) and YouTube for updates, mapping airfields and assessing the ground situation.

Back in India, coordination with multiple agencies was essential. Dr Pradeep Singh Rajpurohit, Joint Secretary (West Asia and North Africa) at the MEA,[32] and AVM Srinivasan integrated the efforts of the MEA and Ministry of Defence, providing invaluable inputs and directives. The prime minister, external affairs minister, the Chief of the Air Staff and the Vice Chief of the Air Staff closely monitored the operation.

The Air Force pilots and crew charted their operational routes using data compiled by the JPC. The Garuds devised daily

---

32 'Transcript Of Special Briefing by Foreign Secretary On Operation Kaveri', Ministry of External Affairs of the Republic of India, Press Release, *Public,* 27 April 2023, https://www.publicnow.com/view/3B3C2735A2207BBC6DE22ACCC682AAB502BBC227?1682628322.

contingency and backup plans. In this dynamic situation, continuous adjustments were essential as new information emerged.

Initially hopeful for the reopening of Khartoum Airport—where many Indian nationals were stranded—the focus soon shifted to finding alternative airfields.

Meanwhile, Indian Navy ships and both C-130J aircraft continued evacuating Indians who managed to reach Port Sudan, to the International airport from where those evacuees were further airlifted by C-17 Globemasters straight to India in back to back many hour sorties. The Globemasters subsequently undertook operations to streamline the rescue chain.[33]

The JPC continued to wait as Sudanese airspace remained closed, and the situation deteriorated further. Many Indians were still trapped in Khartoum and surrounding areas. The distance between Khartoum, the epicentre of the conflict, and Port Sudan was approximately a two-day journey by road.

Indian embassies spared no effort, arranging around sixty to seventy buses to transport stranded Indians from Khartoum to Port Sudan for evacuation. Distressed Indian citizens reached out through MEA helplines and social media, with embassies coordinating to gather them at designated locations before boarding them on to buses.

This massive logistical operation was fraught with challenges at every step, from ensuring safety during transit to overcoming communication hurdles in the conflict zone.

The role of the Defence Attaché to Sudan, Lt Col Gurpreet Singh,[34] was especially commendable, as he managed, coordinated

---

33 https://timesofindia.indiatimes.com/india/operation-kaveri-first-batch-of-278-indians-evacuated-from-sudan-to-jeddah/articleshow/99769545.cms/April, 26 2023/

34 Lt Col Gurpreet SIngh : https://x.com/EoI_Khartoum/status/1654830450848718850 // India in Sudan @EoI_Khartoum

and negotiated amidst the chaos—even when his own pregnant wife was caught in the same dire situation.

Ghan Sham, who was eventually brought safely back to India along with his brother, recalled the harrowing experience:

> We were travelling in five buses, and ours was the last one without the Indian flag. Suddenly, we came under a hail of bullets. The windows shattered, and we all ducked for cover. Militia members boarded our buses, demanding money. They kicked and hit us with their rifle butts. When we revealed we were Indian citizens, they eventually let us go.

Being an Indian citizen in Sudan proved an advantage compared to citizens of other countries, whose governments were less actively involved. Even under grave threat to their own lives, officials at the Indian Embassy in Sudan acted as a liaison with all parties to ensure the safe passage for Indian nationals. However, travelling from Khartoum to Port Sudan remained extremely challenging. Many evacuees faced beatings, threats, and had to pay bribes to avoid dire consequences. Extortion at every checkpoint—whether controlled by the RSF or the military—was rampant. There was a severe scarcity of food and water, and airstrikes and reckless hailstorms of bullets were common occurrences.

Long-term Indian residents dealt with additional hurdles with expired visas and passports, increasing the workload on MEA authorities and delaying military evacuation efforts.

During the first flights into Port Sudan, the Indian Air Force was uncertain about the ground situation, given the rapidly changing situation. There was palpable apprehension. So, on those initial flights, the aircrew—including pilots and co-pilots—donned bulletproof jackets and helmets for protection.

The Garuds on board meticulously verified the Indian credentials of passengers before allowing them to board. They were prepared to respond to any contingency, securing and surrounding the aircraft to deal with any possible threats.

Meanwhile, the loadmaster[35] maintained vigilant oversight of the entire boarding process, while the maintenance crew diligently attended to their duties. The pilots often disembarked to scan the area.

Amidst the chaos, reports emerged that approximately 150 to 200 people, including Indian Embassy staff, remained stranded in Khartoum. By then, the road to Port Sudan had become off-limits due to the escalating intensity of the civil war, adding to the complications faced by those trying to escape.

Despite waiting for two to three days, warnings continued about the extreme dangers of attempting to land at Khartoum Airport, which lay at the centre of the conflict. Reports spoke of burning airplanes on the runways and significant damage, including craters caused by heavy blasts, posing a serious risk to the Indian rescue mission.

Flying to Khartoum was extremely dangerous.

Wing Commander Uniyal, who was involved in the mission shared:

> When operating in foreign territories, we're keenly aware of India's global reputation. The world looks to us, and the safety of our aircraft and crew is non-negotiable. Any compromise would be a major setback for Indian and military diplomacy. That's why we meticulously plan every mission. During the Sudan crisis,

---

[35] The loadmaster is responsible for properly loading, securing, and escorting cargo and passengers before a flight.

initial information was scarce, and ground reports were constantly changing.

Distressing videos kept surfacing, showing stranded Indians amidst the chaotic exodus from besieged Khartoum. Nations struggled to evacuate their citizens, with some videos even depicting civilians carrying weapons while attempting to escape. This was alarming and posed additional challenges as it became difficult to distinguish between genuine evacuees and potential threats.[36]

Despite ongoing attacks, evacuations continued from the safer coastal city of Port Sudan. However, entering the Sudanese mainland airspace remained perilous amidst the turmoil of various nations trying to evacuate their citizens.

The joint planning cell, growing increasingly concerned, took proactive measures to identify an alternative airfield while continuing to closely monitor the situation at the Khartoum airfield. Fortunately, they discovered an abandoned World War II–era military base—Wadi Seidna—in the desert near the Nile, just twenty-two kilometres from Khartoum, where many embassy staff and others were stranded. Once communication was established with the embassy staff, they confirmed that they could travel to the Wadi Seidna Airbase from Khartoum.

The discovery of an alternative air route brought relief, but it also placed heavy responsibility on the Air Force to ensure the success of the rescue mission. The airfield at Wadi Seidna was being used by the Sudanese military to carry out air strikes against the RSF. Reports indicated that RSF fighters, travelling in about twenty trucks, were

---

36 Some civilians hid weapons on their person, especially knives, which can pose a serious threat in the enclosed environment of an aircraft, particularly once airborne. Securing the aircraft was therefore amongst the top priorities of Garud operatives.

positioned east of the Nile and attempting to cross a bridge to reach the Wadi Seidna airfield.[37] The risk of an attack on the airbase was very real.

Meanwhile, news broke that a neighbouring foreign nation had brokered a deal between the Sudanese military and the RSF for a seventy-two-hour ceasefire—reportedly invested substantial financial incentives to persuade both sides.

Nevertheless, the ceasefire provided a crucial window for nations to swiftly evacuate their citizens. Sudan announced it would neither assist nor fire upon foreign aircraft during this period dedicated to evacuation efforts.

The Indian Air Force swiftly mobilized for evacuation operations. More and more people trapped in Khartoum began their arduous journey towards Port Sudan, where the Air Force would commence their rescue. The Defence Attaché in Sudan was working tirelessly on the ground, coordinating efforts.

Despite the ceasefire, renewed clashes erupted between the Sudanese Army and the RSF. Militias attacked American and other convoys. The Indian convoy also faced similar threats as it moved from Khartoum to Port Sudan.

The evacuees rescued from Port Sudan—bewildered and traumatized—were quickly flown back to India via non-stop flights by the C-17 Globemaster. Operations at Port Sudan continued in this manner during the seventy-two-hour ceasefire, while awaiting final approval to evacuate those stranded at Wadi Seidna.[38]

---

[37] Zeinab Mohammed Salih, 'Sudan conflict: Army fights to keep Wadi Saeedna airbase, residents say', BBC, 21 May 2023, https://www.bbc.com/news/world-africa-65662939.

[38] This included Indian nationals who were unable to join the convoys to Port Sudan but were able to reach Wadi Seidna.

While one C-130J Super Hercules continued with its sorties as planned, another was placed on standby for the potential mission to Wadi Seidna. However, the MEA withheld clearance, citing concerns about the aircraft's safety due to the ongoing dangers of flying over Sudanese airspace. Time was also needed to coordinate ground logistics.

Defence Attaché, Sudan was tasked with gathering as many Indian nationals as possible and facilitating their safe movement to Wadi Seidna ahead of the aircraft's arrival. This complex operation also included the evacuation of his own pregnant wife. One can only imagine the immense mental strain he must have endured—navigating a deteriorating ground situation, arranging vehicles, ensuring safe passage and coordinating the evacuation of every Indian citizen, all while working closely with the Sudanese authorities and carrying the additional worry for his wife's safety.

Finally, on the morning of 27 April, the green signal for Operation Wadi Seidna arrived. The ceasefire was set to end at midnight. This was their only chance to evacuate 118 Indian from the area.

It was now or never.

~

Wadi Seidna Airbase
Sudan
April 2023

The crew of the other C-130J aircraft, which had been kept on standby, received an urgent call from their Commanding Officer. Among them was Wing Commander Rajneesh Chandra Uniyal. The

CO informed them of a new operation requiring them to fly to Wadi Seidna to evacuate Indian nationals. Although the exact number was unclear, it was estimated to be around 150-200 people. He also briefed them that the Wadi Seidna Airbase might be damaged, under attack and that, given its proximity to Khartoum, they could encounter airstrikes while airborne.

The aircrew immediately began extensive mission planning, knowing they had to depart in the evening.

The pilots first addressed potential threats. There were many unknown variables they could face on the ground after landing, including the risk of being shot at or captured. The pilots discussed the aircraft self-defence system procedures with the combat systems operator to prepare for such contingencies.

They devised a clear plan for the controlled use of flares and chaff as a last resort to evade a missile strike. Next, they conducted a terrain analysis. There was no clarity on the condition of the runway.[39] Information about Wadi Seidna Airbase was scarce; they could only gather limited details from Google Earth, which showed it to be a basic, barren airstrip with a short runway and minimal air force infrastructure or ATC facilities. There were no fences, no ground crew and no guidance—just an old hangar.

Using coordinates from Google Earth, they planned how they would approach, land and park the aircraft safely. The pilots completed their terrain analysis with mission planning computers, charting the safest and quickest route to Wadi Seidna. To avoid potential airstrikes, they ruled out flying over cities or major roads

---

39 A lot of crashes and mishaps occur during landing.

in Sudanese airspace. The landing area was thoroughly examined for hazards such as mountains, hills, trees or buildings near the hangar that could pose crash risks on the short runway.

Their meticulous plan was then relayed to the CO, who in turn briefed his seniors. They also coordinated with the Defence Attaché, Sudan and shared their intended landing patterns. The Defence Attaché was tasked with initiating the evacuation only after the aircraft was safely parked.

Meanwhile, the Garuds were briefed on landing orientations and instructed to disembark quickly, bringing Indian nationals on to the aircraft from the ramp side within a strictly limited time frame. Any delay on their part could jeopardize the mission and potentially leave citizens behind.

The departure was scheduled for 1700 hours. Wing Commander Uniyal was assigned as the co-pilot alongside the legendary Group Captain Ravi Nanda,[40] the Commanding Officer of the Veiled Vipers No. 77 Squadron and captain of the aircraft for this historic flight. The mission plan was communicated to the Garuds, who immediately began preparing their gear.

Squadron Leader Pritam Singh Jaitawat, Commanding Officer of 612 Garud Flight and the Garud mission leader for Wadi Seidna, knew that his real mission would begin the moment the ramp opened. The operation ahead was unlike anything he had ever faced.

He shared with me:

---

40 https://www.aninews.in/news/national/general-news/group-captain-nanda-led-daring-rescue-ops-in-sudan-had-conducted-similar-action-in-kabul20230429225945/

I've operated in the valleys of Kashmir, facing life-and-death situations. But there, a safety net always existed—a brotherhood that ensured contingencies were handled. Backup would arrive if needed, military hospitals stood ready to treat the wounded, and in the worst-case scenario, my brothers would carry me home.

Even amidst danger, there was a structure, a system at my back. But here, in a foreign, war-torn land, those comforts were gone. [There were] no reinforcements waiting to swoop in, no familiar terrain to exploit, no guarantee of evacuation if things went south. The only certainty was uncertainty.

This was the ultimate test—an operation so risky it bordered on madness. The stakes were higher, the risks amplified and the isolation absolute.

He needed to brief his boys. They began preparing for the mission, discussing their course of action for when the ramp opened. Their precision, training and motto made them lethal, effective and fierce. Jaitawat exchanged radio frequencies with the aircraft captain to ensure secure communication lines.

At 1700 hours, the entire aircrew and the Garuds boarded the powerful C-130J Super Hercules. None of them knew the dangers that lay ahead in the conflict-ridden, collapsing state, yet they were ready to risk everything for their countrymen, their mission, the Air Force and the nation.

Their unwavering courage and selfless service immortalize them in the chronicles of the nation's history.

Later, I asked Squadron Leader Jaitawat if he had faced any qualms about embarking on such a risky mission on foreign soil, with no guarantees and no assurance of their safe return if anything went wrong. He replied:

There was absolutely no regret while boarding the plane because even if we could save a few families, it was worth every oath and every bit of training we've undertaken over the years. We are conditioned from the beginning, that the nation comes first! The Air Force comes first!

When I posed the same question to Wing Commander Uniyal, asking how it felt to fly such a risky mission with a wife and children waiting for him at home, he smiled and said:

My wife is braver than me. I know if anything happens to me, she [will] manage everything I leave behind. She is a pilot's wife whose heart hangs by a thread almost every day when I am up in the sky with my aircraft. I knew she would manage. She has always been a source of strength for me.

As the ramp was closing, preparing for take-off into unknown territory, dusk was approaching. *We will be landing in the dark*, the pilots thought.

Just as they were about to take off, an emergency call from the MEA forced them to delay the flight by half an hour.

Important coordination efforts for the safe evacuation of the Indian nationals were still underway—the evacuees had not yet reached Wadi Seidna, and parking the aircraft at the desolate airbase would have been too risky. This real-time information sharing stands as a testimony to the cooperation and professionalism of various departments.

As soon as the second clearance signal came, the pilots immediately took off.

The lone C-130J Super Hercules ventured into uncontrolled airspace through uncharted routes to reach Wadi Seidna. With no precise information on navigating Sudanese airspace under such volatile conditions—no established protocols, reliable routes or fixed drills—the situation was fraught with uncertainty.

During mission planning, however, the crew had discovered an open-source document that provided critical guidance. It detailed the optimal flight altitudes, operational frequencies and recommended routes for entering and exiting the perilous Sudanese airspace. This proved to be their best strategy to avoid potential collisions.

Driving a car requires skill and strict adherence to traffic regulations to prevent accidents. Similarly, aircraft rely on structured systems to ensure safe navigation in the skies. Flying in uncontrolled airspace, without substantial ground support or ATC monitoring, is akin to venturing into a cauldron of chaos.

Yet, the courageous IAF pilots willingly embraced this risk for the sake of their fellow countrymen.

They had prepared their flight plan based on open-source data, assuming that any other aircraft in the zone would also be following the same protocols. It was the best available option under the circumstances. The pilots still hoped to establish communication with other airborne platforms and Khartoum ATC to gather essential air traffic information. Upon reaching Port Sudan air space, they attempted to contact other aircraft using the frequencies provided in the open-source document:

'Any aircraft on this frequency, this is India Foxtrot Charlie 007.'

No response.

Despite several attempts, they were unable to establish contact with anyone. By then, they had flown a considerable distance from

Port Sudan and had also lost communication with the Port Sudan ATC.

It was a perplexing situation. The pilots' hearts raced as they navigated uncontrolled airspace blindly. Any aircraft could approach from any direction, risking mid-air collision. With no communication channels open, they were also vulnerable to missile attacks.

To make matters worse, they faced deteriorating weather conditions, with clouds reducing visibility and turbulence shaking the aircraft. As they gained altitude, temperatures dropped and ice began forming on the aircraft's leading edges and windshield. An aircraft cannot exceed its design limits; the pilots increased engine power to generate hot air to melt the ice but doing so reduced aircraft performance.

Amidst constant warnings of Level One and Level Two icing, pressure mounted. In desperation, they tried once again to reach Khartoum ATC but received no response.

Despite Sudanese assurances that rescue aircraft would not be targeted, there was no guarantee of assistance or even confirmation that Sudanese ATC personnel remained available during wartime.

The Indian pilots persisted:

'Khartoum ATC, this is India Foxtrot Charlie 007.'

Silence. They began making frantic blind calls to any aircraft in the area:

'Any aircraft, this is India Foxtrot Charlie 007 on this frequency.'

After several attempts, they finally reached another aircraft within range. It was the first contact they had made since becoming airborne, and brought them some relief.

'India Foxtrot Charlie 007, this is UK 2043. Go ahead.'

'UK 2043, this is India Foxtrot Charlie 007. We are proceeding to Wadi.'
'India Foxtrot Charlie 1007, confirm Wadi?'
'Affirmative,' the Indian pilots replied.
'India Foxtrot Charlie, Wadi Airbase is damaged …'

And then, abruptly, silence on the radio.

The pilots were left bewildered. They tried reconnecting on the same frequency but received no further response. It seemed the other aircraft had moved out of range again. It was a grave situation—flying blind, with no communication, and now, the one contact they had briefly established hinted that the airfield they were heading towards was damaged. It was a tense and uncertain moment.

Wing Commander Rajneesh Chandra Uniyal shared:

I've flown many challenging missions, but Wadi Seidna was unmatched. Everything seemed against us. Turning back felt like the safer choice, but the plight of the stranded Indians and our duty drove us to take tough calls. The Indian Air Force's rigorous training proved invaluable, equipping us to stay composed and handle the situation. As pilots, staying sharp and current is crucial—it's not just about us but managing the entire aircraft with precision, matching its speed and responses to the millisecond.

During the course of writing this book, I came to deeply understand that the failure of even a single mission is far more than a loss of resources—it affects the morale of the entire nation, undermines national security and hampers international diplomacy. Images of burning aircraft tarnish the reputation of a nation, leaving a lasting stigma on the global stage for decades. An advanced aircraft like the C-130J is a priceless national asset and a symbol of pride—the officers entrusted with these machines are the crème de la crème.

The pilots decided to refer to the open-source document once more. It stated that aircraft were required to contact Khartoum ATC before reaching Wadi Seidna, and if there was no response, the aircraft must not land but return. Eventually, both pilots agreed to follow the protocol but also decided to assess the ground situation at Wadi Seidna one last time. If conditions were favourable, they would land; if not, they would return.

Wing Commander Uniyal recounted:

We were flying at high altitude. Despite the uncertainty in airspace, there was a hunch that if we hadn't been shot down yet, no one would shoot us, at least in the air. We wanted to give this mission one last attempt. We were desperate to save those families. That's what we take an oath for—serving the nation.

As luck would have it, the UK aircraft once again came within range briefly and contacted the Indian crew:

UK 2043 to India Foxtrot Charlie 007, UK-C130 is operating on the ground in Wadi.

Wing Commander Uniyal grinned, his eyes sparking bright while talking to me:

'If the British could land there, then so could we. The news that a UK aircraft had successfully landed at Wadi airfield further boosted our confidence.'

Since Khartoum ATC had still not responded, the pilots made a tactical decision to change their route. Knowing no help was coming, and relying solely on training and instinct, they had to act decisively.

Even though there was no response to their calls, they knew others could have heard them, could possibly be waiting for an opportunity to target the aircraft. It could have been fringe elements, the militia, or even someone in control of the ATC at that moment.[41]

Multiple aircraft had already been shot down during the civil war. So, the pilot deviated from the pre-planned route and flew straight to Wadi Seidna—it was their best option.

When they reached Wadi Seidna, it was completely dark. There was no moonlight, no starlight and no illumination from nearby areas—the lights had likely been turned off for safety. The crew activated advanced night vision systems of the C-130J, which cast a green glow across the cockpit screens. Even with these systems, visibility remained severely limited.

Landing required careful movements—slowing down and braking at just the right moment—but it was tough to see clearly. The combat systems operator (CSO) took control. Using his equipment and training, he guided the pilots, staying alert for any threats or obstacles. His expertise helped bolster the team's confidence in the aircraft and in the crew's abilities.

'Fifty miles to land,' the CSO's voice resonated in the cockpit. The pilots swiftly executed drills appropriate for that altitude.

---

[41] Zeinab Mohammed Salih, Ruth Michaelson and Michael Savage, 'Sudanese army blocks Britons from boarding last rescue flights', *The Guardian*, 29 April 2023, https://www.theguardian.com/world/2023/apr/29/sudanese-army-blocks-britons-from-boarding-last-rescue-flights#:~:text=Britons%20are%20feared%20to%20have,war%2Dtorn%20country%20on%20Saturday.

'Twenty miles to land… Ten miles to land,' the CSO continued, prompting immediate action from the pilots.

Despite being only eight miles out, neither the runway nor any lights were visible through the night vision goggles (NVGs) or the naked eye. Uncertainty loomed until the CSO's voice broke the tension once more.

'Pilots, CSO—LZ[42] twelve o'clock.'

A wave of relief swept through the cockpit as the pilots realized they had a clear path ahead. Communication continued over hot mics as they manoeuvred through the landing approach, guided by the CSO, who used the C-130J's sophisticated equipment to map a safe landing path.

'Runway okay, minor irregularities, degraded runway, anticipate rough landing!' came the CSO's next update.

Despite the runway's imperfections, knowing that they could land the aircraft boosted the pilots' confidence. Descending in total darkness, the runway remained invisible even at two miles out. Only at 300 to 400 feet above ground level did patches of the runway become faintly visible. With no guiding lights, they prepared for touchdown, needing to execute the flare manoeuvre[43] to slow the aircraft's descent and avoid a crash landing.

Once again, the CSO played a crucial role. Guiding them on altitude, he cued the pilots to flare at the right moment. The aircraft

---

42 Landing zone.
43 The purpose of the flare manoeuvre is to reduce the vertical speed of the aircraft to ensure a smooth and controlled landing.

touched down safely. It was only when they felt the wheels meet the ground that the rest of the crew realized they had successfully landed in pitch-black conditions.

The pilots immediately taxied and parked the aircraft with engines running, minimizing the risk of mechanical issues and reducing turnaround time. With the night vision system still active and the ramp open, it was time for the Garuds to begin their ground operations.

~

As soon as the ramp opened, the Garuds leapt onto the ground. Bulletproof helmets fitted with Picatinny rails and mounted night vision devices adorned their heads. Elbow and knee pads protected their joints, while tactical vests[44] were strapped tightly over their digital camo-patterned uniforms.

Squadron Leader Pritam Singh Jaitawat, CO 612 Garud flight checked his Garmin GPS watch—they had only two hours to complete the mission and safely escort the Indian nationals back to the aircraft. Surveying his boys, he saw calm, focused faces.

Good, he thought.

The CO was acutely aware of how, during Operation Devi Shakti in Afghanistan just a few years ago, herds of people had rushed towards the aircraft. He needed to secure the perimeter quickly. He immediately formed buddy pairs and assigned some of them to perimeter security.

Then, Jaitawat and his buddy, Sergeant Vikas Tiwari, moved out for reconnaissance. In the pitch-darkness, devoid of even distant light, they felt disoriented. There was no designated contact person

---

44 A tactical vest is a protective vest, often bullet-resistant, worn on the upper body by soldiers or law enforcement personnel to safeguard the chest and back.

on the ground, no one to guide them to the evacuees. Relying on their NVGs and torches, they moved forward uncertainly. After walking some distance, they spotted a flicker of light about 400 to 500 metres away.

Ray of hope. Could be a threat. Need to inform the Captain, Jaitawat thought.

He radioed Group Captain Nanda, requesting him to exit the aircraft. Returning to the C-130J, Jaitawat briefed the Group Captain about the distant light and the need for further investigation. He also updated him on the Garuds deployed to safeguard the aircraft and outlined their contingency plans.

Taking two more Garuds with him, Jaitawat set out to search for the evacuees. Adjusting their approach in accordance with the Rules of Engagement applicable in a foreign nation, they left behind heavy gear and carried only essential equipment in their backpacks—radio sets for communication.

On the other side of the story, Defence Attaché, Sudan Lieutenant Colonel Gurpreet Singh had undertaken a challenging journey to reach the airfield with the group of Indian evacuees, one of whom was his pregnant wife. They crossed numerous checkpoints, navigating firefights and other threats along the way. Having coordinated at multiple levels to ensure the safety of their convoy of buses, they were expected to arrive just moments before the C-130J.

Air HQ was monitoring both the aircraft and the evacuees to ensure their arrival was synchronized under these precarious conditions. However, upon reaching the Wadi Seidna airfield, the indian evacuees were stopped by local authorities. The airfield was being jointly managed by the British and Sudanese military, and neither party was willing to allow them entry due to overcrowding.

After a tense half-hour delay, Lt Col Singh's persistence paid off, and he was able to get the convoy inside. This delay was the reason for the temporarily stalled flight clearance for the C-130J,[45] as permissions were withheld until the situation on the ground was confirmed.

Eventually, senior officials from the MEA and the IAF back home were able to coordinate with all parties involved in the evacuation and align them within a unified time frame.

It is worth noting that their Indian identity played a crucial role in convincing both the British and the Sudanese authorities to allow the evacuees through. We must thank the excellent work of the MEA under Dr S. Jaishankar and the global image of India in today's times.

Meanwhile, Squadron Leader Jaitawat was approaching the distant light. Tactically, this move carried risks, but time was running out—only a few hours remained before the ceasefire was set to end.

There was no one in sight, and their phones had lost connectivity. Contacting the source of the light was crucial to assessing the situation swiftly.

As they drew closer, they realized the light was coming from an aircraft. Without knowledge of its radio frequencies, they couldn't initiate contact using their radio sets. Jaitawat decided to signal with his torch, flashing it tactically towards the aircraft. It was crucial to avoid triggering a defensive response.

The response came in kind—two flashes, signalling acknowledgment. This was repeated several times, after which Jaitawat and his team cautiously approached the aircraft, ensuring

---

45 There was no question of the aircraft waiting for the evacuees, given the risk of remaining airborne during an active civil war. Several aircraft from different nations had been shot down during this period.

both sides recognized each other as friendly forces before closing the distance.

It turned out to be the same UK aircraft that had come within radio range during their inbound flight.

The Garud CO approached a foreign soldier to inquire about their identity.

The officer replied:

'We're UK Special Forces. This is our aircraft, and we're waiting for our citizens to board. There are some issues with their passports and visas, and the necessary clearances haven't been issued yet. We plan to depart as soon as possible.'

At that time, the British were managing the airfield under an agreement with the Sudanese military and had assisted with airbase repairs.[46]

The UK Special Forces briefed the Garuds on the ground situation. They explained that a large crowd had gathered about 600 to 700 metres ahead. Some British soldiers were manning a small checkpoint in that area, followed by another checkpoint controlled by the Sudanese military. Temporary tactical barriers had been erected, and amidst the chaos were people of various nationalities, making it difficult to locate their own citizens. With the ceasefire nearing its end, there was no assurance that gunfire wouldn't erupt before then.

The air was thick with tension and urgency.

---

46 'UK Operation POLARBEAR – Wadi Seidna Air Base NEO – UPDATED', Joint Forces, 30 April 2023, https://www.joint-forces.com/uk-operations/63877-uk-operation-polarbear-wadi-seidna-air-base-neo.

After the briefing, the Garuds proceeded towards the UK checkpoint, located some distance from the aircraft. The British soldiers stopped them, refusing to allow further advancement.

One of them stated firmly,

'We cannot permit you to proceed. It's too risky. We're the last friendly checkpoint. Beyond us, you'll encounter the Sudanese military, who aren't in the best mood, and then there are hundreds of people desperate to board any aircraft they see. It's too dangerous to proceed.'

The young Garud CO persuaded the officers, and they eventually agreed to let him pass, on the condition that two Garuds remained behind to coordinate with the aircraft in case of an emergency—ensuring communication over the same radio frequency. Jaitawat left one buddy pair at the UK checkpoint and continued ahead with his buddy only. His objective now was to locate the Indian evacuees within the sea of people.

He informed Group Captain Ravi Nanda of the new arrangement via radio, knowing that timely updates were critical. With time running out, it was vital for the aircraft captain to remain aware of all developments to manage any potential crisis.

Squadron Leader Jaitawat and Sargeant Vikas Tiwari soon arrived at the checkpoint manned by the Sudanese military. Some soldiers were stationed behind temporary barriers, with hundreds of people spread out beyond. The military had strategically funnelled the crowd using barricades and trenches, leaving only a narrow passage leading towards the tarmac.

It was a scene of utter chaos.

In the night, among the sick, elderly, women, children and young people scattered over a kilometre or more, Squadron Leader Jaitawat and his buddy, Sergeant Tiwari struggled to identify their countrymen. He focused on individuals with South Asian features—who might be from India, Pakistan, Bangladesh or neighbouring countries—but, in the pandemonium, locating them seemed nearly impossible.

Suddenly, Jaitawat spotted a man in a yellow T-shirt with a long beard and a headlamp, waving feverishly at him. It was Lieutenant Colonel Gurpreet Singh.

Though Jaitawat did not know who he was at that moment, the sight filled him with hope. He immediately requested permission from the Sudanese military personnel to cross to the other side. Reluctantly, and only after he asserted his nationality and clarified that he had permission from the Indian Air Force to rescue Indian citizens, they allowed him through.

Crossing that narrow, chaotic stretch amidst the frenzied crowd was a daunting task, but the Garud eventually managed to reach the man in the yellow T-shirt. Upon reaching him, Jaitawat quickly spoke to him in Hindi[47] about other Indians. The Defence Attaché confirmed he had a list of their names and mentioned the difficulties in keeping them together. Jaitawat urgently requested him to gather the group and begin moving towards the aircraft with him.

Despite the stern Sudanese military personnel, and a chaotic crowd, they managed to navigate through the barricades and reach

---

[47] Squadron Leader Jaitawat wanted to be absolutely sure he was dealing with an Indian citizen, so he deliberately spoke in Hindi.

the tarmac. While preparing for the mission, Jaitawat had reviewed footage from Khartoum showing individuals carrying weapons. The presence of even a single armed person could jeopardize the safety of the aircraft. There was also the risk of panicked, distressed individuals boarding the aircraft and potentially causing harm—such as running towards the engine or causing other damage.

Moreover, there was a real possibility of radicalized individuals or enemy operatives posing as evacuees with the intent to sabotage. These scenarios not only endangered other evacuees but also the aircraft itself, risking the entire mission and potentially leading to a tragic outcome on foreign soil. Any damage to the aircraft would not just be a loss for the institution but also a blow to national pride.

'We need to frisk them,' Jaitawat instructed his buddy.
Returning to the UK soldiers' checkpoint with the group of evacuees, all four Garuds began a meticulous screening process. The list that Lieutenant Colonel Gurpreet Singh had given them indicated 118 Indian nationals. As the evacuees stood in a queue, each individual was verified against their passport and thoroughly frisked. They could not afford to mistakenly evacuate individuals of other nationalities and cause embarrassment for Indian diplomats. When one operates on foreign soil, the rules of engagement are strict.

Among the evacuees, several rudimentary weapons—such as knives—were found. While understandable, given they had fled a conflict zone, these posed serious risks inside the aircraft. Throughout the screening process, Squadron Leader Jaitawat maintained constant communication with Group Captain Ravi Nanda on board the C-130J, who urged him to expedite the process due to escalating safety concerns.

The ceasefire was about to end.

The Garuds took a firm stance with the crowd, demanding they voluntarily discard any weapons or face stricter consequences. This ultimatum had an immediate effect, prompting those still concealing arms to relinquish them.

Despite the urgency, the Garuds continued the painstaking screening. They scrutinized facial features, focusing on prominent South Asian traits, as many in the line were of various nationalities, seeking to escape the conflict. Questions about India, their families, and detailed cross-verification with the passport list helped identify and extract the 118 legitimate Indian evacuees.

Many foreign nationals were removed from the queue. Those left behind pleaded and shouted, as they were waiting for evacuation by their own governments. [48]

During this process, Squadron Leader Jaitawat learnt that the man in the yellow T-shirt was none other than the Defence Attaché, Sudan—Lieutenant Colonel Gurpreet Singh—who had been eagerly awaiting their arrival and was aware of their arrival so could locate Garud and waved his hands to them.

Amidst the chaos, a member of the Sudanese military approached the Garuds, pleading to be evacuated. He had his pregnant wife

---

48 It is important to acknowledge India's global standing today. Beyond the extensive humanitarian missions carried out during the COVID-19 pandemic, India is increasingly recognized as a rising world leader in both diplomacy and military capability. Many countries were unable to evacuate their citizens during the Sudan crisis—either due to lack of will or insufficient resources to operate under such grave conditions. A government is, at best, under a moral obligation to repatriate citizens who have voluntarily left the country. While some nations abandoned their citizens, the Indian government risked everything to bring its people back. That is worthy of appreciation.

with him and was desperate to leave Wadi Seidna. Squadron Leader Jaitawat quickly informed Group Captain Nanda and the Defence Attaché, both of whom approved the family's evacuation on compassionate grounds. This shows the compassionate side of Indian officials and their work ethics.

The embarkation process commenced, captured in striking images that later circulated widely on social media during the Sudan crisis. These photos showed Garud Special Forces scanning passports under the glow of torchlight. The mission garnered international praise, including from External Affairs Minister Dr S. Jaishankar, who lauded the Indian Air Force's daring rescue.

Following the operation, Dr Jaishankar stated:

This has been an operation where people have risked their lives. Most of the embassies left when the fighting started, but [the] Indian Embassy stayed. The challenges they faced were daunting, and eventually, an Indian Air Force plane landed at a rudimentary airstrip where a plane had been shot up, and yet these people took the risk of landing there with an almost non-existing air traffic control. The courage shown by the Air Force was matched by the embassy staff on the ground.[49]

The heartfelt appreciation by the then CAS warmed the hearts of air force personnel further.

Air Chief Marshal V.R. Chaudhari said:

---

49 'Operation Kaveri: EAM Jaishankar explains the toughest evacuation process for Indians in Sudan', *Economic Times*, YouTube, https://www.youtube.com/watch?v=pMYk160_zxM

I think the IAF displayed its core capability of being able to carry out operations in the most difficult of situations and my kudos to the aircrew who executed this mission so flawlessly. I want to assure the nation that whenever the time comes, we will do it again and again.

Reflecting on the experience, Sergeant Vikas Tiwari remarked,

> We didn't feel the impact until we landed in India. It was when we saw the Chief of Air Staff's joyful appreciation that we realized we had accomplished something heroic.

With the embarkation complete, the Garuds conducted a final area scan before boarding the aircraft themselves.

The pilot exhaled deeply, unleashing full power as the aircraft soared away. Crossing the Red Sea and leaving the dark terrain behind, they knew they had escaped danger.

During the flight, the evacuees were overwhelmed, shouting, 'Bharat Mata ki Jai' at the top of their lungs. Elderly women approached to touch the feet of the young Garuds and crew members, who felt awkward but were showered with blessings. Each person was immensely grateful to the Air Force personnel, offering heartfelt thanks.

Ghan Sham later told me:

> I have no words to describe how we felt when we saw the Indian Air Force. Frankly, we never hoped we would be rescued. We had seen the worst of the war and witnessed the horrible fates of many before our eyes. We crossed countless threats to reach Wadi Seidna, and the situation was so grim that we had lost hope. But the moment we saw our forces, a big feeling of relief washed

over us. Our saviours had come. Our gods had arrived. We knew nothing would happen to us now. We would be saved.

The news of the daring rescue spread quickly—especially after a Turkish C-130 J aircraft was fired upon shortly after the Indian C-130J had departed.[50] The incident highlighted the gravity of the successful airlift.

This remarkable evacuation made headlines across the world. Amid the tension surrounding Operation Kaveri, it brought immense relief to Indian families anxiously awaiting the return of their loved ones from Sudan.

Later, the evacuees boarded the impressive C-17 Globemaster, operated by No. 81 Squadron, the Sky Lords, under the command of Group Captain Sameep Nijhawan, the brave officer whose inspiring leadership pushed squadron to give their best at testing times when they had to fly non-stop flights.[51]

The Globemaster aircrew were also sensitive to the fact that these passengers had endured distress and trauma. Though the aircraft was configured for military rescue—where survival equipment takes precedence over the aesthetic sensibilities of commercial planes—the crew did everything they could to make the evacuees feel comfortable.

The Commanding Officer personally stood at the ramp to ensure an efficient boarding process.

He shared:

---

50 'Sudan crisis: Turkish evacuation plane fired on', BBC, 28 April 2023, https://www.bbc.com/news/world-africa-65423962.
51 Rahul Bedi, 'The Aircraft Powering IAF's Rescue Missions in Sudan', The Wire, 6 May 2023, https://thewire.in/security/iaf-c17-aircraft-rescue-mission-sudan.

There had been many instances where our mettle had been tested but the heart-warming one would be the faces of some of the elderly women who were incapable of boarding the aircraft; when we somehow arranged four wheelchairs and helped around fifteen such elderly women board the aircraft, their faces lit up and they would not stop showering their blessings.

The co-pilot of that particular globemaster was Flight Lieutenant Har raj Kaur Boparai,[52] a newly-wed officer whose mehendi was still fresh on her hands. At the time of Operation Kaveri, she was the only woman pilot flying the gigantic C-17 Globemaster. (By the time I wrote this story, we had more women flying these giants.) A photograph of her in her green uniform, evacuating citizens in distress, went viral during that crisis—giving wings to thousands of young girls in villages and cities alike.

During the course of writing my book I had the privilege of meeting her and Group Captain Sameep Nijhawan, who proudly walked me through the halls of No. 81 Squadron, adorned with photographs of their heroic rescue missions across the globe. The C-17 Globemasters, aptly nicknamed 'Globe Trotters', stood as a testament to the squadron's versatility and strength. He shared how operating in such challenging situations fills them with a deep sense of satisfaction.

Later, standing beside the iconic C-17, its cockpit towering at the height of a double-storey building and its cavernous interiors stretching out before me, I felt humbled. I wondered how they

---

52 PTI, 'IAF's Only Woman Pilot Of C-17 Aircraft Brings Back Indians From Sudan', NDTV, 27 April 2023, https://www.ndtv.com/india-news/iafs-only-woman-pilot-of-c-17-aircraft-brings-back-indians-from-sudan-3985544.

managed to fly something so massive, let alone cross seven seas to carry out daring rescues.

At No. 77 Squadron, the Veiled Vipers, meeting Wing Commander Rajneesh Chandra Uniyal and the other officers involved in the operation—including the Combat Systems Operator and Flight Commander—felt like stepping into a real-life *Top Gun* moment. I say this without bias—their badges, hard-earned in impossible terrains and unimaginable situations, gleamed upon their green overalls, while their ever-present smiles and Ray-Bans only added to their aura. Truth be told, these Indian pilots looked far more dashing than Tom Cruise himself.

And the Garuds?

The fearless daredevils greeted me with wide grins and shared souvenirs from their respective flights. Among them was a framed map of Africa with Wadi Seidna's topography highlighted, and a Colombian dagger inscribed with '612 Garud Flight', commemorating their heroic operation. Today, it proudly graces the walls of my living room.

By the time the interviews concluded and the magnitude of the mission truly sank in, I found myself wondering: Could I do justice to the story of these real-life heroes, whose bravery might otherwise have been overshadowed by the enormity of an international crisis?

This story needed to be told to remind the nation that saving lives is as heroic as taking down enemies' lives, and the next time you see a massive Indian Air Force Aircraft soaring across the skies during an international emergency, remember those inside are risking everything for each one of us.

Author's note

This story is based on interviews conducted with those at the very heart of a daring rescue mission—Air Vice Marshal S. Srinivasan, then ACAS

Operations (Transport and Helicopter) and the nodal officer for the overall mission; Wing Commander Rajneesh Chandra Uniyal, co-pilot during the Wadi Seidna operation; the Combat Systems Operator involved in the mission; the current Commandant of the Garud Regimental Training Centre, who oversaw Garud operations during Operation Kaveri; Squadron Leader Pritam Singh Jaitawat, who led the Garud team in Wadi Seidna; his G1, Sargeant Vikas Tiwari now promoted to Junior Warrant Officer; and Brigadier Gurtej Singh Grewal, then the Defence Attaché to Saudi Arabia. I am deeply grateful to each one of them for offering their insights and helping bring this vital story to life.

While this narrative captures only a few key protagonists, it represents the countless unsung heroes whose contributions remain behind the scenes due to operational sensitivities and the vast scale of such missions.

2

Deoghar Cable Car Rescue: A Legendary Ropeway Rescue Mission

Trikut Hills
Deoghar District, Jharkhand
10 April 2022

THE CABLE CAR glided smoothly along the steel ropes of the Trikut ropeway, the setting sun casting a warm glow over the lush green expanse below. Rakesh Kumar, seated inside the cable car with three female relatives, marvelled at the breathtaking view from 1,200 feet above the ground. The occasional swaying of the car only added to the thrill.

Suddenly, the thrill turned to terror.

A loud jolt rocked the cable car, snapping it violently out of rhythm.

Rakesh barely had time to grasp the metal railing before the trolley plummeted several feet, the sheer force of the falling cable car slamming the passengers against its walls. A horrifying metallic screech echoed across the valley. A split second later, the car came to a bone-rattling halt, swinging wildly in mid-air. The initial silence was deafening. Rakesh's head throbbed as warm blood trickled down his temple, his vision blurring momentarily. His companions cried out in pain—a fractured leg, a bruised back, a bleeding scalp—but there was no time to tend to injuries. All they could do was cling to the sides of the trolley, praying it wouldn't fall further.

Outside, the situation was grim. Twelve cable cars hung precariously along the 766-metre ropeway, frozen in the amber light of the fading sun. As the minutes ticked by, the soft glow gave way to darkness. The sky turned an inky black, and the winds began to howl with a sharp, relentless ferocity.

Through the window, Rakesh could see nothing but shadows—the outline of dense forests far below and the faint silhouettes of the jagged Trikut peaks. The occasional cloud drifted past, blotting out the dim moonlight, making their suspended prison feel like a void in the sky.

Inside, fear was palpable. The metal cage creaked ominously with every gust of wind. The women huddled together, sobbing and whispering prayers. Rakesh gripped the edge of the seat, his mind racing. They were stranded hundreds of feet above ground, locked inside a trolley that only opened from the outside.

No escape. No help.

Hours dragged on. Hunger gnawed at their stomachs, and thirst burnt their throats. The rhythmic swaying of the trolley was a cruel reminder of their helplessness. With every sway, they feared the cable might snap and send them plunging into the chasm below. The cries of other stranded passengers echoed faintly through the night—some shouted for help, others wailed in despair.

By now, the cold was merciless, the sharp winds howling like tortured spirits. The sound was eerie, amplifying the sense of isolation. The forest below looked like an abyss, its shadows shifting and writhing under the flickering moonlight. Every creak of the cable or sway of the trolley felt like a harbinger of doom.

Then, faintly, a beam of light cut through the dark. It was distant but unmistakable—a sign of hope. Moments later, a loudspeaker crackled to life, the voice of the civil administration breaking through the silence: 'Do not lose hope. Rescue is on the way.'

But as the hours stretched on, that hope dimmed. For those stuck at the highest points—like Rakesh and the women with him—the idea of rescue seemed impossible. They were too high up, too remote. The chill of the air was rivalled only by the chill in their hearts. Despair sank in.

Rakesh looked at the terrified faces of his companions and the infinite void outside the window. He whispered to himself, 'If this is it, then so be it. If Baba Baidyanath wills it, we will go. If not, he will work a miracle.'

And, indeed, a miracle was on the way.

It roared through the cold, dark skies in the form of the Indian Air Force's Mi-17V-5[1]—one of the world's most advanced transport helicopters—carrying the fearless pilots, crew and the IAF's elite Special Forces: The Garuds.

When the ground falters, the heavens rise to the occasion.

---

1 Mi-17V-5 is a military transport variant in the Mi-8/17 family of helicopters, produced by Kazan Helicopters, Russia. It is a modern, multipurpose, NVG-compatible helicopter, designed to carry up to thirty-six personnel, cargo and equipment either inside the cargo cabin or on an external sling (up to 4,000 kg). It can be used to deploy tactical air assault forces, reconnaissance and sabotage teams, destroy ground targets with rockets and bombs, and evacuate the wounded in its ambulance configuration. The Mi-17V-5 is equipped with an advanced autopilot system, as well as state-of-the-art avionics and navigation equipment.

This was no ordinary rescue. It would etch its name into history as the Deoghar Cable Car Rescue—a feat never before attempted on such a daunting scale, perhaps anywhere in the world. The only precedent was the Timber Trail rescue[2] of the 1990s, which involved the rescue of ten people from one cable car. The mishap had occurred at the Timber Trail resort in the scenic town of Parwanoo, Himachal Pradesh.

Here, forty-eight survivors were stranded across twelve cable cars.

Deoghar District Headquarters
10 April 2022

The holy city of Baba Baidyanath was alive with vibrant Ram Navami celebrations. Devotees filled the streets in jubilant rallies, singing and dancing to devotional bhajans. Temples overflowed with Vaishnava Hindus offering prayers and fasting, while charitable events and community meals fostered a spirit of unity. The grand ratha yatra, featuring elaborately adorned chariots of Rama, Sita, Lakshmana and Hanuman, wound through the streets, echoing chants of, 'Jai Shri Ram'.

However, the district management was on high alert due to the risk of communal unrest during the processions. The magnitude of the festival and the chariot processions amplified the risks of clashes. Every law enforcement officer remained on edge, ready for any disruption.

---

2 Suchet Vir Singh, 'Throwback to fabled 1992 rescue op as tourists saved from dangling cable car in Himachal', The Print, 20 June 2022, https://theprint.in/india/throwback-to-fabled-1992-rescue-op-as-tourists-saved-from-dangling-cable-car-in-himachal/1004640/.

At the district headquarters, District Magistrate (DM) Manjunath Bhajantri—known for his swift and decisive actions—stood vigilant alongside the Superintendent of Police (SP), Deoghar. Their watchfulness was abruptly interrupted by an urgent call reporting a cable car disaster.

By 1845 hours, the magistrate arrived on the scene to a harrowing sight. Cable cars hung perilously from the ropeway, their occupants crying out in panic. A crowd of about 300 locals had assembled—some attempting to help, others standing by in shocked silence. The arrival of local leaders and the relatives of the trapped passengers, their faces etched with fear and grief, compounded the chaos as night fell.

Amid the growing tumult, the DM swiftly ordered additional police forces to manage the crowd and secure the area. He moved among the distressed families, offering words of comfort and assurance. 'DM sahab, *bacha lo*,' they pleaded, clinging to the hope that rescue efforts were underway.

As the head of the District Disaster Management Authority, Mr Manjunath mobilized all available resources. He contacted the National Disaster Response Force (NDRF), State Disaster Response Force (SDRF), Indo-Tibetan Border Police (ITBP), the Indian Army, and even reached out to state ministries.

Each call was a lifeline, a desperate bid to bring more hands into the rescue.

Tension spiked when a local leader, misunderstanding the complexity of the situation, suggested restarting the cable cars to reset the system. Manjunath quashed this idea before it could escalate into another crisis. Another wave of pressure hit when whispers spread that the rescue must be completed by nightfall, adding to the already immense strain.

By then, the young district magistrate knew that only an aerial rescue could avert disaster—something impossible to initiate in the dark. Undeterred, he coordinated with the Prime Minister's Office

(PMO) to extend the operation timeline, all while absorbing barbs from impatient and fearful relatives accusing him of inaction.

This chaos was not new to Manjunath. His journey from the rural village of Sureban in Karnataka—where he was the first to break through to IIT Bombay and later, the Indian Administrative Service—to his current posting had made him resilient. The struggles of his past had honed his ability to stay calm and assertive under pressure.

As night fell, the rescue operation intensified. The district administration, led by the resolute DM, had mobilized every possible resource. Aska inflatable tower lights illuminated the darkened landscape, casting long shadows on the anxious faces of the people on the ground while serving as a beacon of hope for those stranded in the air. A makeshift camp was established at the site, complete with a temporary helipad in anticipation of the aircraft that would soon arrive for the rescue. Drones delivered food and water to stranded passengers wherever they could reach. Loudspeakers blared frequent announcements, assuring the trapped passengers that help was on its way and urging the gathered crowd to remain calm.

Meanwhile, the DM's phone buzzed incessantly with calls. Important ministries, concerned authorities and media houses—both national and international—sought constant updates. Social media, fuelled by random clips captured and shared without context, only added to the panic. Misinformation spread by some media outlets further heightened the chaos. Bhajantri swiftly ensured effective media management to prevent unconfirmed reports from fuelling further distress. With multiple forces arriving—each with specific demands—the challenges mounted. He made the call to activate the Deoghar Aerodrome immediately.

By 2300 hours, realizing the need for continuous on-site coordination, Manjunath decided to stay at the camp. He called his wife to explain the situation. She understood the gravity of what he was facing.

The relatives of the trapped passengers had grown increasingly impatient. 'You keep telling us the Air Force is coming, but where are they? Why haven't they arrived yet?' they demanded.

Reflecting later, Sri Manjunath Bhajantri, who is currently serving as District Magistrate, Ranchi city, shared with me:

It was an unprecedented emergency, with no clear protocols. Lives were in grave danger, and the pitch darkness made assessment difficult. Hundreds had gathered—some helping, others disrupting. Passengers and relatives cried out, and many threatened the administration. We had to manage the night until the Air Force arrived.

Then he paused before adding:

'You know what our biggest fear was? That the cable cars might fall before the Air Force arrived.'

～

Air Force Station, Barrackpore
West Bengal
10 April 2022

Group Captain Yogeshwar Krishnarao Kandalkar, the Commanding Officer of the 157 Helicopter Unit based at Barrackpore, had just settled into a rare evening at home. It was 2230 hours, and he was helping his wife, Shweta, wind down the birthday party for their son, Sharvay, who had just turned ten. Although Sharvay's actual birthday had been the day before, Kandalkar had been busy with a crucial inspection, and the celebration had been delayed by a day.

As the wife of a helicopter pilot, Shweta was accustomed to these interruptions in their lives, the long absences and the constant juggling of responsibilities. She knew she couldn't afford to burden her husband with every small concern, understanding that his job demanded undivided focus and a clear mind. Despite his busy schedule, she appreciated that they were able to celebrate their son's milestone together.

Her family meant everything to her. Sharvay had just entered double digits. Their parents and relatives had gathered to celebrate. Life seemed to be unfolding in the most peaceful of ways. She felt she couldn't ask for more. But, as they say, in the life of an Indian Air Force pilot—especially a helicopter pilot—peace is always fleeting.

At that moment, the shrill ring of Kandalkar's phone broke the tranquillity of the evening. He glanced at the screen—it was a call from Eastern Air Command. *Odd*, he thought. *A call from Command at this hour?*

'Kandy,' the senior officer's voice came through the line, 'I've shared some photos and links of a ropeway accident. Go through them and let me know. Launch a helicopter so you can reach the location before sunrise.'

Kandalkar quickly checked the time—2230 hours. Grabbing his phone, he watched the breaking news flash across TV:

'Many stranded in a hanging ropeway. One dead. Rescue attempts underway. Trikut Ropeway in Deoghar, Jharkhand.'

Without wasting another second, Kandalkar called his second-in-command, his trusted flight commander.

'Hi, awake?'

'I'm having dinner, sir,' he replied.

'No worries! You eat, I'm coming over,' Kandalkar said, already heading out the door.

When he arrived at his flight commander's quarters, the scene was almost comical. Clad in a mundu and dark-blue half-sleeve shirt, the

Tamil officer was seated with a plate of sambar rice in his hands—clearly less than thrilled by the interruption. Despite the awkwardness of the moment, he greeted his CO with a smile.

Kandalkar wasted no time and showed him the report. As the flight commander scooped the last bit of rice into his mouth, the two officers studied photos of the incident.

'What do we do?' Kandalkar asked, almost to himself.

Without missing a beat, both said nearly in unison, 'Timber Trail Rescue!'

They were referring to a legendary operation carried out by the IAF on 13–14 October 1992—an unprecedented and daring rescue after a cable car malfunctioned at Timber Trail, Parwanoo, near Chandigarh.[3] The Mi-17 crew led by Flight Lieutinent Paritosh Upadhyay of 152 Helicopter Unit (HU), based at Sarsawa in Uttar Pradesh, alongside 1 Para Commandos, led by Major Ivan Joseph Crasto, had rescued ten stranded passengers.

Now, the reports spoke of forty-eight passengers stranded mid-air in the Trikut ropeway, spread across twelve different trolleys suspended at varying heights, ranging from 300 feet to 1,200 feet above the ground.

The pilots searched for any reference to a rescue of this scale but found none.

In fact, the data showed numerous tragic ropeway accidents worldwide. There were forty-three deaths in the 1976 Cavalese cable car disaster in Italy, seven in the 1983 Singapore cable car disaster, and twenty in the 1999 Saint-Étienne-en-Dévoluy disaster in France. In India, the 2017 Gulmarg cable car mishap claimed seven lives when a tree fell on the line. The statistics were grim, and the pilots knew this would be a one-of-a-kind rescue operation. There were no

---

3 https://puneetspage.wordpress.com/2020/11/03/the-daring-cable-car-rescue-at-timber-trail-1992/

established references, no standard operating procedures (SOPs). The only guidance they had was from the pilots involved in the Timber Trail rescue operation in 1992.

Coincidentally, the 152 Helicopter Unit[4]—the same unit that had carried out the Timber Trail rescue—was the first unit Group Captain Kandalkar had served after his commissioning. The stories of that operation—how the Mi-17 helicopters and commandos had worked in perfect synchronization to save lives—had stayed with him throughout his career.

Now, decades later, it was his turn to make history.

'Get the birds ready,' Group Captain Kandalkar said, firm resolve settling in his voice.

As the helicopter unit prepared for the daring operation, another urgent call came through—this time for twenty-seven-year-old Flight Lieutenant Tejpal Yadav,[5] the newly appointed commanding officer (CO) of the Garud Flight at Kalaikunda Air Force Station,[6] located approximately 151 kilometres from the Barrackpore Air Force Station.[7] He had only just completed his training at the Garud Regimental Training Centre (GRTC) and had taken command of the flight two weeks prior.

∼

---

4 'No. 152 Helicopter Unit, IAF', Wikipedia, https://en.wikipedia.org/wiki/No._152_Helicopter_Unit,_IAF.

5 https://www.bhaskar.com/local/rajasthan/alwar/behror/news/the-terrorist-jumped-from-the-window-and-threw-a-grenade-bled-but-stacked-130855302.html/ हेलिकॉप्टर से लटककर बचाई थीं जिंदगी, अब शौर्य चक्र

6 Anchit Gupta, 'IIT Kharagpur's Lesser Known Indian Air Force Neighbour', IAF History, 22 November 2023, https://iafhistory.in/2023/11/22/evolution-of-kalaikunda-airbase.

7 https://www.bharat-rakshak.com/indianairforce/database/units/6+Wing/ 6 Wing/Bharat Rakshak

Air Force Station, Kalaikunda
Kharagpur, West Bengal
10 April 2022

At twenty-seven, Flight Lieutenant Tejpal Yadav was the youngest commanding officer at Kalaikunda Air Force Station. That night, he was enjoying a casual party with a coursemate who had recently been posted to the same station. The evening was winding down when his phone buzzed at 2300 hours.

'Flight Lieutenant Yadav,' he answered, only to hear the urgency in the voice of the Chief Operating Officer (COO).[8]

'Garuds are required for a rescue operation in Jharkhand,' the COO began without preamble.

'What are the initial inputs, sir?' Tejpal asked, his tone instantly professional.

'There's been a cable car malfunction in Jharkhand. Twenty cable cars with seventy-six passengers were operational, but now they're stranded in mid-air. The NDRF, SDRF, Indian Army and civil administration have rescued twenty-eight passengers from eight cars at lower heights. The remaining cars, suspended at higher altitudes, are beyond their reach. The civil administration has formally requested support from the Indian Air Force.'

The COO paused briefly before continuing. 'Helicopters from Barrackpore will arrive at first light to pick up your team. I'm forwarding you some links with details. For further information, contact the CO of 157 HU. Prepare your men.'

---

8 The Chief Operating Officer is a senior officer at an Air Force Station responsible for facilitating and coordinating all operations carried out by the various units in that station.

Tejpal reviewed the forwarded reports, but they were vague—no concrete data, no precedents and no established SOPs. Without wasting a moment, he summoned JWO Ranjeet Kumar[9] and ordered the entire 627 Garud Flight to assemble.

Within thirty minutes, the Garuds were ready. Many had been woken abruptly from deep sleep, but their expressions remained sharp and focused, their eyes reflecting the silent resolve of warriors.

Tejpal stood before them, keenly aware of the stakes. He was still settling into his new role as CO, grappling with the enormity of leading one of the most lethal units in the Air Force.

The CO laid out the situation:

> This is unprecedented. Never in the history of the Garuds—or any Indian Special Force—has there been an operation to rescue people from multiple cable cars suspended in mid-air. The task will require landing on those cars to evacuate passengers. We have no references, no SOPs and incomplete intel. It's a high-risk mission with no guarantee of our own safety.

Despite the gravity of the briefing, when Tejpal asked for volunteers, every hand shot up without hesitation. The sight filled him with pride. After deliberation with his G1, he selected a team, combining experienced veterans with young blood.

As the team began their preparations, there was no room for doubt. The risks were staggering, but for these men, duty was paramount. Somewhere in Jharkhand, lives were hanging by a thread—and it was up to the pilots and Garuds to bring them back.

~

---

9 The senior-most Garud of airman rank in a garud flight, who is responsible for overseeing the operational aspects of that flight.

Ops Rooms, 157 Helicopter Unit and 627 Garud Flight
Barrackpore and Kalaikunda, West Bengal
11 April 2022
0200 hours

By 11 April, twenty-eight passengers from eight trolleys had been rescued by the NDRF, SDRF, Indian Army and ITBP forces, but no further rescues were possible. With all ground-based efforts proving futile for those stranded higher up, the DM made a desperate request through the state government, which led to a call for assistance from the Indian Air Force.

Air Headquarters in New Delhi wasted no time, issuing orders to the Eastern Air Command. By 2200 hours, Air Marshal A.P. Singh, then the SASO[10] of Eastern Command, after discussion with the AOC-In-C AM Dilip Kumar Patnaik, AVSM, VM who had been a famous Kargil hero, took charge of the operation. Messages swiftly spread across the region, summoning the best teams and aircraft for this challenging mission.

By the time Group Captain Kandalkar of 157 Helicopter Unit received the orders, the night was half gone. An aviator with twenty-two years of service and over 4,500 flying hours across platforms like the Mi-17V-5, Cheetah and Mi-8, Kandalkar understood the enormity of the challenge. The aircraft had to be meticulously prepared; even the smallest oversight could prove catastrophic. Kandalkar and his flight commander rallied their teams to ready the chopper.

Speaking later, Kandalkar recalled the mission with a mixture of pride and gravity:

---

10 Senior Air Staff Officer, the second senior-most officer in command after AOC-In-C.

People say India is from Kashmir to Kanyakumari, but to me, it's from Indira Col to Indira Point.[11] I've flown across this entire span—rescuing flood victims in Kerala, evacuating injured soldiers under fire in Kashmir, operations in Nagaland and Mizoram, even forest fires in Tamil Nadu. But this? This was unlike anything we'd faced before. No SOP, no reliable intel, no landing zones. Just a team, a helicopter and a belief that we could do it.

The rescue's complexity was compounded by the need to hover—holding the helicopter stationary mid-air while conducting winching[12] operations. This manoeuvre demanded extreme precision and skill. He paused before continuing:

The closest reference we had was the famous Timber Trail rescue operation. As I read the reports, it struck me that we would need to execute the Timber Trail operation twelve times over, at twelve different heights and under twelve unique circumstances.

By then, my flight commander[13] had activated the co-pilots. We had very little information about the terrain, so we used Google Earth for assistance, while the ground crew prepared the Mi-17V-5 for take-off at 0400 hours. We charted several plans but, in the end, one thing was clear to us: The only way to carry out the rescue was through winching.

---

11 The northernmost point of India is Indira Col in Siachen and the southernmost point is 'Indira Point' in the Andaman and Nicobar Islands.
12 A winch is a mechanical device used to lift heavy objects or people during rescue operations. It consists of a drum around which a rope or cable is wound.
13 Equivalent to the second-in-command of an Army Unit.

To ensure the aircraft was ready for the 0400 hours mission, preparation had to begin by 0300 hours. This meant technicians were on the tarmac by 0200 hours. Meanwhile, messages from Air HQ and Headquarter Eastern Command kept pouring in, leaving no one able to sleep that night.

Group Captain Kandalkar shared with me:

> There were numerous requirements for a rescue operation of this magnitude, and we had no time. We needed our most experienced pilots, refuelling capabilities, landing spots and servicing for such a complex mission. Approximately forty to fifty people were stranded on the ropeway, so multiple sorties were required to evacuate them all. The civil administration had set up a makeshift helipad in an open ground five kilometres from the target location, but we needed a proper aerodrome[14] with at least some basic facilities. Fortunately, we identified Deoghar Airport, about fifteen kilometres from the site. Although it wasn't operational and its facilities were minimal, we needed to establish a temporary command centre for facilities like communication, space to land extra aircraft, etc.

Understanding the magnitude of the mission, the CO made a conscious decision to lead the operation himself.

They anticipated that the operation would require multiple sorties, so a request was made for a refueller.[15] Confirmation soon came through that it had departed from Panagarh Military Station and was expected to arrive at the target location by 0700 hours.

---

14 Aerodrome is an area, including its associated buildings, where aircraft can land, take off and access basic aviation-related facilities.

15 A refueller is a tanker-type vehicle with specialized equipment, used to refuel aircraft.

In the meantime, they also had to pick up the Garuds from Kalaikunda Air Force Station before proceeding to Deoghar.

At one point, Group Captain Kandalkar received a call from Headquarters asking whether the rescue team would comprise Garuds or NDRF personnel to assist the stranded passengers in the cable cars.[16] His response was firm:

'Garuds would be the better choice any day, sir. They train with us regularly on our helicopters and are well-versed in winching operations.'

Thus, the course was set for what would become an iconic cable car rescue—destined to be etched into history.

Meanwhile, Flight Lieutenant Tejpal Yadav, along with his G1 JWO Ranjeet Kumar, was grappling with challenges of his own.

Despite their best efforts, they had no concrete information about the terrain or the situation. In response, the commanding officer assigned two local boys from Bihar and Odisha to monitor every news report on local TV and social media, and report back. One of them, from Odisha, came across detailed coverage on an Odia news channel. The footage revealed the desperate nature of the situation—people waving frantically from the windows of dangling cable cars, the precarious state of the cars swaying in mid-air—and gave a rough sense of the altitude and topography.

Upon seeing the terrain, the Garud realized the immense risks ahead. Every rescue mission has its unique difficulties, but this one posed extreme challenges. Armed with the new information, the team adjusted their weaponry, equipment profiles and team structure accordingly.

Flight Lieutenant Tejpal Yadav later shared with me:

---

16 For such rescue operations, every possible course of action and probable team composition is thoroughly discussed by senior Indian Air Force officers.

Ma'am, as Garuds, we were the ones tasked with landing on those pendulum-like cable cars, dangling in mid-air at such heights. Missions like these always fall under the high-risk category, and there was little input. We had to dangle from thin cables to rescue people. As team commander, I needed an area reconnaissance. I needed to know the load-bearing capacity of the cable cars and the cables they were attached to. We didn't know what impact our movements would have. What if the cables were already at their maximum load capacity? One jump, and the system could collapse.

The risk was compounded by the helicopter's hovering, which puts significant load on the cables. The wind speed could exceed 100 knots when the helicopter approaches, and we needed to operate on those cables in those conditions. And we had no confirmation if the cables could handle that kind of stress.

He paused, then added:

And that was just one problem. Another critical challenge was movement. A helicopter is a moving platform. Landing on a static platform, like during flood rescues, is easier. But here, we had to jump onto trolleys stranded in mid-air, which were swaying like pendulums. The airflow from the helicopter and the trolley's movement created a scenario where you're jumping from a moving helicopter onto moving trolleys, balancing your every move amidst the strong air current. There was always the risk of falling.

Throughout the night, the Garud's and the crew of the 157 Helicopter Unit worked tirelessly in preparation for one of the most challenging missions of their lives, unaware that this was just the beginning. The real tests would begin only upon reaching the target area.

The Garuds' orders were clear: Report to the runway by 0300 hours sharp to board the aircraft at 0430 hours.

Trikut Parvat
Deoghar, Jharkhand
11 April 2022
0615 hours

Located in Deoghar, the Trikut ropeway stood as a marvel of modern tourism, a gateway to the summit of the main peak. Towering at 2,470 feet above sea level, the three-peaked hill offered an irresistible lure to adventurers, with the 766-metre-long ropeway serving as its crowning jewel.[17] The route wound through rocky terrain and dense forest, revealing breathtaking views of Deoghar and the sacred Trikutachal Mahadeva Temple nestled below.

Yet, on 10 April, this serene attraction turned into a harrowing spectacle.

What began as a day of awe-inspiring rides soon spiralled into chaos.

Without warning, the ropeway malfunctioned, leaving seventy-six passengers suspended mid-air in twenty trolleys. The tension was palpable as state and national forces launched a rescue operation, but their efforts could only reach those passengers stranded at lower altitudes. Those dangling at higher heights seemed beyond help. While the administration had deployed drones to deliver food and water, even those mechanical lifelines faltered against the jagged boulders and dense undergrowth, unable to reach the upper trolleys.

---

17 'Trikut Pahar', Deogarh Tourism, Government of Jharkhand, https://deoghar.nic.in/tourist-place/trikutpahar/.

As desperation mounted, a bold decision was made: Aerial rescue was the only option.

An urgent plea to Air HQ in New Delhi set the Indian Air Force into motion.

The skies above Trikut Pahar reverberated with the hum of rotor blades as Mi-17V-5 helicopters roared into view. Their imposing five-blade rotors and distinctive grey silhouettes blended seamlessly with the overcast sky. Designed for high-risk missions, the advanced twin-engine Mi-17V-5 stood as a lifeline in this crisis.[18]

Inside the cockpit—fortified with metal plates —sat Group Captain Kandalkar and Flight Lieutenant Aakash Aggarwal, his skilled co-pilot. Junior Warrant Officer (JWO)[19] Rashpreet Singh served as the vigilant flight engineer. At the rear, near the entrance door, Flight Gunner Junior Warrant Officer Venkatesh G. and Master Warrant Officer[20] Satish Kumar remained laser-focused on their roles, each ready for action.

As part of the 157 Helicopter Unit's fleet, the Mi-17V-5 reached the target area, where the crew conducted an aerial reconnaissance before proceeding to Deoghar Airport to begin the actual mission. Along the way, they had also picked up the Garuds from Kalaikunda Air Force Station, who had been waiting on the runway.

Group Captain Kandalkar recalled the conversation he had with the young CO of the Garud Flight.

'Good morning, youngster! Hope you've had experience with rescue operations before?'

---

18 https://www.airforce-technology.com/projects/mi-17v-5-military-transport-helicopter/?utm_source=chatgpt.com/ Mi-17V-5 Military Transport Helicopter/April 3, 2020/Airforce technology.com

19 A Junior Warrant Officer is the equivalent of a Naib Subedar in the Army and a Chief Petty Officer in the Navy.

20 A Master Warrant Officer is the equivalent of a Subedar Major in the Army and a Master Chief Petty Officer (First Class) in the Navy.

Flight Lieutenant Tejpal Yadav responded, 'Sir, I've just finished my training from GRTC and took over command fifteen days ago.'

Kandalkar chuckled, *'Kar lega na tu?'*

The Garud replied with enthusiasm, 'Sir! *Josh pura hai!*'

Kandalkar later shared warmly:

You see in operations like these, no matter how many hours we may have worked before, what truly matters is the josh and the intent to get the job done. This was a new kind of mission for all of us, but I really liked the young man's attitude.

As the pilots scanned the rugged terrain through the helicopter's transparent cockpit panels, they executed precise manoeuvres over the landscape. In the rear cabin—spacious enough for around thirty-six passengers—the Garuds, seated and alert, had their binoculars trained on the dangling cable cars, assessing the feasibility of landing atop them.

It was then that Tejpal, peering through his binoculars, noticed something alarming: There was grease everywhere, not just on the cables but also on the roofs of the cable car trolleys where they needed to land.

Meanwhile, the pilots faced their own challenges. The entire area was surrounded by towering hills and a steeply inclined ropeway. At first, they struggled to even locate the cables, as they were so thin. The cable cars, roughly 4x3 feet on top—about the size of four floor tiles—and just five feet in height, were difficult to spot from the air. To get a clear view, Kandalkar, captain of the aircraft, had to make three low passes, flying close to the hills. To approach the target area properly, he had to guide the helicopter between two small humps in the terrain. Getting close to the cables also carried serious risk.

During the first sortie, he asked his crew over the intercom, *'Dikha?'*

'*Nahi*, sir! We'll have to get closer!' the co-pilot replied.

He flew closer. Then the gunner shouted in excitement, '*Dikh gaya*, sir, first pillar *dikh gaya! Thoda aur paas lo.*'

The crew finally spotted the cable cars—painted in different colours—and were even able to identify the numbers marked on them. The gunner and flight engineer quickly noted these details for the upcoming rescue.

The crew also observed that the ropeway ran through steep hills, with obstacles and high terrain on both sides. Two main cables stretched between two pillars, one at the bottom and the other at the top of the hill. There was another set of cables for maintenance trolleys. Because of the steep slope, the helicopter would need to hover significantly higher than the cable cars, making the task that much harder. Variable wind speeds added to the challenge, constantly shifting the hover direction. Low clouds and haze further limited visibility, making the flying conditions even riskier.

Through the trolley windows, people could be seen waving and shouting, desperate for help. The sight was both intense and heartbreaking.

By the time the Garuds and the crew had finished assessing the challenges of the upcoming rescue, the helicopter was running low on fuel. The captain decided to land and refuel. On the way back, he reflected on his earlier decision to bring two gunners on board. He now saw how crucial they would be during the operation—while Venkatesh, the main gunner, would handle the winching and the pilots focused on controlling the helicopter, the second gunner would assist in ensuring the main rotor remained at a safe distance from the ropeway cables.

~

Deoghar Airport
Jharkhand
11 April 2022
0900 hours

On the ground, from Deoghar Airport to Trikut Parvat, the situation was one of utter chaos. Two teams from the NDRF—one from Deoghar and the other from Patna—along with the ITBP, the Indian Army and the civil administration were working tirelessly to evacuate passengers and provide medical assistance.

The scene was overwhelming: People running frantically, ambulances waiting for victims, stretchers being carried through rugged terrain and temporary tents erected by the civil administration to serve as logistics hubs. Despite these relentless efforts, it wasn't enough. Everyone was anxiously waiting for the Indian Air Force to begin rescue operations, hoping for a miracle.

Finally, the IAF arrived. By 0600 hours, the Mi-17V-5 from 157 Helicopter Unit, carrying the elite Garud Special Forces, had landed, awaiting refuelling before beginning operations.

At 0645 hours, another Mi-17 helicopter from Ranchi touched down and launched the first aerial rescue sortie. The crew began with the cable cars suspended at lower altitudes, where the incline of the ropeway cables was flatter, believing this would allow them to hover closer to the gondolas and offer better visual references. However, the plan quickly began to unravel. As the Mi-17 neared the gondolas, the ropeway began swaying violently. A series of technical challenges emerged, forcing the pilot to abort the mission and return to base.

When the first helicopter returned without a successful rescue, the atmosphere shifted from hopeful to desperate. People began to wonder aloud: If even the Indian Air Force couldn't succeed, then how could the forty-eight passengers still stranded on the ropeway possibly be saved?

Group Captain Kandalkar later recalled a conversation with a policeman stationed at the scene.

The policeman had said, 'Sir, if you can't save them, at least deliver food to them.'

Kandalkar asked, 'How do you expect me to deliver food?'

The policeman replied, 'Just hang from a rope and take it to them.'

Kandalkar smiled, 'If I can hang from a rope to deliver food, then our Special Forces can reach them the same way, right?'

'Yes, sir,' the policeman agreed.

'Then,' Kandalkar continued, 'if my Garuds can reach them, we can bring them back too.' He added with determination, 'Let me go. I'm a senior officer, and if I can't do it, perhaps no one else can.'

As rescue efforts continued, a Cheetah helicopter from Bagdogra arrived for reconnaissance. Meanwhile, a new problem surfaced: The refuelling vehicle expected to refuel Kandalkar's helicopter had lost its way. While the aircraft was ready, the refueller was still en route, instead of having arrived in the early morning, as planned. The crew quickly established contact with the drivers, provided updated directions, and anxiously awaited the vehicle's arrival so they could launch their first rescue sortie.

The atmosphere around the site was charged with tension. Relatives of the trapped passengers were consumed by anxiety, while thousands of onlookers from nearby villages had gathered, hoping to witness the rescue. The district magistrate had requested additional police forces, but they struggled to control the swelling crowd, which grew increasingly unruly by the minute. The media was present in full force, covering every detail of the unfolding crisis, while a significant portion of the government machinery focused on managing both the crowds and the media.

Despite an appearance of order, the situation remained precarious. The threat of riots, arson or further casualties loomed. Many relatives wept inconsolably; women fainted and the children whose parents were trapped in the cable cars were visibly traumatized.

Group Captain Kandalkar and his crew began by analysing the situation with the NDRF and the DM. The NDRF personnel, already on the ground for hours, shared crucial observations from their efforts to rescue passengers stranded at lower heights. Their expertise, honed through countless disaster management operations, offered invaluable insights into navigating the treacherous terrain and understanding the structural behaviour of the cable cars.

Kandalkar also requested the DM to provide 360-degree visuals of the ropeway and its surroundings to better assess the terrain and identify obstacles. Though the initial rescue sorties had been unsuccessful, they proved vital as they brought back information that helped guide the subsequent attempts.

Every piece of feedback pointed to a pivotal tactical shift: Instead of starting at the lower altitudes, it would be more effective to conduct the first sortie at a higher altitude. This decision had a humanitarian rationale as well—while passengers at lower heights had received food and water via drones, those trapped at the higher altitudes had been without sustenance for over twenty-four hours.

The success of the mission—and the culmination of all the deliberation, planning and efforts by the civil administration, the Indian Air Force and disaster response teams—now hinged on whether the Garud Special Forces could successfully operate from 1,200 feet, rather than the initially planned 300 feet above the ground level.

The urgency was intense, and the risks were overwhelming. Though the Garuds were trained to operate in extreme adversity, this operation would test them like never before. The lives of those trapped depended on their courage—and the cost of failure would be catastrophic.

Group Captain Kandalkar decided to speak to the Garud CO.

Flight Lieutenant Tejpal Yadav stood near the command post, absorbing the latest updates from the NDRF, SDRF, Army and other agencies. The early morning reconnaissance had revealed critical details—like the grease coating the tops of the cable cars—which helped shape the final rescue plan. After a quick briefing, he dismissed his team to gear up. Time was of the essence, and he didn't want to waste a second once the helicopter was ready.

As he entered the makeshift tent to grab his kit, he was met by Kandalkar, who briefed him on the updated plan.

Tejpal paused to consider the request and replied, 'Give me some time. Operating at 300 feet and 1,200 feet above ground level are entirely different scenarios, requiring completely different techniques. Let me assess the feasibility. Besides, this is the first rescue—we have no SOPs for this, and the risk is significantly higher.'

He then stepped out to brief his team about the revised plan.

'Look,' he began, 'the pilots believe there's a better chance of success at 1,200 feet. But can we operate from that height and carry out the rescue?'

Flight Lieutenant Tejpal later recounted the moment to me with a smile:

> I got an interesting response from one of our LACs,[21] a sardar. Jokingly, I asked him, *'Oye, kake, thik hai na?'*
>
> The LAC replied, 'Sir, whether we fall from 300 feet or 1,200 feet, we'll die either way. What difference does it make?'
>
> Surprised, I asked, 'Why are you saying that?'
>
> He replied, 'Sir, there are rocks below. If we fall, we're dead anyway.'
>
> That reply cleared any lingering doubts. It showed me my boys' determination and readiness. I went straight back to the captain and confirmed—we were ready.

---

21 A Leading Aircraftman (LAC) is an airman equivalent of the Naik rank in the Indian Army.

When I later asked Tejpal, 'It's scary just to look down from that height, let alone jump onto a moving trolley dangling beneath a helicopter in violent winds. Weren't you or your team afraid?'

His response moved me deeply:

> At the Garud Regimental Training Centre, we train for 11 months—the longest of any Special Forces unit in India. The reason is that we are not just trained to be lethal but also to become the men entrusted with the safety of national assets. We go wherever the aircraft goes. We slither, winch and jump from various aircraft, and much more all year round. Even though there was no precedent for an operation like this, fear never entered our minds.

The refueller finally arrived around 1045 hours, and the Garuds began kitting up. Tejpal was brimming with determination. Though he was their commanding officer, he was also the youngest on the team, Yet, he made a conscious decision to go first. The senior LACs,[22] some of whom had been part of other rescue operations, offered him the opportunity to let someone else lead the jump initially. But he declined.

He was the leader of their pack, and he remembered what his instructors at GRTC had drilled into him: You are a true commanding officer only if you lead from the front.

'I'll go first,' he replied to the others. 'This type of operation is a first for each one of us.'

Flight Lieutenant Tejpal Yadav, just twenty-seven years old, hailed from a lower-middle-class family in Rewana, a small village in Alwar, Rajasthan. He was the first in his family to clear the tenth standard, and the first from his village to become an Air Force officer.

---

22 Senior airmen with many years in service.

Financial struggles were constant. He had taken up odd jobs to fund his education, as the money his father sent was never enough. There were times when his father—bedridden for years after an accident—couldn't work, and it was him and his brothers who kept things going for the family.

Life was far from easy, but sports and athletics sustained him during those years. The scholarships and prize money he earned, along with the odd jobs he worked, helped him continue his education. One thing was always clear to him—he desperately wanted to achieve something big.

He later shared with me:

In a middle-class family like mine, the biggest challenge is the lack of guidance. There was no one to tell me what was right or wrong. But I wanted to do something so badly that I never stopped trying, no matter the odds. When you come from a village, you know you need to settle down quickly—otherwise, financial instability follows. That fire inside me never let me settle for the ordinary.

Tejpal excelled at sports, representing Rajasthan University at the nationals several times, and had dreamt of joining the armed forces since Class Twelve. Without the money to enrol in coaching classes, he attempted multiple SSBs exams unsuccessfully. Then finally, in 2017, he cleared the AFCAT and completed his training at the Air Force Academy (AFA) Dundigal in 2018, becoming an Indian Air Force officer.

He chuckled as he recalled:

You know, my parents are humble people and not educated. When I told them I had cleared AFCAT, they didn't seem very excited—they didn't even know what it was. The few acres of land my father owned were their whole world. My younger brother, however, was happy for me.

After a few years in service, Tejpal yearned for more action. He volunteered for the Garuds. During the pre-selection phase, forty officers applied, but only nine made it through the training. By the time the passing-out parade arrived, only two had earned the proficiency badge and the maroon beret, officially becoming Garud officers. He was one of them. And he was certainly not going to give up today.

He quietly began gearing up. First, he tightened the straps of his full-body harness, ensuring every buckle was secure and snug. Next, he slid his knee and elbow pads into place over his uniform with practiced ease. The radio communication set came next. He clipped the compact device to his harness, threading the mic close to his mouth and tucking the earpiece securely into his ear. From his belt, he pulled out a gleaming combat dagger—its black blade meant for emergencies—and slid it into the sheath attached to his harness. He pulled his helmet over his head and adjusted the straps, then tugged on his tactical gloves. Finally, he reached for his ballistic goggles and slipped them on.

Alongside Sergeant[23] Pankaj Kumar Rana, his buddy, he began walking towards the aircraft. Fully geared, they exuded an aura of invincibility.

This was their call of duty. This was what they had trained for.

∼

---

23 As a non-commissioned officer, a sergeant is responsible for supervising and guiding a team of airmen, ensuring that they adhere to the strict standards of the Indian Air Force.

Trikut Ropeway
1130 hours

The massive Mi-17V-5 hovered approximately 1200 feet above the ground level and about 80-100 feet above a tiny 4x3-foot trolley platform—a feat of exceptional difficulty. Hovering over such a small area was an immense challenge. Once directly overhead, the pilots lost visual contact with the platform, forcing them to rely entirely on the crew's guidance, all while carefully maintaining adequate distance from the ropeway cables to prevent the massive rotor blades from making contact. A single miscalculation could cause the blades to strike the cables, with disastrous consequences. It was a high-risk manoeuvre.

Flight Engineer JWO Rashpreet Singh monitored the aircraft's system parameters, while co-pilot Squadron Leader K.K. Singh assisted in maintaining a steady hover. Meanwhile, Gunner JWO Venkatesh G. provided precise guidance:

'Okay, slow down. Approaching the spot. Slight left … five metres to go … two metres … one metre left, one metre right … over the spot, hold steady hover.'

Their superior piloting skills and teamwork enabled them to successfully execute a difficult manoeuvre in helicopter aviation.

Now, it was time for the Garuds to take the leap of faith.

As soon as Flight Lieutenant Tejpal hooked himself to the winch cable, Sergeant Pankaj Kumar Rana—a seasoned Garud with years of experience—asked again,

'Sir, should I go first?' Tejpal calmly replied, 'We're both new to this. You stay in the aircraft. If something goes wrong, you'll need to take charge.'

With that, Tejpal began his descent. Secured by the winch cable, he carried a bag of food, water and harnesses for the evacuees strapped to his shoulders. Extra rope and carabiners hung from his waist. His helmet was tightly fastened, ballistic goggles protected his eyes and his gloved hands gripped the cable firmly.

The team had planned carefully—landing on the trolley, even handling a fall or the helicopter stalling. But just ten metres into the descent, the powerful downwash from the helicopter's rotors caused the entire ropeway to shake violently. Each time he touched the metal winch cable, sharp static shocks surged through his body.

He muttered under his breath, 'Great, one more challenge to deal with,' as he prepared to leap from the hovering helicopter onto the swaying cable car, dodging the network of cables all around.

From that vantage point, he had a clear view of the entire ropeway—the vibrating lines, the swaying cable cars and the helpless people frantically waving from the windows. He couldn't help but remember what his instructors at GRTC had often said: 'You'll be tested when the time comes.'

Well, this was it—just not quite how he'd imagined it.

Apparently, the twenty-seven-year-old's 'test' came with an adrenaline rush and a front-row seat to a disaster movie all while the world placed its hopes on his courage. Just staring at the earth below from that height would be unnerving enough to stop the hearts of many—let alone dangling from a thin rope beneath a helicopter.

The gunner continued lowering Tejpal, and when he was about fifteen feet away from the cable car—at the same altitude—he tried using his RT set to request a slight shift in the helicopter's position so he could be dropped directly onto the trolley.

However, the deafening roar of the Mi-17V-5's rotors and the overpowering downwash drowned out all communication. Frantically, he resorted to hand signals to communicate his intent to the gunner JWO Venkatesh and Garud Pankaj Kumar Rana, who were standing at the aircraft's door.

He signalled back—this was the best position the helicopter could hold. Any further movement risked the rotors touching or cutting through the cables.

Now a new challenge awaited Flight Lieutenant Tejpal Yadav: He would have to swing his way onto the cable car, covering the remaining fifteen feet between him and the trolley at a parallel distance on his own. Hanging in mid-air, he began to generate momentum, swaying back and forth on the winch cable. Soon, he realized he was swinging in two motions—circular, with the winch as the axis, and pendulum-like, towards the trolley. He worked hard to control the circular motion, spreading his arms and legs. Once steady, he started swinging forward like Tarzan to cover the distance.

Tejpal silently thanked his instructors, who had pushed him to swing, roll, crawl and endure endless punishment during training. Without their persistence, this moment might have broken him.

After nearly twenty exhausting minutes, Tejpal managed to grab one of the ropeway cables, near the trolley just slightly above the trolley roof, which could be used to reach the trolley roof by adjusting the winch. But a new problem arose.

As he tried to land, the trolley began to sway, and his body repeatedly slammed into its frame. His hands, stomach and waist were scraped against the rough iron. Injuries piled up—sharp cuts and bruises. The pain was intense, but Tejpal gritted his teeth and pressed on, knowing there was no room for failure in this high-stakes mission.

Finally, battling the rotor downwash and navigating through the tangle of cables, Tejpal landed on the roof of the swaying cable car. And now, a new challenge awaited him: How to enter the trolley. Gripping the edges to prevent himself from falling to a sure death, Tejpal realized everything now depended on his judgment and skills.

Carefully, Tejpal detached himself from the winch cable and used the rope he had brought to secure himself to the trolley's support cable—the same cable connecting the trolley to the main structure. With no support from the helicopter, he was now completely on his own. His only safeguard was the 9-mm rope tied to the trolley cable, which would hopefully prevent a fatal fall should anything go wrong.

The next task was to unlock the door and enter the cable car.

Inside, five passengers—stranded for over twenty-four hours—watched helplessly as Tejpal manoeuvred across the roof. The Garud team had focused so intently on planning the landing that they hadn't fully considered how to work the knobs on the locking mechanism. At those altitudes and in those winds, the knobs had jammed.

He realized he would need to hang head-down, like Spiderman, to get a firm grip and unlock the door. He tied a knot in the rope for leverage and took a Spiderman-like leap—legs up, head down, relying entirely on his upper body strength.

The wind was strong. The trolley rocked under its force, but Tejpal managed to stabilize himself by anchoring his boots against the structure. In this precarious position, he finally managed to open the lock.

Tejpal later recounted:

I remember the view of the ground and hills while hanging upside down, 1,200 feet up. At that moment, you can't help but look down. I can't describe how terrifying the sight was—it was beyond anything my brain had ever processed. But I held my nerve and focused on my task.

With the door now unlocked, it was time to enter the cable car. However, the moment the doors swung open, the passengers—who had felt secure in their enclosed space—were overwhelmed by the sight of the 1,200-foot drop below them. Their fatigue and fear took over, and they began to panic, shouting and moving around frantically.

Still outside the cable car, Tejpal acted quickly. As he began manoeuvring to enter, he shouted repeatedly, 'Move away! Move away! Hold on to something! Hold on to something!'

Using the 9-mm rope tied to the trolley cable, he swung into the cabin. Despite the chaos and the dizzying height, he managed to secure himself and calm the frightened passengers. The most critical part of the mission was now complete—he had successfully entered the cable car. He thanked his stars.

High above, Group Captain Kandalkar felt the weight of concern pressing down on him.

The helicopter had been hovering in one position for over twenty minutes. When helicopters fly, airflow helps cool the engines and other systems. But during prolonged hovering, this airflow is disrupted, causing the systems to overheat. To prevent a potential crash, the helicopter would soon need to fly a circuit.[24]

However, they couldn't abandon the Flight Lieutinent Tejapal Yadav below without confirmation of his safety. Communication with him had been nearly impossible due to the deafening rotor noise and the strong winds.

Just as the tension peaked, the gunner relayed the long-awaited news: The Garud had successfully entered the cable car. The captain let out a deep sigh of relief.

Inside the swaying cable car, the passengers were in a state of panic. The family of five—a mother, father and their three sons—sat huddled together, bruised and terrified. Trapped for over thirty hours without food or water, they were weak, disoriented and unsure if stepping out of the cabin would lead to safety or disaster.

---

24 A circuit is a flight manoeuvre or pattern flown by an aircraft to position it correctly in three-dimensional space for landing, while avoiding obstructions and potential collisions with other aircraft.

When Flight Lieutenant Tejpal appeared, the family's emotions were a mix of relief and fear. The sight of the Garud reassured them, but survival instincts and exhaustion clouded their judgment. Calmly, he took out food and water from his bag, and offered it to the family. He reassured them, patiently explaining what would happen next, encouraging them and praising their bravery.

As he spoke, he closed the open door of the car to make them feel safer.

After much reassurance, the family finally agreed to step outside. Tejpal handed them the extra harnesses he had brought and asked who would go first. The family pointed to the mother, hoping she would handle it first and they would take a leap of faith after her. However, after assessing the risks, Tejpal decided to start with the youngest son, a thirty-two-year-old man. The eldest son was paralysed by fear and refused to move. With great patience, Tejpal secured the harness on the youngest son and guided him to the edge.

The winch cable, thrown from the helicopter swung wildly across the fifteen-foot gap to the cabin. Each time, Tejpal had to catch it in mid-air and hook it securely to the survivor. It was no easy task. It took six or seven attempts to retrieve the cable each time, his body half-extended outside the swaying car.

But, the real challenge was psychological—convincing the frightened passengers to step out. Tejpal couldn't force anyone, so he motivated them with calm and reassuring words. Finally, the passengers mustered the courage to trust the harness and be winched up.

Once they reached the helicopter, they were swiftly pulled inside.

The evacuation of the first cable car took time. As the last passenger—now calmer—prepared to step out, he asked, 'What is your name, soldier?'

'Tejpal,' came the reply.

With a faint smile, the man said, 'Thank you very much for saving us,' before being lifted away.

For the first time since the distress call, Flight Lieutenant Tejpal smiled. That simple gesture of gratitude reignited his resolve. He quickly prepared to assist the remaining forty-three passengers.

The helicopter had been hovering for nearly forty-five minutes, and its systems were dangerously overheating. There was no time to winch Flight Lieutenant Tejpal back up. The aircraft needed to break hover and complete a cooling circuit immediately.

With the five rescued passengers aboard, the helicopter departed, leaving Tejpal behind in the cable car. A message was relayed to him: Wait for the V-5's return. However, the initial panic had given way to confidence and hope. Tejpal didn't mind staying behind—he was happy—and ready for whatever came next.

~

Trikut Ropeway
0050 hours

The helicopter swiftly dropped the five survivors at the makeshift helipad before returning to the first trolley, where Flight Lieutenant Tejpal Yadav was waiting. A wave of relief and joy spread across the site—the mission had succeeded. The media began flashing positive news. Though the operation had started on a sombre note due to a casualty,[25] the successful rescue brought renewed hope.

---

[25] There was a casualty on first day of the rescue operation when one person died due to serious injuries sustained when some of the trolleys collided. TimesofIndia.com, 'Deogarh ropeway accident: One dead, 48 stranded; rescue operation on', 11 April 2022, *Times of India*, https://

When the helicopter—piloted by Group Captain Kandalkar and co-piloted by Squadron Leader K.K. Singh—returned to the first trolley, instead of winching Tejpal up, he reattached himself to the helicopter's cable, and they flew directly to the next cabin, which held three passengers—bruised, frightened and traumatized. He once again repeated the entire process, successfully evacuating all three victims.

By then, the helicopter's fuel levels were critically low. The crew dropped the evacuees with the civil administration, where the DM and the NDRF teams quickly transported them to hospitals and administered aid. Meanwhile, the helicopter crew and the Garuds returned to the Deoghar aerodrome for refuelling.

The rescuers were greeted with heartfelt gratitude upon landing. Flight Lieutenant Tejpal recalls an elderly man approaching him with a plate of food, urging him to eat. The crew hadn't eaten in nearly a day, but Tejpal, preparing for the next sortie, politely declined and moved on to brief his boys. By this time, the operation had become more structured.

Tejpal's daring actions and calculated risks, taken at great personal peril, had set a precedent for others to execute the winching operations more swiftly and safely.

After completing his briefing, Tejpal noticed the same elderly man waiting nearby with the plate of food. Frustrated, he said, 'Uncle, I'm busy. I can't eat right now. Why are you following me?'

The man replied, 'The boy you just saved is my relative. You must eat something.'

Tejpal was taken aback. Though he had no appetite, he quietly ate a few morsels.

---

timesofindia.indiatimes.com/city/ranchi/jharkhand-ropeway-accident-one-dead-operation-on-to-rescue-others-stranded-in-cable-cars/articleshow/90774200.cms.

He also recalled how, on day one, while hanging between cable car number 13 and cable car number 14 (they had decided to clear 14 first), a small child had waved his hand out of the window and called out, 'Uncle, *pahle hume nikalo* (Uncle, please rescue us first).'

Tejpal had wanted desperately to follow that voice and save the child first, but he knew that in a combat zone, there is no room for emotions—they can jeopardize not only the mission but also cost more lives.

During a quick break between sorties at Deoghar aerodrome, Tejpal finally checked his phone and saw at least twenty missed calls from his father. When he called back, his worried father immediately asked him, his voice shaking, 'Where are you, beta?'

Tejpal, not wanting to worry him, lied, 'I am at my base, Papa.'

His father replied, 'No, you are lying … I just saw you on TV.'

Tejpal tried again. 'That must be someone else,' he said, and quickly ended the call.

He then walked over to an area where a TV was playing. On every news channel, footage of the Deoghar cable car rescue was flashing—and so was his face.

He shared later:

'*Zoom kar karke dikha rahe the* (They were zooming in on my face). I had no way out but to call my dad again.'

He called home and explained his role, still trying to downplay it. His father said, '*Beta, gaon se bees-pachees log ghar par hi aa gaye hain, aur hum sab mil ke tumhe TV par dekh rahe hai. Sabko bacha ke lana, par apna bhi dhyan rakhna* (Son, twenty to twenty-five people from the village have come home, and we're all watching you on TV. Bring everyone back safely, but take care of yourself too).'

Word had spread through his village.

Tejpal laughed as he shared:

'I told him, *aapne bahut ghee khilaya hai, aap tension mat lo* (you've fed me enough ghee over the years, don't worry).'

I smiled. No matter who you are, how many awards you win, how many people you save, or how great a soldier you become, when it comes to your father, you will always be the little child trying to win in his eyes. That day, Tejpal's simple, humble father finally understood who his son truly was and felt proud of it.

The rescue operation continued into the following day. The Indian Air Force deployed Cheetah and ALH helicopters to assist the Mi-17V-5 crew. On 11 April, the V-5 crew rescued twenty-two people from seven cable cars, though the day ended on a sombre note due to a casualty reported during the ALH operation.

That night, Sergeant Pankaj Kumar Rana decided to remain in one of the last cabins, which housed an injured child who couldn't be evacuated that day. The daring Garud, who had also saved many lives, felt it was his moral duty to stay and comfort those still waiting to be rescued.

Though it was the right decision, it also gave Flight Lieutenant Tejpal, his commanding officer, a sleepless night as his boy would be spending the night suspended mid-air in a cramped car.

Using a satellite phone, Tejpal managed to reach Rana. The sergeant said light-heartedly, 'Sir, the view here is amazing. I'm enjoying the ride—just make sure to buy a ticket. I got on without one.' He said it mostly to ease his CO's concern.

Such is the indomitable spirit of a Garud—they never give up!

The helicopter crew, too, displayed extraordinary courage, risking their lives while managing those complicated hovering operations back to back and setting an example in helicopter rescue operations.

Group Captain Kandalkar recalled a moment on the night of 11 April when he returned to base and spoke to his technical team, on ground which had been working tirelessly to keep the helicopters operational. Concerned, he asked if they had managed to eat or rest.

Their response stunned him: 'Don't worry, sir. Just save the people. We'll eat later.'

He reflected:

As the Commanding Officer, I was the father of the unit. It was my responsibility to look after their well-being. Had they complained about circumstances, it might have distracted me. But they showed dedication to the cause. I felt lucky to have such a team by my side.

∼

Trikut Ropeway
12 April 2022

The next day dawned with a renewed sense of determination as the Indian Air Force continued their rescue mission. They managed to save thirteen more people stranded in three cable cars, but the operation was fraught with challenges. The trolleys reeked of urine and excreta, compounding the distress of the passengers. Without child-specific harnesses, the Garud Special Forces had to secure children with tactical belts and carry them in their arms during high-risk manoeuvres.

On the ground, managing the crowd was becoming increasingly difficult. The Garuds had to repeatedly request the authorities to clear the ground beneath the operational zone, fearing that their equipment, such as daggers, might fall, or worse, a cable car could crash on to the onlookers. At times, Garud personnel narrowly avoided fatal falls while jumping from one cabin to another, their survival often hanging by mere inches.

The pilots faced their own set of hurdles, learning and adapting with each sortie as unpredictable conditions tested their limits.

Despite their relentless efforts, the day ended in tragedy when an elderly woman fell to her death after the winch cable became entangled in the ropeway line. Flight Lieutenant Tejpal, who was inside the cabin, risked his life by climbing atop the swaying cable car to untangle the cable. She was dangling precariously in mid-air, beyond his or the gunner's reach—despite his best efforts, he couldn't save her, and she fell.

Reflecting on that day, Tejpal later recalled:

The helicopter then flew back with the other two survivors for repairs and refuelling. I sat atop the car for a moment, overwhelmed. I didn't feel like entering the cabin again—her husband was inside, the last passenger yet to be rescued. I felt exhausted and drained, but I had to complete the mission.

When Tejpal re-entered the car, the woman's grieving husband, devastated by what he'd just witnessed, faced the Garud. Filled with anguish and rage, he accused him, '*Gira diya na*? (You let her fall, didn't you?)'

Those words cut deeply into Tejpal's soul.

He knew the man wasn't wrong to blame him; they had placed their trust in him. Unable to explain the technical difficulties or the inherent risks, Tejpal could only urge the man to wear the harness and gently console him. He talked about how the other two passengers in the cable car had been saved, and that destiny worked in strange ways. Eventually, the man agreed to leave the cabin, and Tejpal winched him to safety.

Tejpal recounted the emotional challenges of rescuing injured, frightened and distressed people. Each individual reacted differently—some were calm, while others were gripped by fear. Convincing each one of them to step out of the cabin was daunting.

He shared a particularly difficult encounter involving a young man in his twenties who refused to leave the cabin. Despite repeated attempts to secure him with the harness, the man blocked the door in fear, delaying the operation. With the helicopter hovering and time running out, Tejpal resorted to stern tactics:

> I told him calmly, 'We're risking our lives forty-eight times for forty-eight people. The helicopters are flying at maximum capacity, which is risky too. If you waste more time, I might just push you out, and no one will know what happened here. The choice is yours.' Within minutes, he wore the harness and almost jumped onto the winch cable, staring at me in disbelief.

Tejpal laughed at the memory.

There were three casualties across different days, but overall, it was a successful rescue mission in which most of the passengers were saved—thanks to the collective efforts of multiple forces.

When the aircrew landed after completing their final sortie, the atmosphere was charged with gratitude and celebration. Some people touched their feet, others patted their backs, offered sweets, or simply cried while hugging them.

These were the real heroes—men who had risked their lives forty-eight times, facing unimaginable odds.

Many wanted to honour them or invite them into their homes, but within hours of completing the mission, the helicopter crew and Garud had quietly disappeared. Exhausted after working tirelessly for seventy-two hours, they needed rest. For them, saving lives was the greatest reward.

Flight Lieutenant Tejpal Yadav and his team returned to base by 1800 hours on 12 April, where they were met by the AOC of Kalaikunda Air Force station and several senior officers waiting on the runway to welcome the young soldiers. The AOC personally shook hands with each member and invited them to a mess party scheduled for 1900 hours. Tejpal attended the party in his grease-stained uniform and quickly became the star of the evening. The AOC spent a good fifteen minutes praising the heroism displayed by the 627 Garud Flight during the operation.

While concluding my research for the story, I also had the opportunity to speak with the then NDRF Deputy Inspector General Manoj Yadav, who had overseen ground operations. He praised the aircrew wholeheartedly:

> People think the operation was as simple as flying in and picking people up, but such missions are highly technical and require the highest level of skill and preparation. The helicopter's thrust was so strong that it made the cable sway, yet the pilots stabilized the aircraft, maintained precision and approached carefully.
>
> The Mi-17V-5 is a massive aircraft, and its engine cooling depends on continuous flying. Hovering for too long can overheat the engine, posing a significant risk to both the helicopter and the crew. Each sortie required detailed assessment, hovering, and sometimes several circuits.
>
> For each trolley, two to three sorties were often needed. The Garuds had to be dropped and physically enter the trolley to carry

out the rescue at grave risk to their own lives; yet, they did it. I wholeheartedly appreciate the Indian Air Force.

The then District Magistrate of Deoghar, now district magistrate and deputy commisioner of Ranchi, Manjunath Bhajantri, also expressed his gratitude, saying:

> Not just as a government authority, but as a citizen, I am deeply thankful to the Indian Air Force. In the end, everything depended on them. Had they failed, the outcome would have been very different and could have caused significant embarrassment for the nation, even internationally.

~

Aftermath

It was a mission that ended on a perfect note for the personnel involved. Shortly after the rescue operation, Flight Lieutenant Tejpal Yadav and the aircrew received a phone call from the then SASO Eastern Air Command Air Marshal A.P. Singh (now Chief of the Air Staff), who warmly commended their efforts and invited them to the Eastern Command. He was the first amongst the highest authorities to acknowledge their heroism.

They were later felicitated by Air Marshal Dilip Kumar Patnaik, the AOC-in-C[26] at Eastern Air Command Headquarters. On 12 April, honourable Prime Minister Narendra Modi personally addressed all the teams via video conference, congratulating them on their unparalleled professionalism, extending a gesture to acknowledge the valour of brave men by the highest chairs of the nation which made all the forces and civilian authorities involved very

---

26 Air Officer Commanding-in-Chief.

proud. Their names were subsequently recommended for numerous honours.

The crew was showered with record number of awards and commendations for the rescue operation. Among the recognitions were three Shaurya Chakras, awarded to Group Captain Yogeshwar Krishnarao Kandalkar, Flight Lieutenant Tejpal Yadav and Leading Aircraftman (LAC) Sunil Kumar.

The Vayu Sena Medal (Gallantry) was conferred upon Squadron Leader K.K. Singh, Sergeant Pankaj Kumar Rana, LAC R. Singh, Corporal[27] Satyendra Kumar and Corporal A.M. Khan. Numerous commendations from the Chief of the Air Staff and the AOC-in-Chief, Eastern Air Command, were also awarded to individuals who had contributed directly or indirectly to the success of the daring rescue operation.

One of the most memorable moments for the awardees was visiting Rashtrapati Bhavan with their families to receive the honours. They had the privilege of meeting the President of India, the prime minister, the defence minister and other national dignitaries, all of whom applauded their extraordinary efforts against grave odds in Deoghar, Jharkhand.

During the ceremony, Prime Minister Modi even stopped to speak with Flight Lieutenant Tejpal Yadav, remarking, 'How were you swinging by the rope? That was very risky.' Then he said to Gp Capt Kandalkar, '*humne to asha hi chor di thi ki helicopter se nahi hoga to kaise nikalenge logo ko par aapne kar dikhaya.*'

---

[27] A Corporal in the Indian Air Force is a non-commissioned officer who serves as a vital link between higher-ranking officers and junior airmen. The rank signifies a commendable level of experience, expertise and leadership within the enlisted ranks. Corporals are responsible for supervising and mentoring junior airmen, ensuring the smooth execution of daily tasks, and maintaining discipline and order within their units.

For Tejpal, the award ceremony held a personal victory beyond the honours. It became a pivotal moment in his life as he finally introduced his girlfriend to his parents.

Coming from a traditional village background, his family had previously opposed the idea of an inter-caste marriage. Despite his repeated requests, they had refused to meet his college sweetheart. However, during the investiture ceremony, he invited both his parents and his girlfriend to attend. They stayed with him for two days, watched him receive the award at Rashtrapati Bhavan, and spent time together. This shared experience changed their perspective and they finally approved of his relationship.

As Tejpal shared with me:

> I could never have taken my girl to my village; society there is very different. But during the award ceremony, I got the chance for my parents and her to meet. They liked each other so much and eventually my parents gave their blessing.

At the time of writing, Tejpal has been married for a month and a half, and is enjoying newlywed life.

I want to conclude this story with Prime Minister Modi's remark that 'the heroic Deoghar cable car rescue set a precedent for saving lives in similar situations in the future'.

His words ring true. Everyone involved in the operation, whether awarded or not, is a superhero. Not only because they saved lives, along with the countless families, hopes and dreams tied to them, but also because God forbid if a similar situation ever arises again, they have set a precedent for such rescue operations.

Author's note

This story is based on interviews conducted with the heroes who carried out this extraordinary mission—Group Captain Yogeshwar Krishnarao Kandalkar, the Captain of the Mi-17 V5 helicopters; Flight Lieutenant Tejpal Yadav, the then CO 627 Garud Flight and team leader of the Garud detachment; Shri Manoj Yadav, the then Deputy Inspector General of the NDRF, who led the ground operations; and Shri Manjunath Bhajantri, the then District Magistrate of Deoghar. I am deeply grateful to each of them for placing their trust in me. How often do we witness helicopters soaring above floods, disasters and emergencies—yet overlook the silent courage of our helicopter pilots? Through this story, I have tried to honour not only the helicopter stream of the Indian Air Force but also the rare bravery of the Garud Special Forces. What makes this mission exceptional is not just its operational uniqueness, but the seamless coordination, quick decision-making, mutual trust, and efficiency displayed by the Indian Air Force, NDRF and civil administration—working as one for the nation. This synergy was later lauded by the prime minister, Narendra Modi.

The Garud: Indian Air Force's Elite Special Forces

The Indian Air Force's Special Forces, known as the Garud, derive their name from Garuda—a divine, bird-like creature in Hindu mythology, often depicted as the mount of Lord Vishnu. Like Garuda, described in the scriptures as a vigilant protector capable of swift travel and an enemy of serpents, the Garud Special Forces embody dedication and formidable strength.

History

Established in September 2003, while the first batch was passed out in 2004, the Garud is the youngest Special Forces of India. After the Kargil War, and especially after terrorist attempts to attack two major air bases in Jammu and Kashmir in 2001, IAF leaders recognized the need for a specialized force to protect critical air assets and respond to terror threats targeting airfields. Before the formation of the Garud, troops from Indian Army fulfilled some of these specialised tasks for the IAF.

Originally named the 'Tiger Force', the unit was later renamed as Garud Forces. The Garud made their first public appearance during the Air Force Day celebrations in New Delhi on 8 October 2004. However, the 2016 terrorist attack on the Pathankot Airbase shifted the paradigm. Not only were additional Garud flights raised but it also underlined the need for these elite forces in counter-insurgency operations within India.

Role

The Garud is not a covert force but a highly specialized branch of the Indian Air Force, established to undertake a wide range of missions in various environments. Their primary objective is to safeguard India's high-value air assets and conduct special Air Force operations. In peacetime, they support air operations, and participate in counterterrorism and Humanitarian Assistance and Disaster Relief (HADR) missions.

Unlike the Air Force Police and Defence Security Corps, who manage base protection, Garuds are trained for high-risk, specialized missions similar to the Army's Para Special Forces or the Navy's Marcos. They are also capable of operations behind enemy lines, which may require infiltration by air, sea or land. It is therefore they undergo a versatile training programme that equips the Garuds to operate under any conditions—in the air, on land or in water.

Training

Garud trainees undergo an eleven-month intensive training programme—the longest of any Special Forces in India. This demanding training—amongst the most rigorous in the world—pushes candidates to their physical, mental and emotional limits, ensuring only the most resilient join this elite force.

Officer and airmen candidates for Garud are selected from volunteers across different branches and trades. Officers and enlisted personnel face a gruelling seven day pre-assessment and selection before being called for probation training, i.e., the beginning of Garud SF training. The minimum requirement for airmen is in line with any other tradesman entry, like a twelfth-grade education, and applicants are specifically evaluated for their physical parameters. Successful candidates begin their intensive training at the Garud Regimental Training Centre (GRTC) in Uttar Pradesh, which includes a probation period, commando training, parachuting, skill specialization and core competency orientation. The initial three-month probation phase focuses on rigorous physical conditioning and filters candidates for advanced training, i.e. three months of Garud Special Ops Course Commando and six months of further training on MT driving , para descent course, advance SF skill course and advance special ops course. After completing these phases, candidates undergo various specialized training courses, such as military martial arts, low-intensity conflict operations, jungle and snow survival, high-altitude warfare and bomb disposal.

Officer and airmen candidates for the Garud are selected from volunteers across different branches and trades. The Garuds undergo various in-service courses as well, like advanced combat training and collaborative international training. They frequently train with various world-renowned Special Forces such as the USAF STS, British SAS, and Israeli Sayeret Matkal, which enhances their adaptability and equips them with globally recognized best practices.

Their training also includes tech-enhanced skills, such as operating UAVs (Unmanned Aerial Vehicles), advanced communication systems and Laser Designators, providing them with a critical advantage in modern warfare.

Responsibilities

Though their operational journey began with Operation Haran in 2005, Garuds have since participated in various high-profile operations, both in India and abroad. In 2019, they were part of the first deployment of the Armed Forces Special Operations Division in Jammu and Kashmir. They have also been involved in major humanitarian operations and large-scale air shows that demonstrate the might of the Indian Air Force.

Perhaps the most crucial aspect of their work is their ability to operate at the intersection of air and ground power, which is invaluable in an age where hybrid warfare blends traditional combat.

The garud perform multi-faceted critical roles. Their primary responsibilities include protecting Indian Air Force high value assets from sabotage and terrorist attacks. They undertake high-risk missions such as combat search and rescue (CSAR) to retrieve downed pilots from hostile zones, ensure personnel safety, and conduct counterterrorism operations and special reconnaissance .

In destruction of enemy air assets (DEAA) missions, they take direct action to neutralize enemy capabilities, targeting critical infrastructure to disrupt reinforcements. Garuds' niche ability is to expand strategic capability by supporting air operations, including laser designation for precision strikes, integrating advanced technologies, conducting post-strike damage assessments and destroying enemy assets.

Capabilities like Terminal Attack Control (TAC) enables them to guide fighter aircraft on targeting operations. In their Combat Control (CCT) role, they capture and secure airfields in hostile areas, often deploying Combat Free Fall (CFF) for covert insertions, preparing landing strips, and managing air space in the midst of obstacles and hostilities.

Garuds often operate alongside the Rashtriya Rifles in Jammu and Kashmir to gain operational experience. In Kashmir, they are actively engaged in counter-insurgency efforts, neutralizing terrorist groups like Lashkar-e-Taiba (LeT) through direct encounters and intelligence gathering.

Though Garud had been actively deployed since 2004, not a single book on Indian Air force has attempted to feature them with the glory they desreve. So with *Wings of Valour* I have attempted to fill that gap in Indian Military literature. The pride of purpose remains immense that with the help of glorious Garuds themselves, I have been successful in immortalising all their Battle Casulties in one book for them never to fade away from the public memory.

Let the stories begin.

3

Corporal Gursevek Singh, Shaurya Chakra (Posthumous): The Immortal of the Pathankot Attack

IT WAS A cold night at the Pathankot Air Force base, the clock ticking just past 0200 hours. The air was windy and chilly, the ground damp with dew. The base, usually bustling with activity, now lay shrouded in an eerie silence. Somewhere within its sprawling confines, hidden terrorists lurked.

A Gypsy rolled to a silent stop, well short of the target area's perimeter. Its headlights had been turned off before reaching the final stretch to avoid detection. Six figures stepped out silently, clad in the digital print winter uniforms of the Indian Air Force, and tactical vests. Each was armed with an Israeli Tavor CTAR assault rifle, suitable for close combat with its 5.56-mm calibre. The rifles were fitted with a multi-purpose reflex sight and single laser pointers.[1] The men's faces were obscured by helmets and night vision goggles.

---

1 Tavor CTAR Integral, Tavor Assault Rifle, Israel Weapon Industries, https://iwi.net/iwi-tavor-rifle/tavor-ctar-integral/.

These were the elite Garud Special Forces, specially trained for such covert operations. Leading the team was their Commanding Officer Squadron Leader Bhavesh Kumar Dubey,[2] a seasoned warrior with years of combat experience.

Beside him was another Garud, his high cheekbones and strong jawline giving him a fierce, almost intimidating look. His dark eyes were sharp and piercing, capable of assessing threats and opportunities in an instant. The uniform clung to his muscular frame and his tactical vest added bulk without hindering his mobility. His helmet, fitted with advanced communication gear, sat snugly on his head, complementing his battle-ready appearance. Even in full gear, his movements were fluid and efficient, a clear indication that he knew his business.

This was Corporal Gursevek Singh, unaware that he would soon etch his name into history as the first Garud to make the supreme sacrifice for the nation.

The other four Garuds followed the CO and Gursevek, moving with the same tactical precision, every muscle tensed, every sense heightened. They spread out in formation, the sniper taking point, his rifle raised, and scanning for the slightest movement. Slowly and methodically, they advanced, their boots making barely a whisper on the ground.

They encountered a twisted section of the perimeter fence, raising their suspicions. The CO signalled heightened alert with a series of hand gestures. The team moved past the fence and approached a drainage ditch, overgrown with thick vegetation. Without a word, they dropped into it, crawling through the wet, muddy passage. The

---

2 'Squadron Leader Bhavesh Kumar Dubey Conferred Vayu Sena Medal (Gallantry) ', Aviation Defence Universe, 15 August 2016, https://www.aviation-defence-universe.com/squadron-leader-bhavesh-kumar-dubey-conferred-vayu-sena-medal-gallantry/.

thick foliage provided cover but also concealed potential threats. They knew a clear shot from a hidden enemy could come at any moment. Still, crawling through the ditch was the safest way to cross the area.

Emerging from the drainage trench, they encountered another fence, this one with wires cleanly cut. This was no accident. The CO and his team knew they were on the right track.

The CO held the wire as one soldier crawled through, then the second soldier held it as the CO followed. As the third soldier began to cross, his tactical vest snagged on the metal. It was Corporal Shailabh Gaur. He looked ahead; the CO and Corporal Gursevek Singh had already moved towards the military transport (MT)[3] area, where old, damaged Military Engineer Services (MES)[4] vehicles lay scattered. They were now out of sight, and he needed to cover them quickly. Struggling to free his vest, he was caught off guard.

Suddenly, the night erupted with the staccato rattle of gunfire. Muzzle flashes lit the darkness, and the sharp cracks of rifles shattered the silence. A grenade was thrown and it detonated nearby. The rest of the Garud approaching the fence scrambled for cover as the explosion rocked the area, showering dirt and debris around them.

Garud Gaur's thoughts raced to the CO and Corporal Gursevek. They were out of sight and clearly under fire. Despite the continuous gunfire, their training and discipline shone through even in this

---

3   Military transport refers to the movement of personnel, equipment, supplies and other resources by vehicles, aircraft, ships or trains, to support military operations. It is a critical component of logistics and operational planning in the armed forces.
4   The Military Engineer Services (MES) is a branch of the Indian Army responsible for providing engineering and infrastructure support. It plays a critical role in maintaining and developing the infrastructure necessary for military operations.

unexpected attack in the pitch dark, proving that they were fighting back effectively.

Gaur shouted, 'What's happening?'

Gursevek's voice came through, 'Come over!'

Recognizing the urgency, Gaur understood they needed immediate cover. He quickly removed his jacket and moved towards the MT yard, where the CO and Gursevek were engaged in a critical battle.

This was no ordinary confrontation—it was a stand against vicious terrorists intent on damaging and destroying India's precious assets. Their target was the pride of the Indian Air Force: Multi-billion-dollar fighter jets, radars, missiles and more, housed in the technical area[5] of the base. These weren't local militants but highly trained, Jaish-e Mohammed fidayeen of the Afzal Guru squad[6] sent on a special mission to achieve something unprecedented in the history of terror attacks on India. Their aim was to ensure the attack echoed around the world.

It was a fight for survival. The battle was on!

~

---

5 An airbase's technical area is a designated zone where aircraft maintenance, repair and technical support activities are conducted. It includes maintenance hangars, storage facilities, avionics and electronics bays, ground support equipment, technical workshops and other critical infrastructure essential for the operational readiness and efficiency of the airbase.

6 Abhinav Pandya, *Jaish-e-Muhammad: Inside the Terrifying World of the Prophet's Army* (New Delhi: HarperCollins India, 2024), p 338.

Adampur Airbase
Within 100 kilometres of the Indo-Pak Border
Jalandhar, Punjab
1 January 2016

Corporal Gursevek was in a jovial mood. He had just spoken to his newly wedded wife, wishing her a happy new year and a lifetime of togetherness. Though he could not stay on the call for long—he had to return to duty—the memories of their wedding remained vivid.

His brothers-in-arms back at the Adampur Flight[7] couldn't attend the wedding due to leave restrictions, but everything else had been perfect.

Jaspreet Kaur later shared:

> Ours was an arranged marriage, fixed by our grandfathers who were friends. We saw each other for the first time during our engagement in August 2012. I liked him instantly. We knew he was a commando[8] in the Air Force, and I couldn't stop gushing over it. I always thought, if the slightest thing went wrong, he would handle it. But I never imagined that one day, he himself would be taken away. He tried to tell me many times during our three-and-a-half-year-long courtship that his job was risky, but I always dismissed it, thinking, "*Aisa thode na hota hai* (Things like that don't actually happen)".

Even though they had wanted to get married as soon as possible, Gursevek's posting to Srinagar and some personal issues within their

---

7 The Garud unit at the Adampur airbase.
8 Special Forces personnel are popularly referred to as commandos.

families had delayed the wedding until 18 November 2015—just forty-five days before the fateful incident.[9]

Corporal Shailabh Gaur, Gursevek's brother-in-arms, had been with him every step of the way—from their rigorous Garud training to joint postings. They faced the same perilous operation during the Pathankot attack, where both were shot. Only Shailabh survived to tell the story, having had the honour of sharing his journey with the legendary Garud, Gursevek.

Their journey began at the Indian Air Force recruitment rally[10] in Ambala in 2008. Gursevek hailed from the village of Garnala, while Shailabh was from Ambala Cantt, just five kilometres away. The rally, titled 'Indian Air Force Security', attracted thousands of aspirants and was designed to recruit candidates for one of the most rigorous training programmes in India.

The difficulty was evident from the start. Shailabh remembers a rope tied at the entrance gate—only those whose heads touched it were allowed inside for the written test. The test itself was much tougher than those of other forces, demanding a high level of aptitude and intelligence. After the written test, candidates had to run 2.4 kilometres in ten minutes—on the same day. Many succeeded, many did not, but despite the long, exhausting day, both Gursevek and Shailabh were selected for the next round.

It was then that Gaur first met Gursevek. Seeing him walking back from the centre, he offered Gursevek a lift.

---

9 The terrorists attacked on the Pathankot Air Force base on 2 January 2016, in which he made the supreme sacrifice for the nation.
10 The Indian Air Force conducts open recruitment rallies for various technical and non-technical positions (below officer rank). Eligible candidates can register and participate in the selection process as part of these rallies.

The following morning, they had to report again and run an additional five kilometres, followed by an interview to assess their English-speaking skills and then medical tests. Eventually, only a few made it to the final selection list. Gursevek and Shailabh were among those chosen for training, but received their enrolment letters a year and a half later due to recruitment-related delays.

Shailabh clearly remembers 30 June 2010 as the day they began their journey at the Airmen Training School[11] in Belgaum (now Belagavi), Karnataka. They trained there for four months. At every stage, recruits were filtered out, but it was only at the Garud Regimental Training Centre (GRTC) that they realized their real training had truly begun.

The days were long and the nights felt endless at GRTC. They faced the gruelling demands of Indian Air Force Special Forces training, which involved running with heavy logs, crawling over sharp stones with bare chests and bound hands, and performing hundreds of push-ups on their knuckles. Their bodies were marked daily by blood from abrasions caused by sharp stones, bushes and thorns. They crossed drainage ditches, crucial for infiltration training—trenches filled with filth, and reeking unbearably. Yet, each of them would crawl, roll or even stand submerged head-down in the same dirty water for hours.

They also endured survival training without food or water, with sleep only a distant dream. Punishments were relentless, yet they constantly pushed their physical and mental limits—climbing ropes, navigating obstacles, running and performing front rolls over hot, uneven terrain.

---

11 https://indianairforce.nic.in/airmen-training-school/Provides joint Basic Phase Training for all trades of airmen. It has now been renamed as BTI (Basic Training Institute).

'It was mental more than physical,' Shailabh later recalled. 'They tested our limits.'

Many recruits quit. Out of hundreds, only twenty-one remained. Ultimately, just fourteen earned the highest honour—wearing the golden proficiency badge and becoming part of the Garud Special Forces. Gursevek and Shailabh were among them.

Shailabh recalled how Gursevek remained unflinchingly calm and constantly encouraged others during tough times. When someone would say, 'I can't do this,' Gursevek would reply, 'Do you have the option to quit? No, right? You want to become a Garud? Then keep going. Don't overthink it. We're all in this together.'

His resilience was likely rooted in his spirituality. Shailabh shared:

> I remember he would recite the Guru Granth Sahib every day, even if only for five minutes. He was deeply inspired by the stories of the Khalsa warriors—he would tell us how they faced death but never quit. Perhaps this inspiration drove him to become a part of Garud history himself. *Woh kahta tha, "Khalsa warrior mar jate hai par apni pagadi hui jagah kabhi nahi chodte* (He would often say, Khalsa warriors may die, but they will never abandon their turban and position)."

Shailabh vividly recalled the elation of passing their training with flying colours and receiving their maroon berets. After a year of gruelling training, donning the maroon beret marked their elite status. They were now part of a league.

Shailabh and Gursevek were posted to the Air Force Station in Srinagar, Kashmir,[12] where the unique terrain offered invaluable on-ground learning experiences.

---

[12] Anchit Gupta, 'Srinagar Air Base: A Chronicle of Aerial Combat', IAF History, 6 September 2022, https://iafhistory.in/2022/09/06/srinagar-air-base-a-chronicle-of-aerial-combat/.

Shailabh recalled those initial days:

Our first posting in Srinagar exposed us to a different reality. Especially before the abrogation of Article 370, patrolling or even walking the streets as security personnel was incredibly challenging. Mobs could appear out of nowhere, hurling stones at us. We couldn't fire at them, as they were civilians with only stones, not weapons. Even simple tasks like buying groceries in the market were fraught with danger. Locals would be hostile, often recognizing us as security forces and communicating amongst each other in their language, making us wary of potential threats. And we couldn't really do much about it as it could lead to human rights issues and unwanted international attention.

He added:

The locals would stack a lot of fodder and hay on their rooftops, which provided easy cover for snipers. There were open windows where snipers could lie in wait, target security personnel and flee within seconds through the network of underground tunnels built into the houses. Constant vigilance was part of our daily job.

After about two years in Srinagar, the two were posted to the Adampur Air Force Station in Punjab.[13] It felt like destiny had orchestrated that the two remain together.

With a touch of nostalgia, Shailabh shared:

It feels like there is someone out there planning everything for us. We are mere instruments in a grand scheme. He knows what will happen, how it will unfold, and when it will occur. He was on a

---

13 Adampur Air Force Base, Fandom.com, Military History, https://military-history.fandom.com/wiki/Adampur_Air_Force_Base.

path to greater goals, and I crossed that path. Then his marriage just forty-five days before his supreme sacrifice. How does that make sense, even though they were engaged, their marriage was delayed over one reason or the other for a long time.

Gursevek got engaged to Jaspreet Kaur while he was posted in Srinagar in 2012, during one of his leaves. But it wasn't until his posting to Adampur that they were finally able to marry, in November 2015. Their wedding was a lavish Punjabi affair, filled with joy and celebration. Although Gursevek could hardly be with his wife, he planned to secure accommodation at Adampur Air Force Station so Jaspreet could join him. Life seemed complete for him. They honeymooned in Agra, and since Ambala was close to his base, he made every effort to visit her as often as possible.

Shailabh (then a Leading Aircraftsman, now a Sergeant), recalled:

> Gursevek was transformed. The joy of marriage was evident. We teased him a lot, but he was very happy. When he returned after the wedding, he threw a lavish party for the entire flight. We celebrated with drinks and dancing. I remember his excitement as he talked about buying a car so he could visit his wife and show her around. He'd say, "Gaur bhai, you have a bike. I'll buy a car. Since our homes are close, we can use your bike on one leave and my car on the next."

Jaspreet cherishes the memories of their courtship days. She shared with me:

> After our engagement, we would talk endlessly on the phone. He'd tell me about his day, and I'd share mine. During his leave, whenever he visited his family in Garnala, he made sure to meet me. We'd go to Chandigarh, visit Sukhna Lake or the Rock

Garden together. Those days are still vivid. I never imagined the fate that awaited us or how cruel it could be.

These stories, though filled with joy, also weigh heavily on my heart. As an author, it's a rich, yet sometimes painful, journey to encounter stories brimming with beauty and hope, only to confront such tragic ends. Jaspreet and Gursevek's story is one of those wrenching narratives.

Jaspreet also shared that Gursevek rarely got leave, but he managed to come home during Christmas. That was when they discovered they were expecting their first child. Gursevek's joy was boundless. He began making plans for the next fifty years, envisioning how he would support and stand by their child.

Those were the last happy memories Jaspreet holds dear.

∼

Adampur Airbase
1 January 2016
1600 hours

Corporal Gursevek was preparing for his evening games when he received an urgent message:

> *Don full combat gear, collect rations, ammunition and other essentials for a day-long mission, and report to the armoury immediately. An Op Emergency had been declared.*

He quickly donned his tactical vest, loaded with magazines, and pulled his ballistic goggles over his digitally patterned Air Force uniform. He secured his elbow and knee pads, holstered his Glock pistol on his thigh as his personal weapon, fitted his bulletproof helmet with optical equipment, and grabbed his trusty Israeli Tavor

CTAR assault rifle. In his rucksack, he also packed a set of civilian clothes, anticipating the possibility of a reconnaissance mission in civilian areas. Although such last-minute missions were not uncommon, the specifics of this one were still unclear.

When all the Garuds assembled at the armoury, they were briefed on a critical threat to the security of the Pathankot Airbase. Reports indicated that four terrorists had crossed the international border from Pakistan using the Kathua–Gurdaspur route in Punjab on the night of 30–31 December 2015.[14] Suspected of belonging to the Jaish-e-Mohammed outfit, the terrorists were reportedly dressed in Indian Army fatigues and heavily armed with automatic weapons.

On the night of 31 December 2015, they had intercepted a taxi driven by thirty-five-year-old Ikagar Singh near Bhagwal, a remote village on the Punjab-Pakistan border.[15] There were conflicting reports about what followed—some said Ikagar fought back, while others claimed the terrorists used him to travel a short distance until one of the taxi's tyres burst. Regardless, the terrorists slit his throat and continued their escape.

They then hijacked a Mahindra XUV with a blue beacon, belonging to Punjab Police Superintendent (SP) Salwinder Singh. He was travelling with his cook, Madan Gopal and a jeweller friend, Rajesh Verma, to a shrine near the border. The terrorists tied, blindfolded and gagged Singh and his cook, leaving them in a nearby forest. Rajesh Verma was abducted and later found with his throat slit, though he survived and managed to reach a hospital.

---

14 Bharti Jain, 'Pathankot terror attack: 'Fidayeen came in batches, hid in grass', *Times of India*, 5 January 2016, https://timesofindia.indiatimes.com/india/Pathankot-terror-attack-Fidayeen-came-in-batches-hid-in-grass/articleshow/50446226.cms.

15 https://www.ndtv.com/india-news/a-cab-driver-died-fighting-pathankot-terrorists-who-wanted-his-car-1262378/ A Cop Didn't Fight Pathankot Terrorists, My Brother Did'/Jan 6 2016/ Barkha Dutt

Salwinder Singh managed to free himself and trekked to a nearby village, where he used his cell phone to alert his superiors. He reported that the terrorists had stolen his beacon-equipped vehicle and two of his three phones—they somehow missed the third phone, which he used to make the call. He also reported that the terrorists spoke Hindi, Urdu and Punjabi, and had mentioned 'Pathankot' while communicating with their handlers in Pakistan.[16]

This alert initially led the Punjab Police to treat the situation as an armed robbery because of the notorious image of SP Salwinder Singh, resulting in a critical twelve-hour delay before central agencies were involved. The blue-beacon car had indeed facilitated the terrorists' entry into Pathankot, enabling them to pass through several police checkpoints unimpeded, with police personnel even saluting them as they drove through. On 1 January, the same vehicle was discovered parked just 1.5 kilometres away from the Pathankot Airbase. It was feared that the terrorists had either already infiltrated the airbase or were hiding in the nearby Army base.

During this period, several media reports emerged, some speculating that Salwinder Singh may have acted as a courier for the terrorists,[17] given his past involvement in drug smuggling. Reports suggested that Singh had made two covert trips to the Peer Baba Mazar in Taloor village (under the Narot Jaimal Singh police station jurisdiction) on 31 December, accompanied by his cook, Madan

---

16 Barkha Dutt, 'They Came Back To Kill Me, I'm Innocent, Says Cop Abducted In Pathankot', NDTV, 5 January 2016, https://www.ndtv.com/india-news/they-came-back-to-kill-me-im-innocent-says-cop-abducted-in-pathankot-1262294.

17 Anand Kumar Patel, Alok Pandey and Sudhi Ranjan, 'Among Unanswered Questions On Pathankot Attack, Several About A Senior Cop', NDTV, 5 January 2016, https://www.ndtv.com/india-news/among-unanswered-questions-on-pathankot-attack-several-about-a-senior-cop-1262143.

Gopal—said to be his bodyguard—and his jeweller friend, Rajesh Verma.

It was rumoured that Singh received payment in diamonds for each drug consignment smuggled via that route. The proximity of the shrine to the suspected infiltration point for the terrorists raised suspicions that it might have been used by drug traffickers.[18] This speculation was reinforced by the presence of the jeweller, who, it was believed, was there to verify the authenticity of the diamonds. It was possible the Pakistan-based handlers used the same network to launch the terrorists into India.[19]

Further reports questioned why the SP was on the road at an odd hour of the night, unaccompanied by his official security detail, precisely along the route where the terrorists intercepted a ride. While the terrorists killed the driver and attacked Verma, Singh and Madan Gopal were only tied up. Some also suggested that the terrorists may have infiltrated through the unguarded *nallahs* along the India–Pakistan border, where electronic surveillance is less effective. Despite electronic monitoring, infiltration can occur at any point along this extensive and porous border.

Headlines worldwide were abuzz with reports of the terrorists' movements, coinciding with Prime Minister Narendra Modi's historic visit to Pakistan on 25 December—the first by an Indian prime

---

18 Shibhana K. Nair, 'Singh got paid in diamonds for facilitating drug racket, reveals NIA interrogation', *Mumbai Mirror*, 14 January 2016, https://mumbaimirror.indiatimes.com/news/india/Singh-got-paidin-diamonds-for-facilitating-drug-racket-reveals-NIA-interrogation/articleshow/50571154.html.

19 Punjab has long served as a transit point for drugs originating from Afghanistan. Drug money has become a major source of election funding in Punjab, and, over time, a well-organized drug cartel has emerged with the active connivance of politicians, police officers and drug lords. This illicit money is also used to finance militancy.

minister in twelve years. Intended to ease tensions between the two nations, the visit included a meeting with Pakistan's prime minister, Nawaz Sharif. However, it was widely believed that certain elements within Pakistan opposed peace and often orchestrated attacks on Indian soil whenever an Indian premier visited Pakistan in an attempt to sabotage diplomatic efforts.

As the situation escalated rapidly, Indian security agencies were placed on high alert, and the National Security Guard was mobilized to reach Pathankot.

At around 1500 hours on 1 January, the Commanding Officer Squadron Leader Bhavesh K. Dubey[20] of the Garud Flight stationed at Pathankot received a call from the higher headquarters inquiring about the status of available Garud personnel. The CO, who was on leave that day, informed them that only a few Garuds were currently present at the base, as the rest were deployed elsewhere on another critical mission.

He was told that Air Marshal S.B. Deo, Air Officer Commanding-in-Chief of Western Air Command,[21] was en route to Pathankot to coordinate the situation alongside senior leadership. To reinforce the base, he would pick up additional Garud personnel from a nearby Air Force station.

It was then that the Garuds from Adampur, including Corporal Gursevek, were called into action.

Following a briefing, two aircraft were dispatched to transport the reinforcements. One aircraft carried the AOC-in-C along with a six-member Garud team, while the second transported another Garud

---

20 https://www.bharat-rakshak.com/indianairforce/database/29775// Wing Commander Bhavesh Kumar Dubey// bharat rakshak.com

21 Equivalent to an Army Commander appointment in the Army, senior Air Marshals who command the Air Commands are designated as Air Officer Commanding-in-Chief (AOC-in-C).

team to Pathankot as part of the initial response. These teams were the first responders, with additional Garud flights from across the nation mobilized later based on operational needs.

Upon arriving in Pathankot, the two incoming Garud detachments joined the Garud flight already stationed at the base and were promptly briefed by the dynamic CO of the Garud Flight at Pathankot. Known for his extensive field experience, he was highly regarded among his peers as a seasoned professional with a talent for making precise decisions with calm efficiency. He knew his job well.

Addressing the Garud teams, the CO stated:

'As you all know, the terrorists have likely entered the base. We must locate and eliminate them.'

The NSG Counter Terror Task Force (CTTF-1) had reached the base by around 2200 hours on 1 January 2016 and they had a joint meeting with all the authorities responsible for Pathankot, where Pathankot airbase tasks were assigned. Squadron Leader Dubey summarized the objectives of the meeting to his men.

The sprawling Pathankot Air Force base extended over several kilometres, with forested areas and dense elephant grass. It housed a fleet of fighter jets and attack helicopters, along with other missile systems, radars and hardware. Strategically positioned along the main highway linking Kashmir with the rest of India, the base was about thirty-five kilometres from the Pakistan border. This 'mini city' also included family quarters, schools and shops catering to Air Force personnel and their families.

The CO ended the meeting by saying, 'Aerial platform are operational—UAVs and aircraft are all in the air for reconnaissance and observation. Any suspicious movements will be reported to us immediately. Be alert and be ready. Be ready for action at any moment.'

He then divided the two incoming Garud detachments, mixing personnel from Adampur with those stationed at Pathankot to ensure each team had someone familiar with the terrain. One of the teams, including Corporal Gursevek, was kept directly under his command. Another Garud team was deployed to assist the AOC-in-C, Western Command, who had stationed himself at the air traffic control (ATC) tower.

Understanding the gravity of the situation, Gursevek sent a quick message to Jaspreet before heading to his designated Area of Responsibility (AOR): *'Please go to bed, don't wait for my call. There's urgent work to be done. I'll call you myself.'*

Not realizing this would be their last communication, Jaspreet replied with a simple 'Ok'.

~

Pathankot Airbase
Punjab
2 January 2016
0130 hours

The CO's phone buzzed sharply, breaking the silence of the night. On the other end, the AOC the senior most officer in any airbase from the Pathankot Airbase spoke urgently. Unusual movement had been detected by one of their RPAs[22]. The thermal signature showed movements in a densely vegetated area near the airbase's boundary, close to a residential zone. Although wild boars and nilgai often roamed the area, the coordinated movement in the thermal signature suggested something else, at the late hour the late hour.

---

22 Remotely Piloted Aircraft.

The CO quickly assembled his team of six Garuds and took the briefing.

After the briefing, the team readied themselves, loading gear into the vehicles with grim determination. As they drove towards the target area, the night seemed to grow colder, the air thick with anticipation. The CO also instructed the other two Garud teams to converge on the target area immediately. It was a dewy, cold January night, and they faced the challenge of locating potential terrorists in a vast, sprawling area.

The CO stopped the Gypsy at a strategic distance from the target area, the engine softly idling in the cold morning air. They disembarked silently, weapons at the ready, and began their tactical advance.

The silence was palpable, broken only by the occasional rustle of leaves and distant nocturnal calls. The team moved swiftly, their movements smooth and practiced. Forming a line, each Garud instinctively understood his role in the silent ballet of a tactical advance. The CO signalled with a subtle hand gesture, and the first soldier, weapon ready, moved forward. He scanned the darkness, every muscle tense as he edged into the thick vegetation. He paused, listened, and with a quick nod, indicated that the area was clear.

The second soldier followed, weapon sweeping the darkness with disciplined precision. Then the third, then the fourth—each Garud moving forward with methodical caution.

As they pressed on silently through the cold, the Garuds faced numerous challenges. Visibility was low, weather was chilly and the unforgiving terrain made their task difficult. Dense foliage and tall elephant grass provided ample cover and obscured visibility. Proximity to residential areas, messes, schools and other structures further complicated their mission. From a tactical standpoint, it was an ideal hiding place for terrorists.

Finally, they reached the spot indicated by the RPA input, where movement had been detected. The CO assigned Gursevek and Shailabh to advance, and verify the zone before the rest of the team followed. Their task was to cordon off the area. Gursevek provided cover with his gun while Shailabh conducted a careful search.

Although nothing was immediately visible, their instincts warned them that something was amiss. There was a sense that someone had been there recently.

> They returned and reported to the CO: 'The area feels suspicious. We should check it thoroughly.'
> Moving further, they discovered a hidden path through the tall grass leading to an old, abandoned building with two rooms.
> Gursevek asked the CO, 'Should we search this as well, sir?'
> The CO replied, 'Yes. We need to inspect the entire area thoroughly. Leave nothing unchecked.'

They began their cautious approach, advancing through the grass towards the derelict building, senses heightened for any surprises. The thick grass rustled underfoot, but the Garuds moved with a practiced, almost eerie silence. As they neared the perimeter, the CO signalled the team to halt.

In the dim light, they spotted the twisted remains of a fence extending towards the forested area near the boundary wall. The wires were mangled, as if something heavy had forced its way through. Although it wasn't uncommon for wild boars to break through such fencing, it roused their suspicion.

The CO signalled for the team to prepare for a breach.

They surged forward. Leading the way was the CO, followed by Gursevek and then Shailabh Gaur, and the other Garud. The CO, most familiar with the area, cleared the immediate zone with swift, calculated movements. Gursevek followed, his gun sweeping left and right as he scanned the zone for any sign of movement. The third and fourth Garuds covered the flanks, their eyes sharp and fingers steady on the triggers.

As they crossed the fence, the cold air seemed to thicken, and the silence pressed in around them. Their surroundings were shrouded in darkness, with the thick vegetation making it nearly impossible to see more than a few feet ahead. Still, the Garuds pressed on, their senses on high alert and their resolve unbreakable.

They pushed forward along a muddy drainage channel, used to divert rainwater across the base. Its depth and foliage cover made it the safest route, shielding them from potential sniper fire. As they crawled through, they encountered another fence with its wires cut haphazardly. Their suspicions grew stronger, solidifying in the darkness. On the other side of the fence lay the military transport yard of the MES.

The makeshift path they had followed ended here, marking their final destination.

The CO signalled for them to cross the fence. He grabbed the wire, and Gursevek moved into position. Shailabh held the wire next, while the CO crossed. The fourth Garud held the wire for Shailabh, but as he crawled through, his tactical vest snagged on the wire. Meanwhile, Gursevek and the CO had already moved deeper into the MT yard, which was filled with old, unused MES vehicles.

The clock ticked past 0200 hours.

Shailabh looked ahead but couldn't see the others in the darkness—they had likely already crossed the small wall between the second fence and the yard. As he struggled to free his vest, gunfire erupted.

He froze.

At first, he wondered if it might be a misunderstanding or friendly fire from Defence Security Corps (DSC)[23] personnel. But then a grenade blast confirmed that the attackers were terrorists—DSC soldiers don't use grenades in protective fire.

'*Terrorists*,' Shailabh realized, quickly discarding his vest.

The remaining three Garuds quickly fell into defensive formation, ready to face any threat. The last two, working in pairs, provided cover from the rear, while the third soldier covered Shailabh.

Inside the yard, the CO and Gursevek saw it was fenced with barbed wire and lined with two garages, their large pillars facing each other. The yard was filled with old vehicles, and the open space in the middle held larger equipment like JCBs and trucks. They crawled through the barbed wire and, as it was pitch dark, the CO used a night vision device to scan the area—but saw no movement.

By then, Gursevek had moved ahead of the CO as part of their tactical advance. Suddenly, a burst of AK-47 fire—around eighteen or nineteen rounds—erupted, aimed directly at Gursevek. Muzzle flashes lit up like firebolts against the darkness. They did not realize that fidyaeens had already taken positions behind the old vehicles and pillars and were watching their movements through their night vision devices. Gursevek was hit several times, but even as he fell, his tactical training kicked in—he immediately took cover behind a JCB and returned fire.

The CO, just ten metres behind him, took cover behind a pillar and also started firing back. The JCB provided Gursevek some

---

23 The Defence Security Corps (DSC) is a specialized unit of the Indian Army tasked with providing security and protection to military installations and sensitive areas. It comprises retired veterans from the Indian Armed Forces.

protection, but a few bullets still hit him. The terrorist firing from behind a Matador kept Gursevek in his sight.

The CO came under heavy fire from another direction. A bullet grazed his right thigh.

Despite being grievously injured, Corporal Gursevek continued firing, holding the attackers in place long enough for the CO to retreat, use his communication device and alert the others.

The firing continued unabated.

By then, Shailabh had successfully untangled his vest. Amidst the chaos, Gursevek had responded, calling for support. Shailabh advanced tactically, navigating through bullets and grenades. As he entered the yard, crossing the wall, he saw the CO and Gursevek under heavy fire. AK-47 rounds rained down on them. Both had taken protective positions: The CO behind a pillar and Gursevek behind a JCB tire, where his body would later be recovered.

On the other end, Gursevek, in spite of his wounds, continued to retaliate fiercely rather than attempting to retreat. From his position, Shailabh could see the firing positions of the terrorists and opened fire to provide cover to Gursevek. However, Gursevek was almost completely exposed, his position known and Shailabh's distance limited the effectiveness of his support.

Meanwhile, Gursevek made a hoax call for rocket launchers: '*Arey, woh* rocket launcher *leke aa* (Hey, bring the rocket launcher)!'

The CO followed suit, shouting for reinforcements and ammunition. These calls were part of a psychological tactic to unnerve the terrorists—and it worked.

Believing that a larger force was closing in, the terrorists panicked. They had assumed that Gursevek and the CO had already spotted them during their advance. In reality, the two Garuds had unknowingly reached the yard by following a trail, and were unaware of the terrorists' positions until they opened fire.

Had the Garud encounter not taken place, the terrorists might have reached their actual target undetected.

Their goal was not to kill people but to damage and destroy India's valuable defence assets, thereby generating sensational international headlines.

Such an act would have struck a severe blow to national pride and military capability, exposing India's strategic and tactical vulnerabilities on the global stage. From the moment they infiltrated India, the fidayeens goal was clear: Strike the Pathankot Airbase's technical area. This was a suicide mission. Even though their presence was leaked in the media, the terrorists pressed on with their mission, focused solely on their goal—indifferent to their personal safety or their families back in Pakistan. But the encounter with the Garuds changed the course of their action.

Gursevek continued to fire relentlessly, frustrating the terrorists now desperate to escape the yard. Their aim was not to engage in fights but to blast aircraft. The Garud's resistance posed a significant obstacle—they could not advance without neutralizing him. The situation escalated rapidly. The NSG and other Garud dets have started taking position behind them. cordoning off the area and cutting off the terrorists' escape routes.

Realizing they were trapped, the terrorists attempted to establish tactical positions. One fired, while the others moved strategically, in a bid to escape. These were no ordinary terrorists; as revealed later, they were fidayeens, or suicide attackers, of the Afzal Guru Squad of JeM and had undergone rigorous training and were equipped with ammunition to last many days and inflict maximum damage.

It was only because of the Garud teams, the National Security Guard and the Indian Army, who took over the next phase of fighting, that they didn't succeed.

Corporal Gursevek Singh was using every ounce of his strength to fire at the terrorists. Shailabh had managed to come closer to Gursevek, intending to form a buddy pair and advance in tactical order to secure a dominant position.

However, terrorists soon began targeting him as well, and several bullets hit him in the abdomen. Many soldiers have shared that in moments like these, the adrenaline rush can overpower even the intense pain from such injuries, and the same happened with Shailabh—he did not realize he was hit and kept firing.

The CO was also returning fire with fierce intensity. At that moment, a terrorist threw a grenade in their direction. This forced both the CO and Shailabh to retreat and take cover.

The CO grabbed Shailabh, and informed him that the others had arrived and cordoned off the area. It was now critical to relay their exact position to avoid friendly fire. The remaining three Garuds from the original team had already taken tactical cover, ready to engage at a moment's notice. Although they could only see and hear the firefight, they were restricted by their position and couldn't fire for fear of hitting their own comrades.

Despite numerous attempts, the CO and Shailabh were unable to get close enough to Gursevek to provide proper cover. In his exposed position, he was vulnerable to attacks from all sides, yet he continued to fight with everything he had. It wasn't until Gursevek succumbed to his bullet wounds that the terrorists were able to escape the area.

Gursevek's bravery had bought critical time to forces, without him, the terrorists could have easily breached the technical area and achieved their objective. The Garud stood tall, despite all odds, even at the risk of his own life.

The fleeing terrorists headed towards the well-lit residential buildings. They wanted to reach the technical area and were willing to go to any length to make sure they did.

In a bid to create a diversion, they set fire to an empty airmen's billet—a classic decoy tactic to confuse and delay security forces. As the building burned, filling the area with smoke and ash, they also set fire to bikes. The fidayeens then reached the DSC mess and began firing indiscriminately. Having lost their composure, they shot at anyone in their path, keenly aware that their time was running out.

It was here that the terrorists killed Sepoy Jagdish Chand of the Defence Security Corps Jagdish Chand had been working in the mess during the early hours of 2 January when the terrorists struck. Despite being caught off guard, he fought with remarkable courage, disarming one of the terrorists and shooting him before succumbing to a cowardly gunfire from the back by the other terrorist and attained *veergati* in the line of duty. The veteran fought valiantly with his bare hands; had it not been for the other terrorist firing from behind, he might have inflicted further damage.

He was posthumously awarded the Kirti Chakra for his gallantry. He was from Dogra Regiment, he had retired in 2009 and was re-employed with the DSC, responsible for security at military establishments. He had only recently been transferred to Pathankot from Leh and had returned from a ten-day leave the day before the fateful incident. Perhaps he had chosen a soldier's death long before he was born. Who would have imagined that he would be killed by an enemy's bullet even after retirement?

Subedar Fateh Singh, fifty-one, was among the five DSC personnel who attained veergati that day. An accomplished big boar shooter, he had represented India in the Commonwealth Games and earned multiple medals. The DSC suffered a high number casualties—primarily because their personnel were caught off guard, without immediate access to weapons at the early morning hours.

It was only a matter of time before the terrorists met their end—dying a nameless, faceless death on foreign lands among people they considered infidels. Within an hour of the first encounter with the Garuds, the lethal National Security Guards—our federal contingency force for counter terrorism—took charge and hunted them down, killing them one by one.

Their deaths were unacknowledged, their graves unmarked. Unlike those who died for the nation, honoured with the highest accolades and mourned by a billion-strong nation as they were draped in the Tricolour and carried to their final resting place.

As you read this, I hope you reflect on that contrast—on what it means to live and die for India versus against it.

In a final, intense encounter, the terrorists were cornered. NSG's Counter Terrorism Task Force 1, with their specialized weapons and tactics, did an excellent job neutralizing the terrorists in an open, broken ground. The Indian Army also joined the operation. By this time, the Indian forces had established tactical dominance—snipers were in position, light machine guns deployed, drones hovered overhead, and Air Force attack helicopters launched missiles. Eventually, all the terrorists were neutralized.

There remains a dispute over the number of terrorists involved. The National Investigation Agency (NIA) maintains that four attackers infiltrated the airbase, while the National Security Guards reports six. Nine years on, the exact number remains uncertain.

During my research, I also came across reports that Shahid Latif, the mastermind behind the Pathankot attack, was shot dead by unidentified gunmen in Sialkot, Pakistan, on 11 October 2023.[24] Some claim he was killed by Indian security forces. While speculation persists, the full truth may always remain unknown. Perhaps that's for the best—for those of us living comfortable, ordinary lives, to remain unaware of what it truly takes to safeguard a nation.

The body of Corporal Gursevek was evacuated as soon as the situation was under control on the afternoon of 2 January. In such

---

24 PTI, 'Pathankot attack mastermind Shahid Latif killed in Pakistan mosque', *The Hindu*, 11 October 2023, https://www.thehindu.com/news/international/pathankot-attack-mastermind-shahid-latif-killed-in-pakistan-mosque/article67407247.ece.

operations, strict protocols are followed to handle the remains of both soldiers and terrorists. Terrorists are known to booby-trap corpses—by removing grenade pins and hiding explosives under the body—to inflict further casualties. It was this tactic that resulted in the balidan of Lieutenant Colonel Niranjan E.K., a brave NSG officer from their Bomb Disposal Unit. He was posthumously awarded the Shaurya Chakra.

Corporal Gursevek Singh too was posthumously awarded the Shaurya Chakra, and Shailabh Gaur was Mentioned in Despatches while Squadron Leader Bhavesh Kumar Dubey was awarded Vayu Sena (gallantry) on 15 August 2016.

By 7 January 2016, after an extensive combing operation, the Pathankot Airbase was declared secure.[25] A significant cache of ammunition and advanced weaponry was recovered, including under-barrel grenade launchers (UBGLs), modified AK-47s, blue Chinese grenades and MP4/5 submachine guns, as well as Indian currency, maps, dry fruits, medicines and drugs.

They were successful in causing seven initial casualties inside the airbase only because they attacked unsuspecting DSC soldiers in the wee hours, else later they were effectively neutralized and the masterminds in Pakistan were devoid of any spectacle of Mumbai attacks kind that they anticipated with Pathankot airbase attack.

In all other airbase attacks across the globe, some aircraft had been damaged like with the attack on the Mianwali Training Airbase, a high-security facility of the Pakistan Air Force, around 0300

---

25 NDTV.com, 'After 80 Hours, Operation In Pathankot Ends, Say Sources: Live Updates', NDTV, 5 January 2016, https://www.ndtv.com/india-news/terror-attack-at-air-force-base-in-punjabs-pathankot-live-updates-1261436.

hours on 4 November 2023.[26] In that instance, militants breached the perimeter by scaling the walls, just as they had at Pathankot. However, this attack reportedly resulted in the loss of three aircraft and a fuel tank, although some reports suggest Pakistan may be concealing the full extent of the damage. Unlike the Pathankot attack, where terrorists could not even damage one aircraft nor could kill any civilians or the foreign nationals inside.

Reflecting on the actions of the initial Garud detachment, I think what they had displayed is pure bravado and raw courage.

When news of Corporal Gursevek Singh's supreme sacrifice reached his village, Garnala, chaos ensued. Jaspreet, who was pregnant and staying at her parents' home, had been trying desperately to reach him for over a day, only to find his phone constantly out of coverage. It was his brother who received the tragic news. Since that moment, Jaspreet slipped into a state of shock, unable to recall much of what happened next. Gursevek's mother, Amrik Kaur, fainted upon hearing the devastating news.

Despite the overwhelming grief, Gursevek's legacy shone brightly.

His last rites were a powerful testament to his bravery. Thousands gathered to pay their respects, including senior officers from the Indian Air Force, Indian Army, police and civil administration. The then chief minister of Haryana, Manohar Lal Khattar, also came to offer his condolences. Gursevek was cremated with full military honours, his sacrifice commemorated with the dignity and respect he so richly deserved.[27]

---

26 Ankit Kumar, 'Satellite images show more damage at Pakistan's airbase than officially stated', *India Today*, 7 November 2023, https://www.indiatoday.in/world/story/satellite-images-show-more-damage-at-pakistans-airbase-than-officially-stated-2460130-2023-11-07.

27 https://economictimes.indiatimes.com/news/defence/teary-final-farewell-to-martyrs-of-pathankot-terror-attack/articleshow/50438430.

Before I conclude the story of this brave son of India, I want to share a poignant recollection from the Garud who helped evacuate Corporal Gursevek's body and want to remain anonymous. He told me:

His eyes were still open, and his fingers were tightly gripping his Tavor. We had to carefully pry the weapon from his hands. It was as if he was reluctant to part with it, even in death. His gaze remained fixed, and despite our efforts, we couldn't close his eyes. He had emptied an entire magazine—every bullet spent. But he embraced a glorious death, one etched into the history of India.

He paused, then added:

Yes, our brother is no longer with us, but his sacrifice was not in vain. Thanks to him, the security forces learnt about the terrorists' presence. We take solace in knowing that his sacrifice helped avert a tragedy akin to Mumbai. His sacrifice served the nation's cause.

His comrades hold him in the highest regard. They have ensured that his tale of valour will never be forgotten and remains etched into the flight's history.

During my research, I had the privilege of visiting the iconic flight of Corporal Gursevek Singh at Adampur Airbase. Inside the building, near the entrance, stands a small sanctum erected in his memory. While showing me around, observing tradition, the CO removed his shoes before entering, and I followed suit.

Inside, I was deeply moved by the striking bust of Corporal Gursevek Singh, SC (P), dressed in his Indian Air Force blue uniform. The walls are adorned with his photographs, each a testament

---

cms?from=mdr/ Teary final farewell to martyrs of Pathankot terror attack/ Jul 14, 2018/ economictimes.

to his legacy. I spent a long time there, enveloped by a profound sense of purpose, as if he was blessing me before I began the task of immortalizing his story.

The Garuds shared that they start each day by saluting him. The young airmen look up to him with immense respect, fully aware of the monumental footsteps they are following and the legacy they must uphold.

~

Afterword

Jaspreet gave birth to a healthy baby girl on 13 August 2016. Her pregnancy had been difficult, shadowed by the loss of her husband in January. For a long time, she remained withdrawn, locked away in Gursevek's room. Time seemed to stand still for her, and her emotional state was fragile.

It was only after the birth of their daughter—whom she named 'Gurreet Kaur', a tribute that combined her name with Gursevek's—that she found a renewed sense of purpose. She shared with me how becoming a mother gave her a reason to live again.

Today, she works at the DC office in Panchkula. When I visited her there, I found her deeply engrossed in a mountain of files. Jaspreet spoke with appreciation about how the Indian Air Force had helped her through the most challenging period of her life. The CO and his wife remain in touch with her, and the Air Force has never forgotten Corporal Gursevek's family. They continue to assist with everyday problems, and include her in their events.

Regarding Corporal Shailabh Gaur (now Seargeant) who was deeply wounded in the firefight, he was discovered by his comrades after the terrorists fled and were engaged by the NSG. It was then that they found two bullet wounds in his abdomen, with his intestines punctured. He was evacuated and discharged from the

AI-generated visual of the Jaffna University Helidrop-IPKF missions, 1987

An Indian Air Force Apache pilot with the Integrated Helmet and Display Sighting System (IHADSS)

Author with Air Commodore Vishwanath Prakash, VrC (veteran), who was one of the Mi-8 helicopter pilots during the Jaffna Helidrop

Author with Air Marshal Awadhesh Kumar Bharti, SYSM, AVSM, VM the DG Air Operations during Op Sindoor

Author with the Air Chief Marshal Amar Preet Singh, PVSM, AVSM, Chief of the Air Staff, under whose leadership the IAF executed Op Sindoor in May 2025

Author alongside Gp Capt Sameep Nijhawan CO of No. 81 sqaudron during Op Kaveri, 2023

Author alongside Wg Cdr Rajneesh Chandra Uniyal, who was the co-pilot of C-130J Super Hercules during the critical Wadi Sedina evacuation

Author with Air Chief Marshal Vivek Ram Chaudhari PVSM, AVSM, VM, ADC, the then Chief of the Air Staff (June 2024)

Author with Wg Cdr Vyomika Singh, IAF spokesperson during Op Sindoor, May 2025

Author pays tribute at the sanctum dedicated to the valiant warriors of iconic 617 Garud Flight

Cpl Gursevek Singh Shaurya Chakra (P) who made the supreme sacrfice during the Pathankot attack in January 2016

IAF's 3rd Ashoka Chakra awardee Cpl Jyoti Prakash Nirala, who made the supreme sacrifice in Op Chandergeer, 2017

Corporal Gursevek Singh with wife Jaspreet Kaur during their wedding ceremonies

Flight Lieutenant Kambhampati Nachiketa with the then Prime Minister of India late Sri Atal Biha Vajpayee during the Kargil War

Garud SF Cpl Nilesh Kumar Nayan, Shaurya Chakra(P) who laid down his life in Op Rakh Hajin in October 2017

Gp Capt Ravi Nanda, the Captain of the C-130J Super Hercules in the daring Wadi Sedina evacuation, Op Kaveri, photo: X @TroopsComfortsLtd

Sri Rajnath Singh, first Indian Defense Minister to fly in HAL's LCA Tejas along with AVM Narmdeshwar Tiwari, the then project director at the National Test Flight Centre, ADA Bengaluru, Sept 2019

Group Captain Yogeshwar Krishnarao Kandalkar being awarded by the President of India for the Deoghar Cable Car Rescue (May 2023)

Garud SF Flt Lt Tejpal Yadav during winching operations in the Deoghar Cable Car Rescue, April 2022

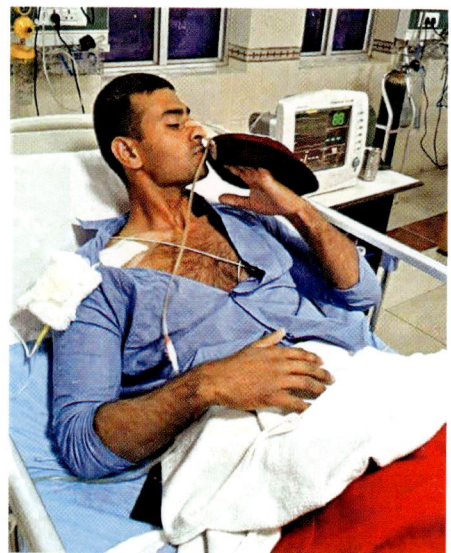

Garud SF Cpl Shailabh Gaur in hospital following injuries sustained in the Pathankot terrorist attack, Jan 2016

Sepoy Gora Singh, the lone surviuor of 13 SIKH LI during the Jaffna Heli Drop IPKF, 1987

Honourable Prime Minister of India Sri Narendra Damodardas Modi at Adampur Air Force Station after Op Sindoor in May 2025

Sergeant Milind Kishor Khairnar, who made the supreme sacrfice in Op Rakh Hajin, Oct 2017

Sergeant Milind Kishor Khairnar with wife Harshada and kids Vedika and Gagan during happier times

The Author with Mrs Jaspreet Kaur, the wife of Cpl Gursevek Singh who made the supreme sacrifice during the Pathakot attack

Wg Cdr Rajiv Chauhan, the Garud CO who led Op Chandergeer and Op Rakh Hajin in 2017, photo: National Defense/YouTube

Sqn Ldr Pritam Singh Jaitawat: The Garud CO who led the Garud team during the high-risk Wadi Sedina mission in Sudan, April 2023. Photo: ANI

hospital after twenty-one days. Now designated a battle casualty, he continues to serve in the Indian Air Force and trains the next generation of Garuds.

Author's note

This story is based on interviews conducted with those who lived through the storm—Wing Commander Bhavesh Kumar Dubey, the then Commanding Officer of the Garud Flight who led the operation, and Sergeant Shailabh Gaur. Both of them have fought shoulder to shoulder with Corporal Gursevek Singh against the fidayeen and frankly, it is only a miracle that they were saved, here to tell the story which must never be forgotten. And then there was Jaspreet Kaur—Gursevek's wife—who opened the doors of her heart with grace and unshakable strength, Meeting her was a bittersweet experience—she deserved a lifetime of happiness with the man she loved, not a lifetime carrying the weight of his absence. Writing this story has been a moving journey—not just because of the unbearable loss, but because of the chilling realization of how close the fidayeen came to their objective and it is only because of the brave men who risked it all that they could not.

4

Sergeant Milind Kishor Khairnar, Shaurya Chakra (Posthumous), and Corporal Nilesh Kumar Nayan, Shaurya Chakra (Posthumous): The Heroic Supreme Sacrifice

Operation Rakh Hajin
Rakh Hajin, Sonawari Tehsil
Bandipora District
Kashmir, India
11 October 2017
0230 hours

THE AIR WAS heavy with tension as the operation commenced in the pitch-black night of Rakh Hajin. The forces had long kept the rickety stone house—a sinister structure with a sloping thatched roof and weathered stone walls—under surveillance. Known as a hub for nefarious activities, and a hideout for both local and foreign

Lashkar-e-Taiba (LeT) terrorists, the house was the focal point of the night's decisive action.

By 0300 hours, the cordon was in place. Now, under the cloak of pitch darkness and with the clock ticking towards 0400 hours, the final move was imminent. However, the terrorists, aware of their precarious situation, made a desperate attempt to break the cordon.

Sergeant Milind Kishor Khairnar and Corporal Nilesh Kumar Nayan, the Garud buddy pair lying prone behind a sturdy log, were only twenty-eight metres from the target—a distance so short that the details of the house's stone structure were clearly visible through their night vision goggles.

Suddenly, chaos erupted as the terrorists, in a frantic bid for freedom, launched two grenades. The first explosion startled the forces, but it was the second grenade that landed perilously close, sending deadly splinters flying towards Milind and Nilesh.

Milind felt the sharp sting of metal slice across his face but pushed the pain aside. His training and instincts kicked in.

'Incoming!' he shouted, already preparing to return fire.

The night vision goggles strapped to their helmets turned the darkness into a vivid, green-hued battleground.

It was difficult to see in the pitch dark but they must be around six to eight terrorists, their weapons blazing. The sound of gunfire filled the air. Despite their injuries, Milind and Nilesh responded with even greater ferocity. Milind, a weapons specialist with an uncanny mastery of firearms, emptied one magazine in a flurry of precise shots. With remarkable speed and agility, he reloaded, his hands moving with the fluidity of muscle memory.

Nilesh, who specialized in navigation, fired bravely alongside Milind, each shot finding its mark. The two soldiers, wounded but undeterred, created a wall of firepower that the terrorists struggled to breach.

'Keep firing! We can't let them get through!' Milind shouted, his voice a mix of command and determination.

'Not till I live!' Nilesh replied through gritted teeth, his focus unbroken despite the pain from the shrapnel wounds on his face.

The terrorists, also equipped with night vision goggles, saw their movements, but Milind and Nilesh's superior training and coordination gave them an edge. Bullets flew in every direction, but the two soldiers held their ground, their minds and movements perfectly synchronized in the heat of battle.

Milind's rifle became an extension of his arm, each pull of the trigger a testament to his skill and experience. He felt a surge of power—akin to Thor wielding his mighty hammer. Nilesh, equally relentless, moved with the precision of a seasoned warrior, his shots as deadly as they were deliberate. Despite their injuries, both of them managed. They took down two terrorists.

As the smoke cleared and the gunfire finally faded, Sergeant Khairnar Milind Kishor and Corporal Nilesh Kumar Nayan of 617 Garud Flight had made the supreme sacrifice. Their bodies lay still, but the impact of their actions resonated through the night.

The echoes of their bravery linger, forever etched in the memories of those who knew them. They were more than soldiers—they were heroes whose names must be eternally honoured and remembered.

~

Apple Orchard
Boon Mohalla
Rakh Hajin
9 October 2017

The early morning mist clung to the lush landscape of Hajin—a place of serene beauty, now marred by the shadow of conflict. Squadron

Leader Rajiv Chauhan,[1] the thirty-three-year-old Commanding Officer of the newly formed 617 Garud Flight, paced within the temporary command post. His sharp eyes, filled with determination and an unwavering sense of duty, scanned the map spread across the table. The call from Battalion Headquarters at Manasbal had been brief but urgent.

'Confirmed intel,' the voice of the CO of 13 Rashtriya Rifle (Kumaon) had crackled over the radio. 'Report to Battalion Headquarters ASAP.'

'We'll leave immediately, sir,' replied Squadron Leader Rajiv Chauhan, whose rank was equivalent to that of an Army Major.

The air in the briefing room was thick with anticipation. Squadron Leader Chauhan, dynamic and dashing, stood as the embodiment of the elite force he commanded.

He was the first CO of the newly raised 617 Garud Flight, established on 27 February 2017 at 12 Wing, Air Force Station, Chandigarh. As he began relaying the message to his men, he didn't yet realize that this fledgling Garud flight was about to etch its name into the annals of the Indian Air Force and the nation itself.

In 2017, Garud flights were asked to volunteer for deployment in the Kashmir Valley, with a rotational policy ensuring that each flight operated there for a few years. The Pathankot airbase attack has shifted the paradigm: It was understood that Garuds needed more exposure in counterterrorism and insurgency operations, along with the need to raise more flights.

Squadron Leader Rajiv Chauhan and his men from the newly raised 617 Garud Flight were among the first to be deployed in Kashmir. They were stationed in Hajin, on the banks of the Jhelum River, approximately 40 kilometres from Srinagar.

---

1 'Wing Commander Rajiv Chauhan', Bharat Rakshak, https://www.bharat-rakshak.com/indianairforce/database/29086.

At the time, Hajin was heavily utilized as a transit route and base camp by foreign terrorist groups such as Lashkar-e-Taiba and Jaish-e-Mohammed. It was infamous, for its hostility towards the armed forces and frequent stone-pelting incidents. Many houses sheltered and accommodated both local and foreign terrorists.[2]

Unlike earlier deployments, where Garuds were attached to Para (Special Forces) units, from 2017 onwards, they were attached with Rashtriya Rifles units. The 617 Garud Flight was attached to the 13 Rashtriya Rifles (Kumaon),[3] whose battalion headquarters was stationed at Manasbal, under the command of an Army colonel. the garud flight operated alongside one of the companies of 13 RR, based along the banks of the Jhelum River in Hajin in the Bandipora district of Kashmir.

In 2017, the 617 Garud Flight and the RR battalion launched a series of cordon and search operations (CASO) in Hajin in response to escalating militant activity.

Just before the deployment of the 617 Garud Flight, on 14 February 2017, during a search operation in Bandipora, terrorists ambushed Indian Army troops. CRPF Commandant Chetan Kumar Cheetah[4] of the 45 Battalion heroically faced the attackers, sustaining nine bullet wounds in the encounter. This incident underscored

---

2 bbc.com/new/world-asia-india-42062192 Hajin: The Kashmiri town that is a 'militant hub'/28nov 2017

3 '13 RR - Battalion Of Rashtriya Rifles—Most Lethal RR Battalion', *The Patriot Brief,* YouTube, https://www.youtube.com/watch?v=e3uVVz5sq6I.

4 Kamaljit Kaur Sandhu, 'Shot 9 times by terrorists, CRPF commandant Chetan Cheetah back in action', *India Today,* last updated 20 May 2018, https://www.indiatoday.in/india/story/shot-9-times-by-terrorists-last-year-crpf-commandant-chetan-cheetah-resumes-duty-1192900-2018-03-19.

the terrorists' dominance and unrestricted movement in the area, necessitating a robust response from the security forces.

Determined to eliminate the terrorist threat, the forces initiated extensive operations. They also compiled a hit list of top terrorist commanders operating in the region.

Garuds would also be part of such raids. These aggressive raids, often involving house-to-house searches, yielded valuable intelligence. Many times during raids, Garuds uncovered cleverly concealed hiding places inside cupboards and even within modified commodes. These commodes, appearing functional from the outside, revealed hidden spaces large enough for two to four people when certain levers were pressed. During these raids, the Garuds recovered foreign passports, caches of cash and mobile phones, despite facing heavy stone-pelting.

One of the Garuds who have operated in the area on the conditions of anonymity shares:

> The mob would appear out of nowhere after most of our raids and incessantly pelt stones at us. Many of us would be injured, but we could not fire at them as they were not armed with weapons. It is only after the abrogation of Article 370 that the situation has normalized. The money pumped in to support stone-pelting has also reduced drastically.

The local police and forces had also kept many houses and mobile phones under surveillance using their human intelligence network, drones and other sophisticated equipment. Often, the Garuds would disguise themselves as local or foreign terrorists to conduct reconnaissance missions. They carefully observed the locals' way of life, their occupations, and, most notably, the vehicles they used for daily commutes. These covert operations proved invaluable in live operations later.

The increased number of raids created chaos among terrorists, forcing them to abandon Hajin as a night-time safe haven and move to the outskirts, specifically Rakh Hajin, which was a nearby village located in Sonawari tehsil of same Bandipora district.

They returned in the morning to Hajin to continue their illegal operations. Despite the upheaval, the Garuds and the RR battalion had not yet succeeded in capturing or eliminating any of the terrorists under surveillance in several months.

But that was about to change.

Squadron Leader Chauhan had just returned from a CASO in Rakh Hajin when he received a call from the CO of 13 RR (Kumaon) to immediately reach Manasbal Battalion HQ. On the night of 9 October, the Garuds had received intel about the presence of terrorists in an apple orchard that lay north of Rakh Hajin, in an area between Hajin and Rakh Hajin. The Garuds were tasked with laying multiple ambushes in the orchard.

The Garud CO assigned his second-in-command, JWO Sandeep Kumar (now retd), to prepare the team for the night ambush, while he instructed Sergeant Milind Kishor Khairnar, his number three, to thoroughly check all the weapons before the operation. Weapons are a soldier's lifeline, and flawless functionality can mean the difference between life and death.

Sergeant Milind, a member of the first batch of Garuds when the unit was raised, was responsible for ensuring every weapon was in perfect working order.

Milind was sharp, intelligent and technologically adept. A tough soldier. Coming from a well-to-do background, Milind cleared the rigorous airmen selection process and enrolled in the Air Force on 16 December 2002. His initial training began at the Airmen Training School (ATS) in Belgaum now Belagavi (Karnataka), alongside 3,500 other trainees, all aspiring to join the Indian Air Force.

The training was designed to prepare them for their future roles as airmen in Indian Air Force. However, Milind's life took a sharp turn when a team of Air Force officers from New Delhi Headquarters visited the ATS campus with a proposal. They were looking for volunteers for a new commando force called the 'Tiger Force'. The officers briefed the trainees about the plans to raise this new force, emphasizing the need for tough, action-oriented individuals.

Seven hundred airmen volunteered for the Tiger Force, but only 100 were selected based on rigorous mental and physical criteria.

Milind was one of the chosen few to begin this elite training. Later, they were informed that the force would be named the Garud Special Forces. Milind thus embarked on his journey as part of the first batch of Garuds.

In June 2003, Milind graduated from ATS as an airman and reported to Air Force Station Mohammadpur[5] in Gurgaon district to begin his training as Garud along with fellow trainees. They would go on to become the OGs of the Garud world—the pioneers, paving the way for future generations.

Many from the first batch now laugh, recalling the earlier days. JWO Sandeep Kumar (veteran), who has since left the service, shared with a hearty chuckle:

> Milind and I were in the first batch of Garuds. When I hear the new generation talking about how tough their training is, I tell them they haven't seen half of what we went through. In our time, the course structure wasn't fixed, the objectives weren't very clear. We just knew we were being raised as a Special Force of the Indian Air Force, but our roles and skill parameters were undefined. So, they made us train with almost every force across India. We

---

5 The first few batches had been sent to Air force station Mohammadpur for training first instead of GRTC.

completed twelve to thirteen courses on various skills, unlike the four to five courses done by the newer generation under a defined structure. We trained with ITBP, NSG and many others. Looking back, I don't understand how we endured it all.

He paused before softly remembering his dearest buddy Milind:

But Milind was the toughest of us all. As the Garud course progressed, many volunteers quit or got injured, but Milind never once complained. In fact, he looked forward to each day and boosted others as well. He was tough, hard to break.

When I asked him which course they found the most difficult, since the initial batches had training exposure with almost all the premier commando institutes in India, he replied:

I would say it was ITBP. Those guys are incredibly tough. I remember they'd leave us exposed in the freezing cold of peak winter, then let our bodies warm up only to throw us back into the bone-chilling cold. We had an instructor called Dharampal, or 'Danda Ustaad', as Milind affectionately referred to him; he was renowned for giving the toughest punishments. The training was intense, and sleep was a luxury we rarely experienced. We rolled, crawled and what not.
  I recall one theory class where Milind fell asleep sitting up. Danda Ustaad saw this and slapped him hard. Milind calmly responded, 'Ustaad, I wasn't sleeping; I was just testing how hard you could hit.' That was Milind for you—always chilled out.

After a year of intense training, only sixty-two out of the original 100 made it to become Garud special froces, and Milind was one of them. Some of the successful trainees were posted to Congo with an Indian Airfield Service unit of the IAF, while the rest formed the first 601 Garud Flight.

Milind was sent to Congo, where he excelled in his duties. He was responsible for securing the Air Force base and the nearby Kindu Airport. After serving in Congo for a year, Milind returned and was posted to the Garud Regimental Training Centre (GRTC), where he served for five to six years in various roles and flights stationed.

Here, I would also like to mention the other protagonist of my story, Corporal Nilesh Kumar Nayan, who sacrificed his life along side Milind. At the time Milind was deployed in Congo, Nilesh was training in GRTC to become a Garud. Milind was about two years senior to him. Little did anyone know at the time that their paths would converge, sealing their fates together as brothers who would ultimately sacrifice their lives saving each other.

The mention of Nilesh would not be complete without his personal life. Nilesh had a love marraige aganst all odds. Minsha was a Christian from Bastar, Madhya Pradesh, and Nilesh was a Hindu from Bhagalpur, Bihar. Minsha had just passed her twelfth grade and was undergoing air hostess training at the Frankfinn Institute when she met Nilesh.

He had recently completed his Garud training and was posted in Chhattisgarh. The Garuds were tasked with monitoring airports in Naxal-affected areas.

It was in 2008, after a chance meeting at Raipur Airport, that Nilesh and Minsha's relationship began to blossom. A mutual friend introduced them, and casual conversations over the phone evolved into a long-distance relationship that lasted over seven years, culminating in their marriage in 2015.

Although Nilesh had proposed to her in 2010, two years into their relationship, both families were initially against the interfaith marriage but Minsha's father passed away in 2011, and eventually, both families accepted the match.

However, Nilesh's side did not attend the wedding—he was accompanied by his Garud family. Then, in 2016, the couple was blessed with a daughter, Himanshi Nayan. The arrival of Himanshi transformed their lives into a garden of roses. Both families came together to celebrate the birth of the grandchild, marking a personal victory for Minsha and Nilesh. Nilesh's parents not only accepted her wholeheartedly but also invited her to their village, where they performed all the traditional rituals and pujas with her for their grandchild.

Minsha shared:

> Today, my mother-in-law is a pillar of support even after Nilesh is gone. We keep in touch and visit often. They see their son in Himanshi.

Nilesh and Minsha had fought hard to create their world together, and they succeeded. But mortals can never foresee what destiny has in store. Neither of them had any inkling of what the future held for them.

Millind and Nayan were part of the Garud team which had left for the apple orchard to lay a cordon based on intel received from the local police about suspected terrorists hiding there. The police had intercepted suspicious communications within a 100- to 200-metre radius of the orchard, leading to the plan for a night ambush. The objective was clear: Lay multiple ambushes, observe through the night and act if anything suspicious occurred.

Squadron Leader Rajiv Chauhan, dissatisfied with the initial Garud strength, called in a nearby Garud flight to ensure the entire orchard was covered. The Garuds, now in buddy pairs, spread out and set up their ambush positions, while other forces searched the surrounding areas.

As the night wore on, the orchard remained eerily quiet. The Garuds maintained their vigilance, carefully scanning every shadow and movement. Milind and Nayan, positioned together, held their ground. This wasn't their first ambush, since arriving from Chandigarh, they had participated in numerous CASO operations.

Milind's wife had been unhappy when he told her about volunteering for a Kashmir Valley posting. They had a comfortable life in Chandigarh, and their children, Vedika and Gagan, finally had a chance to spend time with their father. She had questioned why he would leave again for such a difficult posting. He had explained that he needed to support the Commanding Officer.

Milind's wife, Harshada, shared with me:

> After he left for the Valley, even simple communication with him was difficult. Often, his phone was switched off for days; at other times, the signal would be weak. Sometimes, he would leave for missions and ask us not to call or message, as it could compromise their location during particularly sensitive operations. There were no consistent timings to connect with him. Day or night.

Back to apple orchard, the night had passed without incident and, as dawn approached, the Garud were relieved that their ambush had gone smoothly. In the stillness of the early morning, the Garud Special Forces gathered its gear and prepared to head back. The CO instructed them to search the area one last time before dawn broke. The Garuds scoured the vicinity but found nothing suspicious.

With the area cleared, they packed up and awaited transport. The CO called the Army to arrange for vehicles to pick them up. These vehicles routinely dropped off and collected the soldiers but never stayed with them during the operations. The designated pick-up location was a few metres ahead of the apple orchard. As the Garuds reached the spot, they received a call from the Army informing them that the pick-up would be delayed due to heavy stone pelting en route. Tyres had been burnt and anti-India slogans raised.

It was routine, nothing shocking.

The CO surveyed their surroundings. They stood in Boon Mohalla, on the outskirts of Rakh Hajin village. Nearby, three pucca houses and a few huts were clustered together. The area was partially obscured by the apple orchard on one side, with cultivated fields flanking the other two sides. A mosque stood nearby, adding to the stillness of the early morning.

One house caught the CO's attention. It was adjacent to the main Hajin road and had a prominent dry nala (drainage ditch) at its rear.

Too many male clothes hung outside to dry. The CO decided to set up a mobile vehicle checkpoint (MVC) and position a road opening party (ROP) to monitor passers-by for any suspicious activity. He directed a few of his Garuds to take positions in the nala behind the house until their transport arrived.

The Garuds had been awake the entire night, yet their alertness was impressive. The sleepless training nights had prepared them well. As they settled into position, the early morning sun began to light up the horizon, casting long shadows across the quiet village. The operation had gone smoothly so far, but in this volatile region, anything could happen at any time. They remained vigilant until the Army vehicles arrived.

Unbeknownst to them, the house with the clothes drying outside harboured eight to ten terrorists. As would later be, through the captured phone of one of the terrorists, they had filmed the Garuds conducting their MVC checks. Despite having the opportunity to fire at them, the terrorists chose not to. Their reasons could have included the high number of Garuds, the scattered positions, or simply their own confidence in the security of their hiding spot which they did not want to reveal. Those particular terrorists were highly skilled operatives, having successfully evaded capture despite increased raids in the area over the past several months.

As soon as the convoy reached Hajin, the CO of 617 Garud Flight received a call to report to battalion headquarters at Manasbal. So immediately after, the flight left for the Manasbal at around 1400 hours on 10 October.

∼

Manasbal
Ganderbal district
Jammu and Kashmir
10 October 2017

The atmosphere in the 13 RR (Kumaon) headquarters was charged with a sense of urgency and purpose. The room buzzed with the collective focus of key security personnel, their discussions punctuated by the hum of high-tech surveillance equipment and the rustling of maps and documents. The COs of the Garud Flight, Para (Special Forces), the Superintendent of Police, the DSP (Operations) and other stakeholders had gathered for a crucial briefing.

The meeting had been convened to address recent intelligence breakthroughs. The police, with their extensive surveillance equipment and robust human intelligence network, had intercepted a series of suspicious signals.

Their focus had been on an over ground worker (OGW)[6] who had facilitated the acquisition of a SIM card for a Pakistani terrorist.

---

6 Over ground workers (OGWs), are people who help militants, or terrorists, with logistical support, cash, shelter, and other infrastructure using which armed groups and insurgency movements such as Hizbul Mujahideen and Jaish-e-Mohammed in Jammu and Kashmir can operate. OGWs play a vital role in militant attacks, providing real-time

Intercepted conversations revealed that the terrorist, who had been in regular contact with his local girlfriend, had divulged the location of their hideout during an argument.

The information was explosive.

After analysing the data, it became clear the hideout was in one of the three houses near where the Garud team had earlier set up MVCs. The realization was sobering: The terrorists, suspected to be a mix of local and foreign operatives, were holed up in a location where Garuds were just hours before.

The Garud CO, armed with detailed knowledge of the terrain from the previous night's ambush operation, briefed the assembled team on the operational plan. His insights provided a critical strategic advantage. The terrorists were believed to be high-profile commanders, and it was imperative to act decisively. The plan was to launch a large-scale, coordinated operation, with each unit playing a specific role.

The clock in the Manasbal headquarters ticked past 1700 hours as the high stakes planning session reached its climax. The intense briefing had laid the groundwork for a crucial operation. With the police having departed, the Garud team and Army units remained to launch the operation from this strategic location. The atmosphere grew tense as final preparations were made. Each member of the team absorbed the details of their roles, their focus sharpening with every passing minute. The seamless coordination and cooperation among the agencies was a testament to their shared commitment to the region's security and safety.

---

information and support to the tactical elements. Today, OGWs have also diversified into other roles such as stone-pelting and rioting, apart from providing ideological support, radicalization, and recruitment of militants.

The Garuds were assigned the critical task of establishing the innermost cordon—the closest defensive perimeter around the target house. Their role was pivotal: To ensure the terrorists had no chance of escaping and to secure the area before any further action could be taken.

The Garud CO decided that the team would remain at Manasbal HQ rather than returning to Hajin, to prevent locals from tracking their movements. The plan was to launch directly from Manasbal, using local wood-log transport vehicles to avoid drawing attention.

Given the urgency, the Garuds had not slept since last night. They were tireless, prepared to carry out their mission with precision. Milind, known for his diligence and weapons expertise, double-checked every firearm—his reputation as a meticulous soldier was well-earned.

Wing Commander Chauhan (then a Squadron Leader) shared:

> Milind seemed calm, but he was incredibly professional. Weapons were his passion. Even with two kids, he had volunteered for this mission. He was always eager for action and took immense pride in maintaining his weapons. I trusted him completely, he was my number three, and the loss still pains me.

The CO also recalled a strange moment:

> That night, just before the operation was to commence, I noticed Milind was online despite having been instructed to rest. I messaged him, asking why he was still awake. He said, 'Going into switch off mode.' I still wonder why he said that.

Nilesh, too, had displayed unusual behaviour that day. According to JWO Sandeep Kumar, Nilesh had requested an extra pistol before the mission.

He later told me:

Nilesh asked for one more personal weapon. I told him, '*Abey, tu do-do* personal weapon *kya karega? Hai to* Tavor, Glock … *Aur kitne chaiye* (Hey, what will you do with two personal weapons? You already have a Tavor, a Glock … How many weapons do you need)?' He didn't say anything, just said he had a feeling, and didn't elaborate further.

The CO also mentioned how Nilesh was not originally assigned for the ambush that night. Another Garud, who had fallen ill with an upset stomach at the last moment, had to be replaced.

Then, the CO asked Nilesh to plan the movement and brief him immediately. Nilesh, serving as navigator, meticulously planned the route—he had to coordinate the movements of various vehicles, decide how many personnel would board each vehicle, and determine their stops. The CO reviewed and approved Nilesh's detailed plan, ensuring that everything was set for the operation.

With the final preparations completed, the team launched the operation. Vehicles began moving at staggered intervals to avoid detection. The Garuds, having just laid an ambush the night before, led the operation with the Para (Special Forces) and RR teams following. Each vehicle, carefully chosen to blend in with local traffic, made its way towards the target location, a testament to their meticulous planning and unwavering resolve.

Rakh Hajin
11 October 2017
0230 hours

The night air was thick with tension, and an eerie silence shrouded the dense darkness over Hajin. A convoy of vehicles rolled to a stop at the outskirts of the village, their headlights cutting through the fog like knives. The joint team, led by Squadron Leader Rajiv Chauhan, disembarked. Shadows moved swiftly and silently—the commandos from 617 Garud Flight, 13 RR (Kumaon), Indian Army's Para Special Forces and 31 RR (Commando)—each blending seamlessly into the night. The only sounds were the soft thuds of boots on the ground and the rustle of gears as the men moved with practiced precision to their assigned positions.

Squadron Leader Rajiv Chauhan, directed his men with silent hand signals, each gesture understood and precisely executed. The objective was clear: To establish an innermost cordon around the target house, ensuring no escape for the terrorists within. As the commandos spread out, the night seemed to hold its breath, the suspense thickening with every passing second.

Under cover of darkness, the Garud team demonstrated exceptional situational awareness and navigation skills, swiftly establishing a tight cordon by 0440 hours. The Para (Special Forces) team had secured the front of the house, while the RR battalions covered the left side. Milind and Nilesh, in a buddy pair, had laid an ambush just twenty-eight metres from the house. With no cover available, Milind asked Nilesh to bring a wood log to use as a shield in front of them.

Milind and Nayan were placed between 13 RR parties at the left and another Garud buddy pair to their right—all spaced at calculated intervals. The night was pitch dark, with only an aluminium shed separating Milind and Nilesh from the next pair. The CO personally checked each buddy pair's position, moving from one to another using tactical movements, ensuring he was aware of the exact positions of his men. After confirming the last buddy pair—Milind and Nayan—he returned to his own position to lay an ambush with his buddy.

Once the other units confirmed their cordons, CO Garud established contact with the COB,[7] requesting the rest of the team to commence the search inside the house.

The plan was to first establish a foolproof cordon with a few men to prevent escape and then call in more men, already on standby, to move towards the target house to search it. The target location was the cluster of pucca houses, flanked by an apple orchard on one side and cultivated land on the other two sides.

Though the forces had laid the cordon in complete silence, they were unaware that the terrorists had been observing their movements through advanced night vision goggles—a fact later revealed by OGWs arrested after the operation. The terrorists, realizing they were surrounded, planned their escape such that even if some were killed, others would succeed in fleeing under the cover of darkness. They identified a gap in the cordon, and decided to attack Milind and Nilesh's position to make their escape from that side.

While the forces were setting up their ambush, the terrorists prepared for their escape, arming themselves with weapons and grenades.

Meanwhile, Milind had a motorola radio set to connect with the RR team, while Nilesh's Motorola was set to the Garuds' frequency. Any information Milind received from the RR team, he passed to Nilesh, who then relayed it to the CO.

Nilesh was also observing the house through his telescopic sight. Strategically placed right in front of the house, Nilesh's task was to

---

7   Combat operating base.

detect and relay any movement to the Garuds, while Milind would pass the same information to the Army.

Unlike the other Garuds with their helmet-mounted night vision devices, Nilesh had an advanced, long-range telescopic device mounted on his gun which he used to see in the dark.

Around 0500 hours, the rest of the forces from the COB reached the target area. Just as their vehicle screeched to a halt, a grenade was thrown from inside the house. Within moments, six or seven terrorists, whose exact number could not be guessed due to their rapid movements in pitch darkness, armed and moving in a line, burst out of the house, firing under-barrel grenade launchers, lobbing hand grenades and shooting indiscriminately. One of the grenades exploded right in front of Milind and Nayan, who had only a small log for cover. The splinters injured their faces and inflicted serious wounds.

Despite his injuries, Sergeant Milind Kishor Khairnar displayed exceptional firefighting skills. His accurate fire pinned down the terrorists, creating a momentary stalemate.

However, the intense and concentrated fire from the terrorists' automatic weapons and grenades soon overwhelmed him. And he was struck by a flurry of bullets and shrapnel, causing severe wounds.

Seeing his comrade in peril, Nilesh intensified his fire to provide cover and protect Milind. The terrorists, now aware of the threat Nilesh posed, directed massive fire towards his position. Nilesh too was hit by a volley of bullets, but his resolve remained unshaken.

Despite his grave injuries, Milind displayed extraordinary agility of body and mind. He fired an entire magazine at the terrorists, then swiftly reloaded and continued his assault. In a final act of valour, he killed one terrorist. However, already weakened by multiple wounds, he shifted his position momentarily and, in that instant, a fatal headshot took his life.

Nilesh, demonstrating exemplary courage in the highest tradition of the military, held his ground. He succeeded in killing another terrorist before succumbing to his own injuries. In their final moments, Milind and Nilesh had not only eliminated one terrorist each but had also grievously injured several others, epitomizing unyielding bravery and sacrifice.

The firefight raged on, but the various forces from different units with different set of weapons and mode of operandi were firing cautiously to avoid collateral damage and friendly fire. Soldiers will say casualties in friendly fire happen. Taking advantage of this, some terrorists had managed to flee. The air was thick with the acrid smell of gunpowder and a ghostly silence descended as the firing ceased.

From his position, the CO Garud shouted, 'Is everyone okay?' The tension was palpable. Meanwhile, JWO Sandeep began establishing radio contact with the Garud buddy pairs. There was no response from Milind and Nilesh's radio set. Concern mounted as the 13 Rashtriya Rifles team called the CO, reporting that their night vision goggles revealed four bodies on the ground.

The CO's heart skipped a beat.

He knew it was risky to leave his position with the possibility of remaining terrorists nearby, but the urge to confirm the situation was overwhelming. With a heavy heart, he crawled silently towards the bodies. The reflective bulletproof plates on two bodies, typical of what a Garud donned, confirmed his worst fears—they were Garuds.

Eventually, the bodies were evacuated and transported to 92 Base Hospital, Srinagar.

In the aftermath of the brutal firefight, as the dust began to settle, the full gravity of the situation became evident.

Among the fallen terrorists was a local area commander. He had been the linchpin of the terrorist network who the others had been desperate to protect as they attempted their escape.

Found with a rucksack filled with large stacks of Indian currency, two AK-47 rifles, twelve magazines, hand grenades, cigarettes, drugs, toothpaste and even perfumes ,indicating that the terrorists had really hoped for him to escape alive to load him with extra load. It was also clear that the local area commander[8] had been responsible for the group's escape plan and supplies. Born and raised in Hajin, he knew every alley and hideout, and served as the strategic mastermind, and point of coordination and communication of the organization, his killing was a huge blow to the terrorist network. The other deceased terrorist, while still armed, carried only a gun and some magazines.

The local area commander's death dealt a crippling blow to the terrorist group. Positioned to escape even if others perished, he was the eyes and ears of the terrorists, their leader and focal point.

As the sun rose over the battlefield, the Garud stood solemnly over their fallen comrades. It was the first loss for the 617 Garud Flight, and the weight of their grief was immense. Though some terrorists had fled, the fight had now become intensely personal for the Garud. With burning resolve, they pledged to avenge their fallen comrades.

---

8 The author has deliberately withheld the local terrorists' names to deny them any glorification. Only the names of our men in uniform deserve remembrance—for they are the true heroes future generations must know.

Air Force Station, Chandigarh
12 October 2017

The special Indian Air Force aircraft had landed, bringing back the bodies of Sergeant Khairnar Milind Kishor and Corporal Nilesh Kumar Nayan. The air was sombre as a guard of honour was given in the highest military tradition. The scene was a poignant tribute to the sacrifices made by these brave men.

Nilesh's wife, Minsha, was overwhelmed with grief.

Her voice trembled as she recalled the unbearable days following the news:

> I remember my mother coming to me, urging me to feed our daughter. But I don't remember if I did. I was in shock for a long time. My mother-in-law fainted many times. It was a blur.

Tears welled in her eyes as she continued:

> The Air Force asked me where I wanted the cremation. I told them to take Nilesh to [his village] Udhadih, in Bhagalpur, Bihar. That's where he was born. That's where he should rest.

Harshada, Milind's wife, shared her own devastating ordeal, her voice heavy with sorrow:

> Those days were incredibly tough. Vedika was only six and a half years old, and Gagan was about two and a half. I didn't know what to do. Vedika was so attached to her father, and it took her the longest to come to terms with his absence. She still makes birthday cards for him on his birthday.

Harshada's voice cracked as she spoke of the sacrifices she had to make.

> I tried to find a job, but with no one to look after the children, I had to give it up. Air Force stood by us during our darkest times. The CO and his wife still keep in touch, and their support has been our lifeline.

Visiting the 617 Garud Flight in Chandigarh was a poignant experience. The unit had constructed small busts of Sergeant Khairnar Milind Kishor and Corporal Nilesh Nayan, each proudly wearing their maroon beret and blue uniform. Fresh marigold garlands adorned the statues, a tribute to their heroism. Air Force flags stood tall beside the busts. In front of the busts stood a huge brass diya, casting a warm, golden light. The surrounding walls were adorned with pictures of Milind and Nilesh, their last uniforms, bullets and helmets displayed as solemn memorabilia. Behind the busts, a laminated poster depicted the team that had avenged their deaths, which also included Corporal Jyoti Prakash Nirala in the same picture, who was now also honoured with a bust alongside his brothers.

As I looked at the busts, I felt a profound sense of reverence, knowing that the legacy of their sacrifice would forever be etched in the hearts of those who knew them. But it is equally important for the rest of the nation to know who these brave souls were, and what they did for India and its sovereignty.

Author's note

This story is based on first-hand interviews with Wing Commander Rajiv Chauhan, then Commanding Officer of 617 Garud Flight, who led two of the unit's most defining operations in the Valley, and his senior most warrant officer, JWO Sandeep Kumar who has now retired and works in corporate. Speaking to the KIA's wives, Harshada and Minsha, was emotionally challenging—but it was essential. Despite the page constraints when I could have easily merged Op Rakh Hajin with Op Chandeergeer I chose to highlight the quiet valour of Sergeant Khairnar Milind Kishor and Corporal Nilesh Kumar Nayan seperately to emphasize the weight of their sacrfices. Their story is lesser known as compared to IAF's third Ashoka Chakra awardee Corporal Jyoti Prakash Nirala, who made the supreme sacrifice just days after the sacrifice of Milind and Nayan. At the end we must never forget, award or no award, no sacrifice is bigger or smaller, all blood spilled for the nation is sacred blood.

5

Corporal Jyoti Prakash Nirala, Ashok Chakra (Posthumous): The Valiant Ashoka Chakra Awardee

Operation Chandergeer
Chandergeer Village
Hajin Panchayat Samiti
Bandipora
Jammu and Kashmir
18 November 2017

THE BLEAK NOVEMBER weather had blanketed the Kashmir Valley in a relentless chill. It was the harsh onset of winter, the cold as biting as the conflict that raged within its borders. The wind howled through the mountains, carrying with it a dampness that seeped into the bones, freezing everything in its path. Despite it being around 1500 hours, visibility was near zero, with a steady drizzle reducing the world to a blurry grey haze. The ground beneath the soldiers' boots was a treacherous mix of mud and wet leaves, making each step a battle against the elements.

Through this unforgiving weather, a team of Garud Special Forces moved silently, their forms barely visible against the bleak terrain. Their breaths rose in misty clouds, each movement deliberate and cautious. The daylight was obscured by heavy clouds, casting an eerie gloom over the landscape. The wet ground squelched softly beneath their boots, the only sound in the oppressive silence of the afternoon.

They were on a mission that demanded absolute precision. The cold was unbearable, but the soldiers pushed through, focused on the task at hand. The bad weather was both their ally and enemy: It masked their approach but also made it harder to see, to move, to breathe.

Still, each soldier took up their position with practiced ease, moving with the precision of a well-rehearsed dance, taking advantage of every shadow, nook and cranny that offered even the slightest cover. The Garuds, paired off, spread out around the target house, forming a closely laid cordon.

Behind the house lay a *kaccha nallah*—a crude drainage channel, now choked with a treacherous mix of mud and wet debris. This small, makeshift trench was where most of the Garud Special Forces had taken their tactical positions. Despite being the safest cover available, it was an uncomfortable and precarious spot for laying an ambush. The soldiers, seasoned and resolute, endured the harsh conditions, knowing their position was critical to the mission's success.

Among them was a sturdy, rugged soldier—a light machine gun (LMG) specialist in the elite Garud flight. His gear spoke of his role: Heavy, meticulously assembled and designed for intense combat. Clad in the Indian Air Force combat uniform, he wore a tactical vest layered over a bulletproof plate jacket. The vest was equipped with multiple pockets, holding essentials, including a communication set and additional ammunition. A rucksack on his back held extra supplies, making his loadout significantly heavier than that of his fellow soldiers. A helmet protected his head, while a secondary weapon was holstered at his thigh. His powerful frame and thick beard gave him a dangerous, almost fearsome appearance.

In his gloved hands, he gripped an IWI Negev, a formidable Israeli light machine gun capable of laying down sustained fire with deadly precision. Fitted with a 150-round drum, the weapon was both a tool and an extension of the soldier, and he wielded it with the expertise that only years of intense training and countless operations could bring.

He was Corporal Jyoti Prakash Nirala.

The drizzle had intensified, but the Garud flight remained in their positions, each soldier a silent sentinel in the bleak afternoon. Visibility was poor, but they had no choice—the terrorists were inside the house, and this was the Garuds' only chance to strike.

Corporal Nirala's position on the edge of the nallah was the most precarious. The ground was slick with mud, and the weight of his gear made every movement a struggle. But he was determined. The memory of his fallen comrades, who were killed by these very terrorists these very terrorists, burned in his mind. Today, he would avenge them. The LMG's cold metal bit into his gloves and his tactical vest weighed him down, but he bore it all with the ease of someone who had done this countless times before.

Bracing himself, he adjusted the Negev. The weapon was ready, and so was he.

The mission, executed with unparalleled precision, was wrapped up swiftly. The target was no ordinary group; it was the north Kashmir leadership of the Lashkar-e-Taiba (LeT), a network of foreign-based terrorists with ties to some of the most infamous attacks in history. Among them was the nephew of Zakiur Rehman Lakhvi, mastermind of the 26/11 Mumbai attacks. Their elimination was not just a tactical victory but a significant blow to one of the most dangerous terrorist networks operating in the at that time.

The Garuds succeeded, but at a cost.

Corporal Jyoti Prakash Nirala, who had ensured no terrorist could flee, paid the ultimate price. His sacrifice was the only casualty in an otherwise flawless operation. His bravery is immortalized in the annals of Indian military history. As only the third Ashoka Chakra awardee from the Indian Air Force, and the sole airman to receive India's highest peacetime award, he stands as a symbol of unparalleled valour. His legacy is a testament to the courage and excellence of the Garud Special Forces, and remains a shining example of dedication and bravery in the face of overwhelming odds.

~

Garud Regimental Training Centre
Uttar Pradesh
April 2006

The sweltering heat of the summer sun bore down on the Garud commando training camp, where the air seemed thick enough to cut with a knife. The training ground was alive with the sounds of exertion, as determined young men pushed their bodies to the limit, each one striving to earn the coveted Garud proficiency badge.

A single figure stood out among the airmen—his eyes locked on the vertical rope that dangled before him. It seemed to stretch endlessly towards the sky, but he squared his shoulders and tightened his grip. With a sharp exhale, he launched himself upwards, muscles straining as he pulled himself hand over hand, inching closer to the top. He used only his upper body, his legs hanging motionless as he powered his way up, displaying raw strength and unyielding determination. Every fibre of his being screamed in protest, but he refused to give in, his mind focused solely on reaching the summit. As his hand slapped the top of the rope, he allowed himself a brief moment of satisfaction before descending swiftly, the ground rushing up to meet him.

There was no time to rest. The next challenge awaited—the horizontal rope. Suspended high above the ground, it swayed slightly in the wind, daring the recruits to cross it. The commando grabbed the rope, his body parallel to the ground as he began the painstaking journey across. His arms and legs worked in tandem, muscles burning with every movement. The rope cut into his hands, but he ignored the pain, pushing forward until he reached the other side, his breath coming in ragged gasps.

No sooner had he touched down than the whistle blew, indicating the completion of the task. The otherwise strict Ustaad, known for his rigidity, almost gave a crooked smile. *The boy is good*, he thought to himself. Then he turned to bark instructions to the other recruits, showering them with the choicest of abuses, taunting them that Nirala could climb the rope using only his upper body while they couldn't do it in time even with the help of their legs.

This was just another day at Garud Regimental Training Centre. This was no ordinary military training institute; it was the crucible where men were forged into the elite Garud Special Forces.

And Nirala was determined to emerge stronger than ever.

He had missed the first batch due to a fracture that forced him into several months of mandatory bed rest. After completing his basic airmen training at ATS Belgaum, he had moved to GRTC for the next phase of his one-year Garud training. But within a month, a careless mistake led him to fracture his leg. Rather than quit, Nirala—strong-willed since childhood and determined to see through any commitment—chose to wait. Authorities permitted him to join the next batch, which began in April 2006, after his original batch advanced to the next stage. Nirala rejoined with determination and passed the phase with flying colours in June 2007. It was not easy.

Some days, he would be dangling on ropes; on others, he and his fellow airmen, shouldering a twenty-kilo pittho and a rifle slung across their backs, would speed-march twenty kilometres under the unforgiving sun. The marches became routine—the pittho's weight digging into his shoulders as the distance stretched on, strengthening his legs and hardening his resolve.

They would leap over wide ditches and cross gaping chasms, or be dropped in dense jungles, armed only with a map and a compass to find their way back—learning critical navigation skills.

Weapon-firing drills followed, the crack of gunfire echoing through the air as the trainees honed their marksmanship. First-aid training was also imparted—a vital skill in the field. The trainees learnt how to treat injuries with minimal supplies, how to stop bleeding, how to stabilize a fracture. Nirala's hands would move with practiced ease as he bandaged a mock wound, his mind calm and focused.

But it was communication training that he loved the most. He learnt to operate various communication sets. As the radio crackled to life, he would respond with the calm confidence of someone who knew exactly what needed to be done.

After completing their trade training, the Garud trainees were sent to a military facility under the Ministry of Home Affairs in Sarsawa for commando training. The purpose was to enhance their skills and impart operational training. There, they trained with elite 'Special Groups' known for operating in secrecy, their missions shrouded in mystery and danger. The training was intense, designed to prepare them for infiltrating deep into enemy territory, executing ambushes and surviving in hostile environments.

Physical conditioning was relentless. Full-kit runs were a daily ordeal, with each recruit carrying the weight of their gear as they pushed their bodies to the limit. Instructors, each a seasoned commando, manned every point of the training area, imparting hard-earned operational knowledge.

Cadets learnt the art of room interventions—breaching doors, clearing rooms, searching for hidden enemies and neutralizing them with precision—every movement practiced until it became second nature. Improvised explosive device (IED) demolition was another critical component of their training.

Advanced weapons training further honed the recruits' capabilities. Nirala became proficient with a variety of arms, learning to handle them with the skill and precision required of an elite soldier.

Garud Jyoti Prakash Nirala attended his passing out parade in September 2007, earning his proficiency badge. He went on to complete additional courses, including swimming (learning to swim with uniform and full gear, and perform life-saving tasks) and mechanical transport training to sharpen his driving skills. He also earned his paratrooper badge after completing the basic para jump course at PTS Agra.[1]

After completing all essential courses from India's premier combat training institutes, Nirala was sent for a final twenty-eight-day course at the Corps Battle School (CBS) in Khrew, Srinagar.[2] CBS is renowned for training soldiers from across the country in counter-insurgency and counterterrorism operations, with a specific focus on the challenges in Jammu and Kashmir. Nirala, along with personnel from various services, underwent rigorous training to develop the physical and mental toughness required for operating in the region.

Sergeant Satish Kumar (Retd.), who trained alongside Corporal Jyoti Prakash Nirala, recalled:

---

1 'Paratrooper Training School *Sky Hawks*', Bharat Rakshak, https://www.bharat-rakshak.com/indianairforce/database/units/PTS.
2 Major Gaurav Arya, 'Khrew: The Corps Battle School', *PATRIOT With Major Gaurav Arya*, Republic World, 13 June 2020, https://www.youtube.com/watch?v=mgl3DpM_xCM.

He was incredibly strong-willed and curious. He was physically fit too, with particularly strong hands, which later made him a natural LMG specialist.

The CBS course was an eye-opener. One of the unique aspects was the involvement of surrendered militants as instructors. They provided invaluable insights into a terrorist's mindset—how they think, what triggers them and how they lay ambushes against forces. This perspective allowed us to understand the enemy better.

The Indian Air Force operates across diverse terrains—from deserts to valleys, mountains to snow-covered peaks and dense jungles. The Garud Special Forces, tasked with protecting the nation's most valuable assets, are also deployed in counter-insurgency operations.

By the end of the course, Nirala was fully prepared to serve the nation. He, along with several other Garuds, was then attached to 2 Para (Special Forces) in the Kashmir Valley, operating alongside them. The seasoned Special Forces soldiers were supportive of the freshly trained Garuds, offering them valuable exposure to real-time operations and the unpredictable challenges they presented.

Following his attachment, Nirala received his first official posting at Jammu Air Force Station.

During that tenure, he also completed the programme at the Counter-Insurgency and Jungle Warfare School (CIJWS)[3] in Silchar, Assam, becoming a jungle warfare specialist. The dense jungles of the

---

3 Chaitanya Kalbag, 'CIJWS attains tremendous importance in Indian Army's operations in North-east', *India Today*, 15 November 1982, https://www.indiatoday.in/magazine/special-report/story/19821115-cijws-attains-tremendous-importance-in-indian-armys-operations-in-north-east-772388-2013-08-27.

Northeast, with their relentless rains, were unlike anything he had experienced in the plains or Kashmir.

Training with minimal resources, he learnt to navigate the treacherous terrain, climb mountains using ropes or even bamboo, and survive by eating whatever the jungle offered, including snakes. This training, alongside soldiers from the Assam Rifles and troops from friendly foreign countries, deepened his respect for the agility and endurance of the Assam Rifles soldiers. The course humbled him.

The jungles awed him and the mountains made him feel small. By then, he was married and missed his wife a lot.

~

Rajouri Garden
New Delhi
2005

Sushma Nand softly reminisces about the man she loved dearly, her voice tender as she shares her most cherished memories with me. It's heartbreaking how such profound love stories can remain unfulfilled.

Fathers, husbands and sons must make sacrifices so others can live in peace. Sushma's story mirrors those of countless other military spouses whose husbands have made the supreme sacrifice.

Sushma recalls how Nirala, with his earnest eyes and quiet strength, entered her life unexpectedly. He was about to begin his rigorous Garud training , and his father, Sri Tej Narayan Singh, had accompanied him to Delhi to complete some formalities. During their week-long stay at Sushma's home, she felt an immediate connection, even though they had never met before. Their families hailed from Rohtas district in Bihar, their villages just a stone's throw apart, but their paths had never truly crossed until then.

Sushma's father served in the Electronics and Mechanical Engineers (EME) branch of the Indian Army, an arm renowned for its technical expertise and competitive edge.

At the time they met, Nirala was just about to join the Indian Air Force, ready to embark on his own path of service. The modern, progressive and forward-looking ethos of his EME backgrounds perfectly matched the panache and glory of the Indian Air Force.

Sushma's mother quickly saw potential in the match. The shared service background, caste and village ties made the connection seem destined.

Still, Sushma was hesitant. She was deeply focused on her studies, pursuing a diploma in software engineering from NIIT, and unsure if marriage was the right step at the time. Nirala, however, was immediately drawn to her. But as their conversations progressed, their relationship blossomed. In those days, mobile phones were rare, so Sushma would collect coins to call him from STD booths. Despite his busy training schedule, he would manage to call her once in a while

Their love faced challenges, particularly from relatives who questioned whether Sushma, being an only child, would adjust to Nirala's large joint family. Nirala, the eldest and only son with four younger sisters, carried significant responsibilities. These concerns led his father to call off the match. Yet, by then, the bond between them was too strong to break. Their courtship continued for almost five years. Sushma reflects that they were together for just twelve years—eight of them married. She never imagined she would face such profound grief.

She confided softly, her eyes misty with memory:

> I would tell Nirala that I couldn't be without him, that if I didn't marry him, I couldn't marry anyone else. There was a lot of pressure from my family at that time, since they had started seeing

other boys for me who I would keep rejecting on some pretext or the other. He was aware of this.

Her voice faltered, and she smiled through her tears.

'He would get emotional and console me, saying, "Who told you that I could live without you? Even I cannot be without you."'

Despite his many responsibilities as the eldest son, Nirala couldn't envision life without Sushma. In 2009, they took a leap of faith and married in a temple, knowing their love could overcome any obstacle.

It wasn't an easy decision, but it was one they made together.

Eventually, their families accepted the marriage and, on 6 March 2011, they celebrated their union with full Hindu rituals, a testament to their enduring love. Their life together was filled with joy, and on 3 February 2014, they welcomed their daughter, Jigyasa.

Sushma shares how, after marriage, Nirala's family embraced her wholeheartedly. They affectionately called her 'Baby', a reflection of their warmth. With her four sisters-in-law, Sushma found the sisters she never had. They would sit, eat and chat for hours, as if no rift had ever existed. After their daughter Jigyasa's arrival, life felt more complete, and she became the centre of everyone's affection.

In 2013, Sushma's mother passed away due to complications from diabetes. Although devastated, Sushma found strength in Nirala and his family, who stood by her with unwavering support. Nirala remained by her side through this dark period, and his presence helped her emerge from it.

Nirala was a devoted father. Sushma recalled fondly:

Nirala doted on Jiya. Whenever he was home, he held her, took her out, bought her things. I remember what Jiya's teacher told us after we enrolled her in playschool in Chandigarh. Nirala was there on her first day and checked on Jiya several times, even though the teacher suggested he return after a few hours. She laughed and said she had seen many doting fathers, but none like him.

Nirala was also a devoted son and a fiercely protective elder brother. He dreamt of seeing his four younger sisters happily married.

After his passing, it was his Garud comrades who stepped in to fulfil those dreams, supporting the family with gifts and assistance. They stepped in in other ways too. There is a local custom in Nirala's village which dictates that the bride's feet should not touch the floor during the *vidai*. Nirala's brothers in arms quickly ensured that this tradition continued at his sister Shashikala's wedding, making sure she walked on their hands.[4] The wedding video, which went viral on social media, encapsulates the bond shared by those in the armed forces, which extends well beyond the lives of their comrades. The Garuds repeated this gesture at his other sister Sunita's wedding.[5]

~

---

4 Swarajya Staff, 'Bihar: IAF Garud Commandos Pay For Marriage Of Martyred Commando's Sister, Perform Brother's Duties In The Ceremony', 14 June 2019, https://swarajyamag.com/insta/bihar-iaf-garud-commandos-pay-for-marriage-of-martyred-commandos-sister-perform-brothers-duties-in-the-ceremony.

5 ETV Bharat English Team, '16 Garud Commandos Turn Brothers for Martyr's Sister in Bihar's Rohtas', ETV Bharat, 6 March 2024, https://www.etvbharat.com/en/!offbeat/16-garud-commandos-turn-brothers-on-martyr-jyoti-prakash-niralas-sisters-wedding-in-rohtas-enn24030603444.

Bandipora
North Kashmir
11 October 2017

Nirala's path to destiny began on a day marked by both valour and profound sorrow. His journey, which would see him take on the most formidable terrorists and carve his name into history, commenced with a significant loss. During Operation Rakh Hajin, his comrades, Sergeant Milind Kishor Khairnar and Corporal Nilesh Kumar Nayan made the ultimate sacrifice after eliminating two terrorists. Though the remaining assailants managed to escape.

Camaraderie is at the core of the Indian military, but for the modestly sized elite Garud force, it runs even deeper—coursing through their veins like blood. You cannot harm one Garud and expect the rest to remain passive; they stand united, ready to act as one. The entire flight took Milind and Nayan's loss personally. Nirala too was devastated.

Sushma recalled:

Nirala had surprised us by coming home for Diwali. When he had left for his six-month TD[6] from Chandigarh to Kashmir he had told me he wouldn't be granted leave and would visit only after the TD was over. He joked that I would no longer be troubled by him. I was upset, wondering how we would manage without him for so long. But Nirala had always placed duty first.

Sushma went on:

At the time, Nirala was supposed to help finalize his sister Shashikala's marriage, but he hadn't been able to. During Diwali

---

6 Temporary duty.

2017, he came home unexpectedly, but he looked different—his beard unkempt like any operative's from the Valley—and it frightened Jigyasa. He quickly bathed and shaved, saying he didn't want Jiya to be scared. Later, he took her to the market, buying her toys and chocolates.

I had no idea that was the last time Jiya and I would see him.

His close friend, Sergeant Satish Kumar, was posted in Srinagar when Nirala was deployed in Bandipora. Satish had the rare opportunity to see him just days before his sacrifice. Nirala had flown from Chandigarh to Srinagar and stayed with Satish overnight before heading to Bandipora. Satish recalled their parting at 0300 hours and Nirala's persistent cough. Nirala had requested cough syrup, which Satish sent, unaware it would be their final interaction.

Back in the field, preparations to apprehend the terrorists were in full swing.

Following Operation Rakh Hajin, a significant cache of ammunition, weapons, drugs and mobile phones had been seized—each phone number a potential thread in the web of terror. Advanced technology was employed to trace these numbers, several of which were flagged for surveillance, uncovering a labyrinth of connections.

Soon, one of the numbers was activated, leading the surveillance team to a single elusive target—a foreign terrorist who used the number to communicate with his local girlfriend. The operation was a collaborative effort between the Jammu and Kashmir Police and the Indian military, with both sides exchanging vital intelligence.

A distinct pattern emerged: The number was activated at a specific time each night, with the terrorist moving like a phantom, his location shifting with every whispered conversation across a seven to eight-kilometre radius. Ever cautious, he avoided revealing his exact whereabouts, constantly on the move during calls. The intelligence team listened intently, uncovering crucial details—references to an under-construction latrine, a nearby masjid and more.

The surveillance extended over several days, revealing the terrorist's chaotic yet calculated movements. The man remained elusive, slipping through shadows and staying one step ahead. Yet, the net was tightening.

The gathered intelligence was passed to the CO of the Garud flight, who further intensified the operations. In this high-stakes game of cat and mouse, accurate intelligence was the key. Him along with a soldier of the 13 Rashtriya RIfles (Kumaon), went undercover to pinpoint the terrorist's location. Posing as foreign-based militants, they collected information from locals, while the CO leveraged technology to its fullest.

Drones and UAVs were extensively used to survey the area, peering into houses and gathering additional information. UAVs circled high over Chandergeer, their sensors cutting through the darkness, tracking every faint sign of movement. The CO pushed every resource to its limit, blending cutting-edge technology with raw human intelligence.

Driven by personal loss—the balidan of Milind and Nayan—the Garud CO's determination was unwavering. After extensive surveillance, the terrorist's location was finally narrowed down—all evidence pointed to a specific cluster of houses in the village of Chandergeer.

A fresh obstacle emerged: Chandergeer fell outside the operational area of the company area that Garud flight operated along with. Refusing to let this stop him, Squadron Leader Chauhan sought permission from the battalion CO to conduct the operation. Initially, the request was denied. However, recognizing the Garuds' commitment to seeking justice, permission was ultimately granted.

This mission too unfolded with the same high standards of operation.

As soon as permission was granted and the terrorists' location pinpointed, the Sqn Ldr Chauhan sprang into action. He meticulously orchestrated every detail of the operation with his senior most warrant officer, JWO Sandeep Kumar, weapons specialist Nirala, and the rest of the Garud flight.

Wing Commander Rajiv Chauhan (then a Squadron Leader) later recounted:

> We believe in meticulous planning before leaving for an operation. We drew maps, identified entry and exit points, and marked potential escape routes. Roles were assigned to the Garuds to cover every possible angle. We planned the cordon strategy and anticipated potential problems. Coordination with the police and other forces was arranged, and our contingency plans were set for every scenario.
>
> One significant addition for this operation was the use of large ballistic shields. Having faced casualties in the past, we couldn't afford any more. These shields protected some of our men from a volley of bullets.

He paused, reflecting on the decision-making process:

> There was intense debate about whether to conduct the operation at night or during the day. The target house was near a mosque that drew the entire village during prayer times. In our previous operations, we always moved under the cover of darkness, but this time, we chose daylight—immediately after the evening prayers when the villagers would not be assembled together.
>
> We decided to operate in civilian attire and used common pickup trucks, leaving at staggered intervals. As soon as we

took our positions, we would call for reinforcements to move in promptly.

Wing Commander Chauhan also described the added pressure created by the terrorist's recent silence. The sudden halt in communication with his girlfriend in past few days had raised fears that he might flee. So when intelligence confirmed that the phone had been reactivated after days of inactivity, they decided to proceed immediately. They couldn't afford to wait for nightfall.

18 November was set as the date for the operation.

The exact number of terrorists in the target house remained uncertain, but initial intelligence estimated there were at least two or three oblivious to the fact that number of terrorists were more. With this in mind, the RR battalions were meticulously briefed of the plan. The joint operation was set in motion, with one RR battalion tasked with establishing a cordon and the other designated as reinforcements. The police were to be called in only after the operation concluded, to manage law and order, and ensure a swift exit from the hostile zone.

JWO Sandeep Kumar (veteran), the senior most warrant officer of the Garud flight at that time, shared a poignant anecdote about Nirala:

> Nirala was fearless—a true daredevil. I recall one patrolling mission where he had removed his bulletproof jacket. After the mission, when the CO learnt about this, he reprimanded Nirala sternly, emphasizing that the jacket was never to be removed under any circumstances. Nirala listened quietly, but once the CO was gone, he puffed out his chest proudly and declared to us all, 'I'm not afraid of anyone. If the time comes, I won't hesitate to sacrifice my life, with or without the jacket.'

Little did they know how prophetic Nirala's words would prove to be.

~

Operation Chandergeer
Chandergeer
Hajin Block
Bandipora
34 kilometres from Srinagar
18 November 2017

The village of Chandergeer lay shrouded in a cold, tranquil blanket. On 18 November 2017, the weather was bleak and unforgiving. Heavy clouds blotted out the sun, casting a grey pall over the landscape. Nestled between rolling hills and dense forests, Chandergeer—derived from *chand* and *rahgeer*, meaning 'moonlit walkers'—stood in stark contrast to the turmoil it harboured. Its linear layout, flanked by sprawling orchards and expansive farmlands, rendered it both picturesque and strategically vulnerable. The sole road into the village meandered through the cold terrain, its narrow width and sharp U-turn creating a natural choke point for anyone attempting to enter or exit.

At the heart of the village stood the target house, a rickety structure with a tin roof that creaked ominously in the wind. Four weathered wooden windows, sagging under years of neglect, framed a door that opened directly on to a set of stone steps. Located near a mosque and surrounded by dense apple orchards, the house nestled among three similar homes lining the main road. The setting was ideal for the terrorists: Secluded enough to avoid immediate detection, yet close enough to the village centre to blend in or escape through the orchards.

The mission's success hinged on impeccable timing and precision, as the terrorists, familiar with the village's layout, could easily escape into the forested hills if given the slightest chance.

Back at Manasbal headquarters, the Garud team gathered in high spirits, buoyed by the prospect of avenging their fallen comrades. They joked and clicked pictures, their laughter a stark contrast to the gravity of the mission ahead. Amid the camaraderie, someone said, 'Let's capture this moment—who knows if one of us won't return?' No one guessed the truth of those words. This would be the same picture to be laminated at the walls of the sanctum erected in the premises of 617 Garud flight in the memory of the comrades lost.

JWO Sandeep recalled how Nirala, with his Negev LMG, epitomized meticulous readiness. The Negev was no ordinary machine gun—it was a symbol of firepower and precision. Its heavy-duty barrel, designed for sustained fire, could withstand prolonged bursts without overheating. The LMG's manoeuvrability and ability to fire from different angles meant that only the most skilled operators could harness its full potential

Nirala's secondary weapon, a Glock pistol, was holstered snugly on his right thigh, a trusted sidearm for close engagements. Over his bulletproof jacket, he wore a tactical vest loaded with additional ammunition and a survival kit. Despite the considerable weight of the LMG and his gear, Nirala's efficiency remained unaffected. His strong, calloused hands moved with practiced ease as he checked his equipment.

JWO Sandeep shared:

Nirala could walk or run with that LMG like it was an extension of his arm. Even in the heat of battle, he managed to fire accurately from difficult positions. Handling an LMG requires not just physical strength but a deep sense of responsibility and tactical acumen.

Wing Commander Rajiv Chauhan (then Squadron Leader) added:

> Nirala was more than just a soldier; he was a passionate Special Forces guy who thrived on being at the forefront of every mission. You don't just hand over an LMG to anyone. It's the backbone of the team's firepower. Nirala earned that trust through sheer dedication and skill. He could handle it, and he proved it every single time.

The Garud detachment was a picture of meticulous preparation as they set out for Operation Chandergeer. Disguised in traditional Kashmiri *phirans* over their tactical uniforms, they blended seamlessly into their surroundings. The flowing fabric and intricate patterns of the phirans provided the perfect cover.

A detailed study of the village layout had revealed that the only access point was a narrow road with a sharp bend, forcing anyone entering or leaving to slow down. The convoy of pickup trucks rolled out with purpose.

The first vehicle, containing the Garud CO Chauhan, led the way through the winding roads; seated in front, he reviewed the final details of the operation, his mind focused on the mission ahead.

Suddenly, at a sharp turn, a jolt threw the lead vehicle off course.

The Garud CO's eyes narrowed. The collision threatened their stealth—the noise could attract unwanted attention, drawing villagers to the scene and jeopardizing the carefully coordinated operation. Even worse, the disruption threatened the synchronization between the lead vehicle and the others in the convoy.

Yet, the driver remained composed. With quick thinking and steady hands, he reversed and manoeuvred the vehicle back onto the road. The move was so smooth that the incident went unnoticed by any onlookers. The engine revved, its growl blending into the ambient sounds of the village.

As they reached Chandergeer, the operation's most critical phase began.

The convoy came to a halt, and the Garud sprang into action. They leapt out and swiftly took up positions around the target house. The air was thick with tension, but the Garuds' movements were fluid and decisive. As the team prepared for their assault, the village lay under a dreary sky, the heavy clouds obscuring the sun. Fallen leaves and withered vegetation crunched underfoot, and a light rain further reduced visibility.

The 13 RR (Kumaon) soldiers took up positions at the front of the house, forming a solid perimeter to prevent any escape or interference from that direction. The other Rastriya Rifle battalion secured the surrounding roads, ensuring that all possible exits were covered. The Garuds, positioned at the back of the house, established a close cordon.

As the Garud detachment and the 13 RR (Kumaon) soldiers took up their strategic positions, the scene in Chandergeer unfolded with unexpected intensity. Amidst the meticulous preparation, the rhythm of village life was abruptly disrupted.

A group of women working in the nearby fields noticed the soldiers and suddenly began shouting, their voices piercing the morning stillness. '*Fauj aa gayi! Fauj aa gayi!*' Their alarmed cries echoed through the village. Panic spread as they abandoned their tasks and fled, their screams drawing the attention of the villagers.

At the same time, a few residents emerged from the target house, their movements seemingly casual. They stepped outside, apparently caught off guard by the commotion. The Garuds, quick to react, intercepted them with urgency but calm authority. When questioned, the villagers claimed they had stepped out to answer the call of nature.

The soldiers, however, took no chances.

'Stay here,' CO Chauhan ordered. 'We need you to stay put until we say otherwise.'

Could be OGWs, he thought. *The actual terrorists wouldn't come out unarmed.*

The villagers, faces a mix of confusion and fear, complied without protest. The soldiers positioned themselves strategically around the house, senses attuned to any sign of trouble.

The tension was palpable. The sudden outcry and suspicious movements could only mean one thing—the terrorists had likely been alerted. The intelligence gathered before the mission had been sound, but now the element of surprise was gone. The urgency of the task at hand escalated.

The Garud detachment lay in wait, breaths shallow, nerves on edge.

Suddenly, six terrorists stormed out, firing weapons and lobbing grenades towards the Garud positions behind the house. The chaos was calculated. The terrorists had observed the cordon and decided to run in a single file, one behind the other, aiming to overwhelm a single buddy pair.

The tactic was familiar—exactly how they had operated in Rakh Hajin when Milind and Nayan were killed in action; it was meant to create chaos so that the terrorists could breach the cordon and escape.

But the Garuds had learnt from past mistakes.

The forces were ready, having anticipated such a move. As the terrorists charged, they opened fire with precision, and it was Corporal Jyoti Prakash Nirala who held the line. Armed with his LMG, he was positioned behind a kaccha naala—a crude, muddy ditch that provided little cover and even less stability. The terrain was unforgiving, filled with sludge, half-frozen from the recent snowfall. Visibility was low, and the conditions made it nearly impossible to find secure footing, especially with the heavy kit Nirala carried.

Ignoring the discomfort and danger, he steadied himself, focusing on the task at hand. It was a battle for survival—he needed to perform, even at the risk of his life. As the terrorists approached, Nirala's LMG erupted in a storm of gunfire. The first to fall was the LeT North Kashmir area commander known for his expertise in breaking military cordons. Nirala's relentless assault gave him no chance.

That day, Corporal Nirala was at his best.

He kept firing with deadly precision. The next to fall was the nephew of the 26/11 mastermind Zakiur Rehman Lakhvi—the LeT's 'supreme commander' of operations in Kashmir, and his nephew was Lakhvi's most trusted aide. He was also the son of the deputy to Hafiz Muhammad Saeed, another top terrorist on the National Investigation Agency's (NIA) most-wanted list. Nirala's bullets found their mark, cutting down the Category A++ terrorist[7] in mid-stride.[8]

But the fight was far from over. Some terrorists had escaped the previous operation, which had cost Sergeant Milind Kishor Khairnar and Corporal Nilesh Kumar Nayan their lives. *Not this time*, thought Nirala, as he kept firing, demonstrating his excellent combat skills.

---

7   Category A++ terrorist is the highest classification assigned by Indian security agencies to terrorists who pose an extreme threat to national security. These individuals are top leaders of terror outfits, involved in major attacks, highly trained, and often carry large bounties. They may also have international linkages and are prioritized targets in counter-terror operations.

8   The names of only internationally designated terrorists have been retained for authenticity and clarity. All other names have been deliberately omitted as a conscious decision to deny any space or recognition in our book to those involved in anti-India activities.

In the ensuing chaos, Nirala managed to injure two more terrorists, but the fight was taking its toll. A volley of bullets had struck him, yet he refused to go down. With every ounce of strength he had left, Nirala continued to fire, his resolve unbroken. Then, a headshot and the force of its impact drove him back into the muddy naala.

The effectively led cordon and exemplary valour displayed by Nirala had resulted in killing of rest of the four terrorists by the joint team of Garud SF and 13 RR. This operation was cited as one of the biggest setback to the Lashkar-e-Taiba in media as its entire North Kashmir leadership was wiped off in one go.

The battle had been won, but the cost was heavy. Corporal Jyoti Prakash Nirala had made the supreme sacrifice, fighting with unmatched courage and ensuring the mission's success.

As the last echoes of gunfire faded, a tense silence settled over the battlefield.

Corporal Nirala lay motionless, his uniform soaked with blood and mud. The mission had been a success, but there was no time to celebrate. The CO, JWO Sandeep and one more Garud immediately rushed to Nirala's side, their faces grim. They carefully lifted him up. Despite their combined strength, he felt heavy—his gear and the weight of the moment pressing down on them. They moved cautiously through the kaccha naala, slipping and sliding in the mud, the occasional crack of gunfire keeping them on edge.

The ambulance was only seventy or eighty metres away, but it felt like kilometres. Rain poured down, turning the path into a muddy quagmire. Nirala's weight seemed to increase with every metre, but the Garuds pushed on, their focus unwavering. When they finally reached the ambulance, they handed him over to the waiting medics, their hearts heavy.

Darkness began to fall, the weather worsening as the minutes ticked by. All the terrorists had been killed, but the operation was not yet over. Protocol dictated that each dead body be thoroughly searched before removal. Two Garuds were assigned to check the bodies for hidden dangers—booby traps, IEDs or grenades that could still cause harm. The others remained at their posts, watching and waiting.

Soon, the Bomb disposal experts from other forces arrived, the process took time—two to three hours of nerve-wracking work.

The battlefield was cleared, the dead terrorists loaded into vehicles. Reinforcements and the local police had arrived, but the situation was far from calm. Locals had gathered. Slogans echoed through the streets, and stones began to rain down on the forces. It was a familiar scene—a routine part of operations in Jammu and Kashmir, but no less challenging.

The police, working tirelessly, tried to maintain law and order amid the chaos. They formed a barricade, doing their best to manage the situation. Despite their efforts, the anger of the crowd was unrelenting. The Garud team evacuating Nirala was trapped, unable to move forward or retreat. The situation was critical, and they needed to clear a path.

The police and reinforcement forces worked in tandem, using tear gas and chilli bombs to disperse the mob. Slowly, they began creating a corridor for the vehicles to pass, and the team managed to get Nirala's body to a waiting helicopter at a nearby location. The helicopter, dispatched from the Srinagar base, was crucial for the evacuation.

Once Nirala was safely aboard, the helicopter lifted off, heading towards the 92 Base Hospital. The situation on the ground was still volatile. The remaining forces, now protected by a police convoy, slowly made their way back.

Evacuating the area felt like a scene from a movie—soldiers clung to the back of moving vehicles, one hand gripping the rail, the other holding a gun, brandishing it to intimidate the approaching mob and ensure safe passage. The police too continued working hard to manage the situation.

The Garud forces returned to the base in sombre silence. While some were busy with the afterwork of the operation, others gathered to reflect on the day's harrowing events. Despite the mission's success, a pall hung over them—Nirala was their third casualty. Each loss weighed heavily on their hearts, a reminder of the harsh cost of duty.

They are only a few. Each one of them counts.

Chandigarh,
18 November 2017

In Chandigarh, that same day, Sushma's anxiety mounted as she repeatedly tried to reach her husband, Jyoti Prakash Nirala. On the 17 November , he had reassured her and their daughter over a video call, promising he would return soon—not knowing it would be their final conversation.

As news of the encounter in Bandipora dominated the headlines on TV, Sushma's fears grew. She knew Nirala was operating in that area but clung to hope—until the Air Force personnel arrived at her door.

Then, she knew. Her world was shattered.

The last rites were carried out in Nirala's village of Badladih in Rohtas, Bihar, which became a beacon of pride and sorrow. People from all walks of life, including politicians, bureaucrats and armed forces personnel, gathered to honour the fallen hero.

The Bihta Air Force Station arranged the grand funeral procession. Shok Shastra was performed, and Corporal Jyoti Prakash Nirala was bid farewell following the highest traditions of the Indian Air

Force—a fitting tribute to the son of Bihar and the pride of the Indian Air Force.

In Nirala's absence, the Garuds never abandoned his family. The CO and his wife remained in constant touch, offering support at every step. When it was time for his sisters' weddings—something Nirala had dearly wished to see—his Garud comrades stepped in, going above and beyond what a brother would do.

I was privileged to visit a small yet deeply significant sanctum within their unit—a sacred space to commemorate the brave warriors of the 617 Garud Flight. Inside, the busts of Sergeant Milind, Corporal Nilesh Nayan and Corporal Jyoti Prakash Nirala stand proud.

When I visited, the Garuds were out training. The air resonated with spirited chants of *'Bharat Mata ki Jai'*, '617 Garud Flight *ki Jai*' and their powerful motto, *'Vimshy Mai Yoddha'*—'We are Fighters'. The intensity of their camaraderie and pride was palpable. As I watched the young Garuds practice their daily drills, their voices echoed with an unwavering sense of duty and respect for the legacy they carry.

Corporal Jyoti Prakash Nirala is not only the first airman of the Indian Air Force to be awarded the Ashoka Chakra—India's highest peacetime military decoration for valour, courageous action or self-sacrifice—but also one of only three IAF personnel ever to receive this honour. Flight Lieutenant Suhas Biswas and Squadron Leader Rakesh Sharma are the other awardees.

Hailing from a small village in Bihar, he knew the hardships of poverty and the weight of responsibility—he had four sisters to care for and a family of his own. Yet, when it came to serving his nation, this son of the soil didn't hesitate. This young airman gave his all, earning his place alongside legendary astronaut and icons of Indian airforce.

Author's note

This story is the result of extensive interviews with those who directly served alongside Corporal Jyoti Prakash Nirala—including his then Commanding Officer, Wing Commander Rajiv Chauhan; his coursemate, Sergeant Satish Kumar (Veteran); and Junior Warrant Officer Sandeep Kumar (Veteran), who served as the senior most warrant officer of the flight during the mission. Talking to his wife Mrs Sushma Nand remained difficult as I always find while talking to Amar Balidani's families, but it remains essential to give them a voice too, in the stories of their men whose legacy these women carry forward by raising their children all alone.

Operation Safed Sagar: A Milestone in Military Aviation

May-July 1999

In the spring of 1999, the world began to take notice of Pakistan's incursion into the Kargil-Dras area of Jammu and Kashmir, leading to what would become the Kargil War. This conflict marked a significant turning point in the India–Pakistan relationship. On 8 May 1999, Indian pilots in Cheetah helicopters spotted suspicious movements near the Tololing Ridge in the Dras sector, revealing that intruders had crossed into Indian territory. In the following days, Indian patrols were attacked, resulting in casualties.

Since the 1971 war between India and Pakistan, direct military clashes between the two countries had been rare. However, tensions escalated in the 1990s due to separatist activities in Kashmir and the nuclear tests conducted by both nations in 1998. In an attempt to ease tensions, India and Pakistan signed the Lahore Declaration in February 1999, agreeing to seek peaceful solutions. Despite this, during the winter of 1998–1999, Pakistani military forces covertly entered Indian territory under the guise of mujahideen fighters. This operation, known as Operation Badr, aimed to sever the connection between Kashmir and Ladakh, force India to withdraw from the Siachen Glacier and boost the Kashmir insurgency.

The operation was masterminded by the then Chief of Army Staff of Pakistan, General Pervez Musharraf, with key support from his trusted generals, Lieutenant General Muhammad Aziz Khan and Lieutenant General Mahmud Ahmed. Major General Javed Hassan was responsible for executing the operation, while Brigadier Nusrat Sial, who was later killed during the conflict, led the 62 Brigade involved in the Kargil War. Prime Minister Nawaz Sharif later claimed that Musharraf had not shared the plans with him.

It was only twenty-five years after the Kargil conflict that the Pakistani Army officially acknowledged the involvement of its regular army personnel. In a speech on Defence Day—6 September 2024—Pakistan Army Chief General Asim Munir said: 'Be it 1948, 1965, 1971, or the Kargil War of 1999, thousands of soldiers sacrificed their lives for the country and Islam.'

Although Pakistan's infiltration caught India's political and military leadership by surprise, the intense infantry assaults led by Indian Army officers, the exceptional leadership at junior levels, and the devastating impact of concentrated artillery fire, combined with repeated strikes by the Indian Air Force, proved decisive. These factors gradually eroded the combat effectiveness of Pakistan's Northern Light Infantry.

The Kargil War stands out for the extensive deployment of Indian ground forces and the strategic use of air power, demonstrating that air power can be effective even in the harsh conditions of high-altitude mountain warfare.

On 11 May 1999, the Indian Army launched Operation Vijay to reclaim key high-altitude positions occupied by the enemy. By 13 May, the Western Air Command was on high alert. Jaguar aircraft began long-range photography missions to gather intelligence and Mobile Observation Posts (MOPs) were established.

Communication between Leh and the Kargil helipad was set up via high-frequency radios. On 14 May, a Mi-17 helicopter carried out a reconnaissance mission, followed by a video survey conducted by another Army aviation helicopter. On 15 May, an IAF helicopter was hit in the Kaksar area, damaging its rotor. The enemy's positions on the heights were becoming increasingly dangerous.

A crucial meeting occurred at Air Headquarters on 18 May, but approval for airstrikes was still pending. It wasn't until 25 May, when the Cabinet Committee on Security (CCS) gave the Indian Air Force the green light to strike the infiltrators—without crossing the Line of Control (LoC)—that the government officially authorized air operations. Air Chief Marshal A.Y. Tipnis also made a covert visit to Srinagar and Awantipora to assess the situation, and assured the Army's 15 Corps of air support. This marked the launch of Operation Safed Sagar, the air component of the Kargil War.

Earlier, on 21 May, an IAF Canberra aircraft from No. 106 Squadron conducted a photo reconnaissance mission over the Mushkoh Valley and Batalik. Piloted by Squadron Leader A. Perumal and Squadron Leader U.K. Jha, the aircraft was hit by a Stinger missile, but landed safely. 'The air war began with my flight. It was the first mission over Kargil,' Squadron Leader Perumal later remarked.

This confirmed that the intruders were entrenched along the ridgelines, equipped with advanced weaponry capable of downing aircraft.

The following day, 26 May, the IAF launched its first combat mission. Fighter jets, including MiG-21s, MiG-23s and MiG-27s, targeted enemy positions, supply lines and camps in Dras, Kargil and Batalik. MiG-29s provided top cover, while reconnaissance missions continued to gather intelligence on enemy locations. Despite facing intense missile and anti-aircraft artillery fire, the IAF's initial strikes were largely successful, disrupting enemy supply lines and targeting positions overlooking the critical Zojila-Kargil-Leh highway.

However, 27 May, the second day of Operation Safed Sagar, marked several tragedies for the IAF. Flight Lieutenant K. Nachiketa, piloting a MiG-27, experienced an engine failure during a strike mission. He ejected but was captured, becoming the IAF's first and only prisoner of war during the conflict. That same day, Squadron Leader Ajay Ahuja, flying a MiG-21M, was shot down by a shoulder-fired Stinger missile. Although he ejected, he was captured and later killed by enemy forces. His body was returned to India on 28 May. Additionally, a Mi-17 helicopter was shot down, resulting in the loss of four IAF personnel: Flight Lieutenant Subramaniam Muhilan, Squadron Leader Rajiv Pundir, Flight Sergeant P.V.N.R. Prasad and Sergeant Raj Kishore Sahu.

These losses led to a tactical shift. Helicopters were withdrawn from strike missions, and fighter jets adjusted their tactics to avoid the enemy's missile range. Despite this, the IAF continued precision strikes and reconnaissance missions, weakening enemy positions across the region.

Throughout the conflict, the IAF adapted quickly, deploying additional squadrons to Srinagar and Awantipora, including MiG-21bis, MiG-27MLs, MiG-21Ms and MiG-23BNs. MiG-29s ensured air superiority, while Mirage 2000 detachments were stationed in Punjab, with Jaguar squadrons kept on standby. Mi-17 helicopters provided both attack and logistical support, flying dangerous missions at high altitudes.

Air operations continued for seven weeks, from 26 May to 12 July 1999, when they were suspended to allow the withdrawal of Pakistani forces. During this period, the IAF conducted over 1,700 sorties, including reconnaissance, strike and combat air patrol missions. The IAF also flew more than 2,185 helicopter sorties for logistical support and casualty evacuation. By mid-July, the Indian Army, with nearly a corps-strength force, had recaptured most of the high-altitude positions held by the enemy.

Air operations were coordinated by the Western Air Command, under Air Marshal Vinod Patney, with significant contributions from Air Marshal Michael McMahon and Air Commodore A.K. Singh. Air Marshal Vinod Patney, the then AOC-in-C of Western Air Command, famously remarked, 'On 12 June 1999, when the then Pakistani Foreign Minister Sartaj Aziz raised the point that airstrikes must stop, it gave us great confidence. Air power does get results.'

By the time the conflict officially ended on 16 July 1999, the Indian Air Force had demonstrated immense valour and skill, though not without significant sacrifices. The Kargil conflict saw the IAF achieve a milestone in military aviation. This was the first time air power had been employed at such high altitudes in a rugged, mountainous environment, presenting unique challenges that required innovative strategies and tactics.

No chronicle of the Indian Air Force would be complete without recognizing the air battles fought over the frozen heights of Kargil. While there are countless stories of victories, each filled with daring feats by IAF pilots, one tale stands out—the story of Flight Lieutenant Nachiketa. His resilience epitomizes the courage and determination of an average Indian Air Force personnel who refuses to surrender, even in the face of captivity.

6

Flight Lieutenant Kambhampati Nachiketa: The Kargil Prisoner of War Who Challenged Death Thrice

Muntho Dhalo, Batalik
Eastern part of the Kargil sector
Indian side of the Line of Control
27 May 1999

THE SKY OVER the Batalik sector was an endless stretch of blue, broken only by the rugged, snow-capped peaks that had become the front lines of the Kargil conflict. Nestled among these towering heights lay Muntho Dhalo, a critical Pakistani logistics hub. Unbeknownst to those on the ground, the Indian Air Force was about to strike.

High above, four MiG-27 fighter jets in sleek formation cut through the thin mountain air, approaching the target area. They belonged to 9 Squadron, the Wolf Pack, whose pilots lived by the squadron's motto: 'The wolf is for the pack, and the pack is for the wolf.'

First in line was Boxer-1 flown by Flight Lieutenant Anupam Banerjee , throttling towards the target with precision. The pilot's breathing was steady, eyes locked on the vast sprawl of supply depots and ammunition dumps below. At the perfect moment, Boxer 1 released its payload. Seconds later, bombs screamed earthward and struck with devastating force. Fire erupted from the compound, sending thick, black smoke curling into the sky. Chaos unfolded below as the carefully stacked munitions ignited, detonating in quick succession.

Boxer-2 flown by Flight Lieutenant Bhupendra Khatana followed, banking slightly as the pilot aligned for his run. The target zone, already engulfed in fire and smoke, was still active with enemy forces scrambling in panic. As Boxer 2 released its payload the ground beneath the enemy's feet heaved violently. More explosions rocked the logistics hub, sending massive fireballs into the air. The chaos intensified as parts of the facility crumbled. Flames spread rapidly, devouring everything in their path.

The skies over Muntho Dhalo were stained with smoke as thick black plumes—known as bomb plumes—rose swiftly, obscuring the landscape.

Now, as planned, Hyena-1 and Hyena-2 had to fire rockets.

But Boxer formation had clouded the target so much that Hyena-1 flown by Squadron Leader Ashwini Kumar Mandokhot, the next pilot in formation, was forced to abort. Despite his best efforts, he couldn't see through the thick haze and had to pull up without firing.

Then came Hyena 2, piloted by Flight Lieutenant K. Nachiketa. As he approached, the smoke had thinned just enough for him to see part of the target below. Seizing the opportunity, Nachiketa dived low, targeting the remains of the logistics hub. With perfect precision, he unleashed his 80-mm calibre rockets, mounted on launchers affixed to the underwing hardpoints on either side of the fuselage. They struck with deadly accuracy. The explosion triggered another wave of fire and debris, sending up even more smoke and ash. A thin smile spread across Nachiketa's face as he pulled up, satisfied with the destruction he had unleashed.

Then, suddenly, alarms blared in his cockpit. The engine had failed.

'Mando, Nachi, engine flameout! Relighting!' he called over the radio, his voice calm but urgent. His engine had shut down, and he was attempting a restart.

In the plains, gaining altitude might have bought him more time—but over these mountains, he had precious little time. The hills loomed dangerously close, and every second counted. He tried to relight the engine, but the process was slow. As the seconds ticked by, it became clear that the aircraft wouldn't recover in time. The mountains ahead were approaching fast and, with no other option, Nachiketa made the decision to eject.

He made the second call to Hyena-1: 'Mando, Nachi ejecting!'

His hand gripped the ejection handle firmly and with a sharp pull, the system activated. The cockpit canopy exploded outward and, in an instant, the seat blasted free from the aircraft. The G-forces slammed into Nachiketa, pressing him into the seat, and his world blurred into grey as he slipped briefly into semi-consciousness. As the seat climbed, a small drogue chute deployed, stabilizing him in the air. Moments later, the main parachute unfurled, slowing his descent. The rush of air eased, and Nachiketa began to drift downwards. Even in his fogged state, he heard a deafening explosion—the unmistakable sound of his MiG-27 crashing into the hills. Though his vision blurred, the thunderous crash was a stark reminder of how close he had come to his own death. Now, his focus shifted to his descent into the unknown.

Below, the landscape stretched like a vast white canvas—snow-covered peaks stretching as far as the eye could see, surrounded by desolate, rugged mountains. For a moment, everything was eerily calm, the chaos of battle left behind. But Nachiketa had no idea that he was descending into enemy-held territory—into the heart of Muntho Dhalo.

In a matter of minutes, Nachi would be on the ground, and soon, he would become a prisoner of war.

~

Adampur Airbase
25 kilometres from Jalandhar city
400 kilometres from the international border
Punjab
April 1999

Flight Lieutenant K. Nachiketa was posted at Adampur Air Force Station in 1999, serving with 9 Squadron—the Wolf Pack. His journey to this dynamic base followed three years with 10 Squadron, the Daggers, in Jodhpur. While Adampur, near Jalandhar, offered a different setting, Nachiketa was already a seasoned MiG-27 pilot. By August 1998, he had already mastered bombing, rocket launches, gun firing systems and aerial combat. The desert skies of Jodhpur had shaped him, with endless strike sorties and dogfights sharpening his strike skills and low-level flying precision.

Adampur presented new horizons, with training missions taking him to Awantipora and Srinagar, where mock drills became routine—Indian jets were pitted against simulated enemy strike targets in mountainous regions and against aircraft in high-stakes, hostile environments. Each manoeuvre, each tactic strengthened his instincts, transforming him and his squadron into a seamless, lethal unit.

Off duty, Adampur was a mix of brotherhood and banter. The camaraderie was palpable; bachelors often dropped by married officers' homes, bonding over impromptu meals offered lovingly by their wives. Life as a fighter pilot wasn't just about the craft, it was about family—trust, respect and shared experiences, both in the air and on the ground.

Like all combat pilots of the IAF, Nachiketa was focused, intensely driven and carried an air of confidence that came with knowing his craft well. Still unmarried, he had dedicated himself to the cockpit. The adrenaline rush of flying high-speed jets was matched only by the satisfaction of knowing he was part of something greater than himself—part of the Wolf Pack, whose motto, 'The wolf is for the pack and the pack is for the wolf', symbolized their unity in the air and on the ground.

Yet, little did he know that soon, the skies over Kargil would demand a different kind of test—one that would push his courage, resilience and spirit to the very edge. The next chapter of his life was about to unfold in ways that neither he nor his fellow pilots could have imagined.

By April 1999, news of Pakistani infiltration had begun circulating on Indian TV. By mid-May, 9 Squadron had a sense that deployment to forward locations was imminent. Their operational base was in Srinagar, and by 17 and 18 May, a squadron detachment moved from Adampur to Srinagar. Pilots on duty ferried the aircraft into the Kashmir Valley, and those on leave were recalled. It wasn't just 9 Squadron; squadrons from across the theatre were converging at the Srinagar Airbase. The MiG-21bis[1] fighters were soon joined

---

1 The Mikoyan-Gurevich MiG-21 is a supersonic jet fighter and interceptor aircraft, designed by the Mikoyan-Gurevich Design Bureau

by MiG-27MLs, MiG-21Ms and MiG-23BNs. At Awantipora, squadrons arrived with MiG-21Ms and MiG-29s. A helicopter unit equipped with Mi-17s was deployed for close-range bunker-bursting operations. Meanwhile, Mirage 2000 detachments were stationed at their operational base in Punjab, and Jaguars were placed on standby.[2]

Each aircraft type had a distinct operational role: The Mi-17 helicopters were equipped with rocket pods for bunker-busting; the MiG-21/23 /27 and Jaguars would focus on ground attacks, particularly in the challenging mountainous terrain. The MiG-29[3] and 21bis were responsible for air defence, augmented by the Mirage 2000, which was also involved in electronic and jamming missions. Jaguars and MiG-21 Type 77s, along with Canberras and MiG-25s were to conduct reconnaissance and surveillance.

Eventually, the Mirages and Jaguars focused on precision strikes, causing decisive damage to enemy assets and resources. The

---

in the Soviet Union. Approximately 60 countries across four continents have flown the MiG-21, and it still serves many nations seven decades after its maiden flight. The expansion of the IAF MiG-21 fleet marked a developing India–Soviet Union military partnership, which enabled India to field a formidable air force to counter Chinese and Pakistani threats. In view of the several incidents that have occurred after the 1999 Kargil War, the modernized MiG-21 Bison seems to play, at present, the role of an interceptor and possibly a limited role of a fighter aircraft. The Indian Air Force plans to decommission all MiG-21s.

2 Himalayan Eagles : History of Indian Air force Vol 3 by Pushpinder Singh / Operation Safed Sagar : The summer of 1999 // publisher The society of aerospace studies /march 2007

3 Twin-engine fighter aircraft designed in the Soviet Union. India was the first international customer of the MiG-29, outside of the Warsaw Pact. The Indian Air Force (IAF) placed an order for forty-four aircraft (forty single-seat MiG-29 9.12Bs and four twin-seat MiG-29UBs) in 1984, and the MiG-29 was officially inducted into the IAF in 1987.

transport and helicopter fleet was involved in extensive logistics and maintenance support.

Recalling those days, Group Captain K. Nachiketa (veteran) shared:

> The air was filled with josh and enthusiasm. All the young pilots wanted to prove themselves in the war. After all, it had been almost twenty-eight years since the 1971 war, that airforce had the opportunity to prove its mettle in a full-scale conflict. We were also filled with anger because many of our army soldiers' bodies were being sent back home in coffins or with injuries. We wanted to avenge our brothers.

After arriving in Srinagar, the pilots began intensive training. Over the next five to six days, Nachiketa and his fellow pilots participated in area-familiarization missions to ensure they were comfortable with the terrain in case orders came through. They focused on high-altitude warfare, something no air force had attempted before in such extreme conditions.

The region was marked by ridgelines that were offshoots of the mighty K-2 and Nanga Parbat mountains. These towering heights, reaching up to 5,200 metres, presented a unique set of challenges.

The terrain was harsh, with sheer cliffs on the Indian side and gradual gradients on the Pakistani side. Snow covered most of the region year-round, making habitation nearly impossible. Strategically, the area wasn't suitable for launching major offensives, but it was crucial because the hills offered observation points that could direct artillery fire on the only road link from Srinagar to Leh. It was clear that evicting the Pakistani intruders would take time and effort.

In a book, *Airpower At 18,000: The Indian Air Force in the Kargil War* by Benjamin S. Lambeth, Air Marshal Vinod Patney, then AOC-in-C of the Western Air Command, who oversaw the air operations, said:

On 26 May, we were ready for a full-scale war. Fortunately, we had run an exercise just a couple of months before, but we had not planned for this kind of war. We had to carry out battlefield air strikes and interdiction missions, which yield minimal results for maximum effort. Our training was slightly different, and we had little experience with this terrain. We had to absorb the training rapidly, and in some cases, it took us three days to understand the nuances of the campaign. Our priority was to halt the enemy's tracks and begin rolling them back. We also had to assess their capabilities, resources and deployment of assets.

Flying in such high-altitude regions posed many challenges. The thin air resulted in lower air density, affecting engine performance. Fighter jets couldn't climb as quickly, their performance became sluggish and turning became difficult. Maintaining tactical formations became a real struggle. Even the slightest changes in altitude or temperature significantly affected aircraft handling. Flying at high altitudes required the highest level of skill and focus, but these pilots weren't deterred. They trained day and night, preparing themselves for what was to come.

Nachiketa remembered:

We trained hard. We flew round the clock, then came back to review route maps and tactical documents. We attended briefings, discussed plans and focused on high-altitude flying. We practiced in the range, firing weapons, and familiarized ourselves with the environment. We had to be comfortable flying at high altitudes and understand how to manoeuvre in those conditions. Valley flying was critical. A pilot had to be clear about the routes because flying into the wrong valley could be disastrous. We also had to be extra cautious when firing at high altitudes because handling the aircraft there required precision.

On 25 May, during a high-profile Cabinet Committee on Security meeting, Air Chief Marshal A.Y. Tipnis addressed Prime Minister Atal Bihari Vajpayee with urgency. 'The Army needs Air Force support, and the Air Force can commence operations within twelve hours—six, if absolutely necessary,' he said.

All eyes turned to the prime minister, who responded calmly and decisively, '*Theek hai, kal subah se shuru karo* (All right, start tomorrow morning).'

The Chief of the Air Staff hesitated for a moment before asking, 'Sir, may we have permission to cross the LoC while attacking targets?'

Prime Minister Vajpayee straightened in his chair, his voice firm and clear, 'Please do not cross the LoC. No, no crossing the LoC.'

'Sir!' Air Chief Marshal Tipnis responded, accepting the directive.[4]

With that, Operation Safed Sagar was officially launched. The first air strikes were scheduled for 26 May 1999.

On the evening of 25 May, the directive was clear: The operation would commence at 0600 hours the next morning. The objective was to support the Indian Army in evicting intruders. Group Captain Avtar Singh, Commanding Officer of the 9 Squadron, briefed his pilots: 'Air HQ has given orders to start the operation from 26 May.'

The news spread quickly among the fighter pilots. Nachiketa and his colleagues, who were in the mess, quickly shifted focus from scheduled training exercises to preparing for the imminent airstrikes. For the first time since 1971, Indian air power would be deployed in a major conflict. Excitement ran high.

---

4 IANS, 'Ex-air chief A.Y. Tipnis comments on Vajpayee's orders during Kargil', Mid-Day, 29 June 2019, https://www.mid-day.com/news/india-news/article/Vajpayee-was-firmon-not-crossing-LoC-during-Kargil--Ex-air-chief-Tipnis-21252163.

The air was thick with anticipation as briefings commenced. Army officers arrived to share intelligence updates.

Nachiketa recalled:

> We had a series of briefings—Air Force, Army, you name it. They explained the locations of friendly and enemy troops, the weapons we would carry and the routes we would take. It was a detailed process, and everything had to be meticulously planned.

As a young pilot in 9 Squadron, Flight Lieutenant K. Nachiketa was deeply engaged in the preparations. The atmosphere was charged with a sense of urgency and aggression. The past week had been filled with unsettling sights—injured and fallen Indian Army soldiers, coffins draped in the tricolour. The realization hit hard: It was time to act.

Nachiketa remembered:

> The josh was high. This is what we train for. The aggression and excitement were palpable. We were ready to fire weapons and make a difference.

During this intense period, Nachiketa—like many soldiers—made a call home. Though long queues at the local STD booth made communication difficult, he wanted to reassure his family. In those days, with no mobile phones, a single phone call was a precious comfort to loved ones.

Nachiketa came from a humble middle-class family with strong values. He was the middle child of three siblings, with an elder sister, Vally Maya, and a younger sister, Trisandhya. The bond among them was close, and both sisters doted on their brother. Their father, Mr K.R.K. Sastri, worked in the Ministry of Water Resources and, despite having a transferable job, remained deeply committed to his family.

His elder sister, Vally Maya, shared:

Our father was a learned man, despite our limited resources. He ensured we had a strong value system. I remember how he'd take us to Indian embassy events and encourage our curiosity. Nanna also never compromised on our education.

She also spoke about Nachiketa's early passion:

Nachi was intelligent and had a keen interest in vehicles and aircraft. He was always fascinated by flying. When he cracked the NDA exam and chose the Air Force, it surprised the family. Back then, people weren't very familiar with the armed forces, and it wasn't seen as a lucrative career. Our mother, K.S.M. Lakshmi, was especially distressed as Nachi was her only son. But he was determined. Nanna supported him wholeheartedly, even though Amma was upset.

Nachiketa joined the prestigious National Defence Academy (NDA) in 1990. Filled with excitement and a little anxiety, he joined the Golf Squadron of the 84th course at the Khadakwasla campus in Pune. The next three years were physically and mentally demanding, but, by June 1993, he had made it through. He was ready for the next step: Training at the Indian Air Force Academy in Dundigal.

At the academy, the pressure intensified. Many in the batch did not make it through—many were grounded, unable to realize their dream of flying. Nachiketa wasn't about to let that happen to him. His focus was sharp—he studied hard, trained harder and passed every exam.

Instructors often gave casual advice like, 'Just fly it like you'd ride a bike.' But this was a problem for Nachiketa.

'Sir, I don't know how to ride a bike,' he admitted one day.

The instructor was stunned. 'You don't know how to ride a bike, and you want to fly a jet?' he exclaimed.

But Nachiketa proved his mettle. He passed his solo flight test. A dream come true for any aspiring pilot.

As part of the training, cadets flew solo in the HAL HJT-16 Kiran,[5] an Indian jet trainer known as the 'Ray of Light'. It was a momentous experience, one that pushed each cadet to their limits. Out of the ten cadets in Nachiketa's group, only six managed to pass. The other four were grounded, meaning their dreams of flying were over. Fortunately, they had the option to continue in other branches of the IAF, such as logistics or navigation.

After successfully completing his training at the Air Force Academy, Nachiketa was sent to Bidar Air Force Station,[6] one of the premier training centres of the IAF. The next six months were intense. Here, they didn't just learn to fly—they learnt how to fire weapons, perform tactical manoeuvres and navigate in complex scenarios using an aircraft. Even at this stage, there was the risk of being grounded. Not everyone made it through.

But on 18 June 1994, Nachiketa had done it—he was officially commissioned into the flying branch of the Indian Air Force. His dream of becoming a fighter pilot was within reach. The Air Force has three streams for pilots: Fighters, helicopters and transport aircraft. Through a combination of passion and merit, Nachiketa was selected for the fighter stream.

He shared:

---

5   The HAL HJT-16 Kiran ('Ray of light') is an Indian two-seat intermediate jet-powered trainer aircraft designed and manufactured by aircraft company Hindustan Aeronautics Limited.
6   Bidar Air Force Station, Wikipedia.org, https://en.wikipedia.org/wiki/Bidar_Air_Force_Station.

I always wanted to become a fighter pilot. I loved the idea of flying fast, engaging in aerial combat, firing weapons and serving the nation in the heat of battle. It was everything I had dreamt of—action, adrenaline and purpose.

In 1994, the Air Force primarily flew MiG-21s, MiG-23s, MiG-27s, Jaguars and Mirage fighters. After being selected, Nachiketa and the other pilots were sent to one of two fighter training units. One was in Kalaikunda, West Bengal, where they trained on old British Hunter jets, and the other was in Bagdogra or Tezpur, where pilots trained on MiG-21s. Nachiketa was sent to Kalaikunda, where he joined the Hunter Operational Fighter Training Unit (HOFTU) of 20 Squadron.[7]

Though the Hunters were relics of the past, they remained reliable for training new pilots. Over the next year, Nachiketa and his batchmates honed their skills—learning to fire rockets, guns and bombs, practising combat manoeuvres and mastering tactical flying. The training was rigorous, but it paid off. By April 1995, he completed his Hunter training and was ready for his first operational posting.

Jodhpur was that posting, home to the mighty MiG-27.[8] The Russian-made MiG-27 had wings that could swing to change their angle depending on the mission. It was a powerful machine, capable of both air-to-air combat and bombing runs. Many of Nachiketa's

---

7 'Operational Training Unit', Bharat Rakshak, https://www.bharat-rakshak.com/indianairforce/database/units/OTU.
8 PTI, 'IAF's Mig-27 jets decommissioned after three decades of service; last of Soviet-made aircraft takes final flight from Jodhpur Air Base', Firstpost, 27 December 2019, https://www.firstpost.com/india/iafs-mig-27-jets-decommissioned-after-three-decades-of-service-last-of-soviet-made-aircraft-takes-final-flight-from-jodhpur-air-base-7831111.html.

friends were sent to other MiG squadrons or Jaguars, but he was thrilled to be a part of what was jokingly called the 'swingers club'.

He was ready to touch the skies with glory, to defend his country, and to live the dream that had driven him from the very beginning.

What he didn't know then was that he was destined to write a unique chapter in the history of the IAF—as one of the few Indian prisoners of war (PoWs) to return alive to his homeland.

His sister, Vally Maya, recalled how the news of his capture left them shattered. As she scrambled for information, they realized Nachiketa was unlikely to return. Most Indian PoWs captured in the 1965 and 1971 wars had not returned.

During my interview, Group Captain K. Nachiketa (veteran) revealed how he had defied death thrice. He should not have been alive, but there he was, narrating his story.

At 0630 hours on 26 May 1999, the Indian Air Force launched its first wave of airstrikes over Kargil.

The early morning light had barely touched the rugged, snow-covered peaks when the roar of MiG-21s, MiG-23s and MiG-27s pierced the valley. Their mission: To target and destroy enemy positions, camps, supply lines and ammunition dumps entrenched in the unforgiving terrain.

MiG-29s flew overhead, providing air cover, while the MiG-21Ms of No. 108 Squadron[9] descended to unleash a barrage of 57-mm rockets and cannon fire upon Pakistani troops, mujahideen and mercenaries scattered along strategic points overlooking the vital Zojila-Kargil-Leh highway.

---

9 https://www.bharat-rakshak.com/indianairforce/database/units/list.php?qunit=108+Sqn// No.108 Squadron Hawkeyes

At 1430 hours, the second strike was launched. Reconnaissance missions by both high-flying Canberras and low-flying MiG-21Ms confirmed that significant damage had been inflicted. Fighter pilots faced intense anti-aircraft fire but skilfully evaded it, returning safely to base.[10]

On 26 May, the josh was high after the first wave of successful airstrikes as Nachiketa and the other pilots gathered at the Srinagar base to plan the next bombing mission. The briefing was thorough, with intelligence flowing in from the Army, government and reconnaissance sources. Strict instructions were reiterated: They were not to cross the LoC. The pilots meticulously planned navigation, tactics and coordination with air defence elements. Each pilot knew their role, from executing strikes to supporting the battle damage assessment (BDA) and surveillance teams. In the air, they were brothers, united in their mission.

On 27 May, Flight Lieutenant K. Nachiketa and three other pilots were assigned an early-morning airstrike. The operation was meticulously planned and comprised a strike formation of four strike aircraft, two air defence aircraft and two BDA aircraft.

Nachiketa, call sign Hyena 2, was part of the bombing formation. The team included Flight Lieutenant Anupam Banerjee as Boxer-1, Flight Lieutenant B.S. Khatana as Boxer-2, and Squadron Leader Ashwini Mandokhot as Hyena-1, all tasked with striking the target area at Muntho Dhalo.

Boxer-1 and Boxer-2 would drop bombs on the target, followed by Hyena-1 and Hyena-2, who would launch rockets to maximize damage. It was a well-coordinated attack plan designed for maximum impact. Battle Damage Assessment pilots Squadron Leader Ajay Ahuja and Flight Lieutenant P.G. Reddy, flying MiG-21s, would assess the damage post-strike using high-resolution on-board cameras.

---

10 Puspindar Singh, *Himalayan Eagles*, 'Operation Safed Sagar'.

The bomber formation consisted of MiG-27 aircraft, heavily armed to carry out the air-to-ground attack. As they were equipped primarily for bombing and not aerial combat, two MiG-29s were to provide aerial defence, ready to intercept any enemy aircraft.

The target, Muntho Dhalo, northeast of Batalik, was a vital logistical hub for the enemy, serving as a staging area and supply camp. Destroying it would disrupt the enemy's supply chain, cutting off fuel, ammunition and rations, crippling their operations.

That night, with adrenaline high, twenty-six-year-old Flight Lieutenant K. Nachiketa felt the familiar flutter of nerves as he readied himself for the mission.

~

Muntho Dhalo
Northeast of Batalik
27 May 1999

The next morning, the pre-strike briefing buzzed with anticipation. The mission was set to target Muntho Dhalo. In Balti, 'Muntho' means a small, lotus-like red flower, and 'Dhalo' refers to plateau. At an altitude of 14,500 feet, this bowl-shaped plateau lay nestled between the imposing Ladakh Range to the north, the Kukarthang and Jubar ridgelines to the west, and the Khalubar Ridge to the east. It served as the main logistics and staging base for Pakistan's Northern Light Infantry (NLI) company columns, including the 3rd, 4th and 5th NLI battalions engaged in the Kargil conflict.

After the briefing, Flight Lieutenant Nachiketa approached Squadron Leader Ajay Ahuja of No. 17 Squadron, the Golden Arrows, suggesting they grab breakfast before the mission.

Ahuja smiled and replied, 'Let's finish the mission in forty minutes and then enjoy a hearty meal.'

Nachiketa had never flown with Ahuja before. Squadron Leader Ahuja had arrived from Bhisiana Airbase near Bathinda, Punjab, to support operations in Kargil. A seasoned pilot from Kota, Rajasthan, he had graduated from the National Defence Academy and was commissioned into the IAF as a fighter pilot on 14 June 1985. Over his fourteen-year career, he had piloted MiG-23 and MiG-21 fighter-bombers, and accumulated over 1,000 hours as an instructor. Known for his patience and upbeat demeanour, Ahuja was a respected A2 instructor[11] and the Flight Commander of the IAF's specialist photo-reconnaissance squadron.[12]

Despite being stationed together for a week, Nachiketa had interacted only briefly with Ahuja, who was busy with operational planning, briefings, SOPs, target folders and weather analyses, leaving little time for casual interactions.

On Day 2 of Operation Safed Sagar, Nachiketa's formation was scheduled for an airstrike, with Squadron Leader Ajay Ahuja assigned to conduct the battle damage assessment. It would be their first flight together, none of them knew that they would never meet again.

Reflecting later, with deep sorrow in his voice Group Captain Nachiketa, (then a Flight Lieutenant) shared:

> Fate had different plans. I crossed over without a passport and visa, and was captured as a prisoner of war, while Ahuja sir never returned—he was killed in action. The chance to meet at the breakfast table never came.

---

11 The world of QFI's (Qualified Flying Instructor) has been categorized into ratings. The pinnacle QFI rating is of A1 (instructor of exceptional ability, skill and experience) next comes A2 (very capable, skilful instructor with considerable experience).

12 '1999 Kargil War', Bharat Rakshak, 30 November 1999, https://www.bharat-rakshak.com/iaf/personnel/martyrs/1999-kargil-war/.

After the briefing, everyone hurried to prepare for the mission. Nachiketa, dressed in a green G-suit over his blue overalls, meticulously adjusted his gear in the squadron's dressing room. His green jacket shielded him from the chill, and his standard-issue pistol was checked and securely holstered. The pouches on his G-suit held essential manuals, navigation maps and communication frequencies.

The mission briefing was thorough. Each pilot knew their role, the direction of attack, altitude and initial point. Communication was to be restricted to avoid enemy interception. The sequence was precise: Boxer-1 flown by Flight Lieutenant Anupam Banerjee and Boxer-2 by Flight Lieutenant Bhupendra Khatana would first deploy bombs, followed by Hyena-1 by Squadron Leader Ashwini Madokhot and Hyena-2 by Flight Lieutenant K. Nachiketa dropping rockets—the rockets were for targeted strikes, while the bombs would inflict widespread damage.

The aircraft were parked in blast pens for protection. Nachiketa climbed the ladder into his MiG-27, focused and eager. He fastened his seat harness and connected the pneumatic hose of his G-suit to the cockpit port. A technician removed the ladder, and Nachiketa closed the cockpit canopy. After a quick system check, he lowered his helmet visor and signalled that he was ready.

The engines roared to life as the pilots taxied out from the blast pen to the runway. The formation took off as a tight unit, with Nachiketa the last to leave, marking the start of Day 2 of Operation Safed Sagar.

The sky was clear as they flew in formation, weaving through hills to avoid enemy radar. Cruising at 26,000 feet and at around 1,000 kilometres per hour, the fighters approached the initial point, the landscape shifting from mountains to the target area.

Boxer-1 initiated his dive and released his bombs, followed by Boxer-2. The explosions created a dense plume of smoke, obscuring Hyena-1's view. Unable to see the target clearly, Hyena-1 refrained from dropping his rockets.

As Nachiketa—Hyena-2—approached, the smoke began to clear. He completed his dive and released his rockets with precision. It was followed by gun attack but as he pulled out, disaster struck—the engine sputtered and then fell silent. Temperature and RPM[13] dropped rapidly, and airspeed decreased. Nachiketa knew he had to act swiftly. He jettisoned the drop tank to reduce drag, hoping to buy a few precious moments.

He quickly radioed Hyena-1:

'Mando, Nachi engine flame out! Relighting!' He began the restart procedure.

The engine sputtered back to partial life, but with the hills approaching rapidly and only thirty to forty seconds to spare, Nachiketa knew he had no choice but to eject.

He informed his wingman, 'Mando, Nachi ejecting,' and pulled the ejection handle.

The ejection system activated swiftly: The cockpit canopy blew off and the seat was propelled out of the cockpit by a high-speed cartridge. A small drogue parachute deployed first to stabilize the seat, followed by the main parachute. Everything happened in a matter of seconds.

---

13 Rotations per minute : RPM is a measurement used to determine the rotational speed of an object, particularly in relation to aircraft engines. RPM is a critical measurement in aviation as it directly impacts the performance and safety of an aircraft.

The ejection subjected him to extreme G-forces,[14] causing him to experience a grey-out, where vision blurs and consciousness fades. Though the G-suit helped, it was less effective outside the craft. The descent was swift, landing him on a snow-covered, icy landscape.

As he touched down, he saw his aircraft's wreckage nearby.

Despite the intense pain in his spine from the impact of landing, his survival instincts kicked in. He buried classified documents in the snow to prevent enemy access and dashed across the terrain, seeking cover among nearby boulders.

Suddenly, five figures emerged from the direction of a nearby river. Armed with AK-47s, they advanced, firing at Nachiketa. He fired back with his pistol, but it felt futile.

Group Captain Nachiketa (veteran) chuckled as he reflected:

You know, up in the air, fighter pilots feel invincible. Flying a 20,000 kg aircraft at lightning speed, you can cross from one corner of the earth to another in seconds. We're the warriors of the sky, untouchable and powerful. But then, imagine the sudden shift when you come out of that comfort zone and feel utterly vulnerable. Up there, I was the king of the skies, but on the ground, I was just a mortal. Everything seemed immense and overwhelming. The severe back pain from the rough landing was a sharp reminder of my vulnerability. The sound of gunfire jolted me into action. I scrambled to find cover, drawing my small pistol

---

14 Acceleration in aviation is measured in units of force called Gs, where 1 G equals the force of the Earth's gravity. During steep turns or manoeuvres, a pilot may experience forces of acceleration several times that of gravity. This is especially true in military fighter jets and high-performance aerobatic aircraft, where acceleration forces can reach up to 9 Gs.

and loading it as I took refuge behind a nearby boulder, firing back in desperation.

As his first magazine emptied, he reached for a second, but before he could reload, the enemy closed in and began to beat him mercilessly. As Nachiketa lay on the snow-covered ground, the tension peaked when one of the soldiers pressed the cold barrel of an AK-47 into his mouth, the finger poised on the trigger.

Just as it seemed his fate was sealed, A Pakistani Officer arrived and intervened.

The soldiers were angry. One shouted, 'We're not letting him go. He was dropping bombs from above and firing at us from below.'

With authoritative calm, the officer replied, 'It's all right. He was doing his duty. Now he is our captive.'

Nachiketa recalled:

> That day, death came close to me twice. First, when my aircraft crashed and I had to eject. Second, when the soldiers were about to shoot me, and that officer arrived just in time. Had he been even a moment late or given the order to kill, I would have been dead. I have immense respect for that officer, Captain Qamar of the 5th Northern Light Infantry.

Severely injured and blindfolded, Nachiketa was herded downhill by the Pakistani men—the officer and five soldiers. As they descended, one soldier asked if there were any other pilots with him, possibly mistaking the drogue parachute as belonging to a second person. Nachiketa seized the opportunity to mislead them, replying, 'Yes, there was another pilot.'

Unfamiliar with aircraft systems and focused on finding the supposed second pilot, the soldiers did not question him further.

As Nachiketa and his captors descended the rugged terrain, the relentless pain in his back made each step agonizing. After about forty-five minutes, they reached a makeshift campsite nestled in the icy landscape. When the soldiers removed Nachiketa's blindfold, he was greeted with the sight of forty to fifty armed Pakistani soldiers. He realized escape was impossible, abandoning any hope of evasion.

The camp was modest, with a few tents and scattered military supplies. Nachiketa was guided to a spot to rest. He winced as the snow that had seeped into his shoes caused redness and discomfort, raising concerns about frostbite. A soldier quickly removed his boots and offered some soup to soothe his pain. Another administered a morphine injection, providing much-needed relief.[15]

Soon, a soldier approached with a walkie-talkie and handed it to Nachiketa. A senior Pakistani official greeted him on the other end.

'Welcome to Pakistan,' the officer said.

Nachiketa responded, 'Negative, sir. You are in Indian territory. We're sitting in India. You've crossed over.'

The senior officer laughed. 'Is that so? Well, that's quite a claim.'

'Yes, sir. I'm certain. We're well within our borders.'

'All right then,' the officer chuckled. 'We'll see about that.'

Nachiketa smiled as he recalled the exchange:

'He laughed at the time, but when our army later took control of the area, I wish I could've met him again to discuss who was right.'

---

15 The particular narration filled me with deep anguish when I compared the contrast with which Sqn Ldr Ajay Ahuja was treated and shot down.

While waiting for the aircraft that would transfer him to another location, Captain Qamar—who had intervened to save Nachiketa from the angry soldiers—approached him. Amidst the backdrop of hills and the distant sounds of gunfire, the atmosphere was surprisingly calm. They engaged in a heartfelt conversation, each finding solace in the camaraderie of shared experiences. Qamar, recently married and stationed under harsh conditions, spoke of the isolation and the lack of communication with his family.

It was a brief reprieve where the harsh realities of war were set aside, allowing two soldiers to connect as fellow warriors.

When I asked Squadron Leader Nachiketa if he ever got a chance to thank the officer, he replied with regret that he never did—Captain Qamar was killed in action.

~

Islamabad
Pakistan
28 May 1999

Time stretched endlessly, though it had only been an hour or two since Nachiketa was led to the Pakistani camp. Then the steady thrum of helicopter blades broke the silence. The Pakistani Army helicopter had arrived. They blindfolded him again, and he felt the tug of their hands as they guided him into the helicopter. The hum of the engine vibrated through his bones as they lifted into the sky. After what seemed like an eternity, they landed in Skardu—a city in Pakistan-administered Gilgit-Baltistan, deep within the Pakistan-Occupied Kashmir region.

That night, in a safe house, he was confined to a room. His stomach growled with hunger. He told them he was vegetarian, but the concept seemed alien. One officer, puzzled, asked, 'Vegetarian?

Kya hota hai?' Nachiketa explained he didn't eat meat. After a brief pause, they returned with a plate of vegetables, dal and roti. He ate, grateful, but he knew it was far from over.

Two Pakistani soldiers were then posted inside his room with strict orders: Don't let him sleep. It was part of their strategy, a deliberate attempt to exhaust him, to erode his willpower, to make him vulnerable during interrogation. All night, his mind raced, spiralling into a maze of uncertainty. Where would they take him? What would they do to him? Could he escape? He ran through plans in his head, but none seemed viable.

Reality hit hard—he was now a prisoner of war.

Thoughts of the 1971 war flooded his mind. Many PoWs had never returned. Would he be one of them?

The gravity of the situation sank deep into his bones. Escape seemed impossible. Survival felt like a distant dream. They would not let him sleep—each time he dozed off, they nudged him awake. As the morning light illuminated the breathtaking landscapes of Skardu, a C-130J Hercules descended on the makeshift runway at a nearby Pakistani Army base. Pakistan had acquired these aircraft in 1963 through US military aid. Over the years, arms deals with the US and other European countries had further enhanced Pakistan's air power with advanced aircraft.

Even blindfolded, Nachiketa's pilot instincts remained sharp. He calculated that they must have flown over Lahore. If he could manage to flee from there, perhaps he could reach Amritsar and cross back into India at Attari. The idea offered him a glimmer of hope.

But his estimate was off. The aircraft touched down in Islamabad, not Lahore. His heart sank. Islamabad, surrounded by hills, was much more formidable. Where could he go? How would he navigate the terrain? A wave of tension washed over him, but he maintained his composure, repeating the same fabricated story he'd used earlier at Muntho Dhalo—that he had been on a surveillance mission. This time, though, the interrogation was different. The Pakistani Air Force personnel questioning him were dressed in civilian clothes, making it hard to gauge their ranks. But they were sharp, and they weren't falling for his story.

One of them pointed out the flaw:

'Surveillance missions are flown with trainers, which has two seats. The aircraft we recovered had only one.'

Nachiketa's stomach dropped.

They continued, '*Aapke to dono* trainer *kharab hai* Adampur *mein* (Both your trainers are grounded at Adampur).'

That's when it hit him. They knew far more than he had anticipated.

After a few hours, he was moved by road to a safe house in Rawalpindi, a journey of about an hour. There, the psychological tactics intensified.

'It's better if you cooperate with us,' they insisted. 'Your country has abandoned you. You won't be going back.'

They pushed harder, showing him Pakistani newspaper clippings that falsely reported an Indian pilot's death. The headlines fed into his growing fear.

For Nachiketa, the outside world was now a complete unknown. He had no idea what was happening beyond those walls. His captors continued to press, but he gave them nothing beyond the basics he had been trained to reveal—such as his identification number. Still, doubt lingered. What if they were telling the truth? What if he never returned home, just like the prisoners of war from the 1971 war who never made it back?

What Nachiketa didn't know was that, in the hours following his capture, confusion had spread. The Pakistani media had mistakenly reported that he had been shot dead. The error stemmed from the tragic death of Squadron Leader Ajay Ahuja, who had flown a battle damage assessment mission shortly after Nachiketa's flight.

Ahuja's aircraft was hit by a Stinger missile, and though he had managed to eject, his captors shot him dead. Some media outlets confused Ahuja's fate with Nachiketa's and reported that Nachiketa had been killed. But by the second day, the truth had emerged—Nachiketa was alive, and it was Squadron Leader Ajay Ahuja who had made the supreme sacrifice. BBC reporters stationed in Skardu had even seen Nachiketa during his transfer, and their observations made their way into international news.

Yet, inside the safe house, Nachiketa remained in the dark, haunted by the grim reality of being a prisoner of war.

His captors kept pressing him for information—about Indian troop deployment, aircraft avionics and ammunition types. But he didn't cooperate. He dodged their questions, refusing to give them what they wanted. Until then, they hadn't physically harmed him. Instead, they used a hot and cold treatment, threatened him, and even sent a Maulvi Saheb to brainwash him, trying to break his belief in India and Hinduism.

Nachiketa recalled:

> We all operate on certain beliefs, and they try to break those beliefs. They have experts for it. They know the shortcomings and the negative aspects of any religion or country. When you're sitting comfortably in an air-conditioned room, with tomorrow's day planned, you think differently. But when you haven't slept, when you know death is near and that if you don't cooperate, third-degree torture awaits ... the mind works on a different level.

You become prone to believing a lot of things. They create a world around you, and you're standing on the border between reality and myth, unsure of what to believe. They talk about religion, about leaders, about service … corruption … everything in a way that makes it seem real, makes everything look bad. Ultimately, we are what we believe. Their goal is to erase your will to fight. It's systematic. This happened even in the 1971 war, to weaken the mind and spirit during interrogation.

By 29 May, they had grown frustrated. Declaring him uncooperative, they forced him to sign some documents and handed him over to the ISI. That's when the real torture began.

Those three days in the ISI cell …

Nachiketa doesn't talk much about it. The torture wasn't just physical. It was mental and emotional, a relentless assault on his mind and body. They beat him. They tortured him in ways that were gruelling. They showed him newspaper clippings again—the same false stories about the Indian pilot who had ejected but was shot dead. They changed the narrative as it suited them. It was in their hands, and they used it to break his morale.

'No one cares about you now,' they told him again and again.

'Even if we release you, your nation won't respect you. They'll treat you as a traitor. Your service won't honour you, won't promote you.'

Their words started to take a toll.

He shared:

It makes you question, *Who am I doing this for? Does anyone care?* If you're gullible, you can fall for it. They manipulate you systematically.

But Nachiketa was fortunate. His parents were religious, and he came from a grounded background.

I was only twenty-six years old. But the values my family had instilled in me, the strength of my character, the resilience that the Air Force training had given me … all of that helped. It was what kept me going.

The torture didn't stop. He was blindfolded, moved from one cell to another, tormented in shifts. He was in a terrible situation.

I had to perform our morning rituals in the same room. They gave me dirty, blood-stained clothes to wear. They gave me minimal food. But eating wasn't the priority. Sleep was. After a point, all I wanted was to sleep.

But the body is miraculous—it starts comparing the different pains: The pain of no sleep, the pain of not eating, the physical pain, the pain of being hit on your legs, the pain of not sitting, the pain of the bright lights burning into your eyes and causing headaches. Your body begins to focus on whichever pain is less. That's how you survive.

My head was hot, I had a fever, the high-intensity lights in the cell caused constant headaches … They made me stand, never allowed me to sit. That's when you start to think you won't return.

At one point, they brought up his father.

They knew about my father's bypass surgery three months earlier. One day, they told me he'd had a heart attack. 'Cooperate,' they said, 'or you'll never see him again.' That was the only time I felt weak, that I felt sad. Since they knew about the bypass surgery, I believed them about the heart attack. I didn't know it had been in the news.

Nachiketa paused, his voice growing softer.

> I closed my eyes and said sorry. 'Sorry, Father. I won't be able to see you again.' That was a weak moment.

What Nachiketa didn't know was that far beyond the walls of that cell, an entire nation was rallying behind him. Across India, people were praying for his safe return. The media relentlessly covered his capture, while abroad, over 10,000 NRIs had signed a petition urging President Clinton to pressure Pakistan for his release.

Back home, Prime Minister Atal Bihari Vajpayee took a firm stance. He demanded Nachiketa's unconditional and immediate release.[16] His ultimatum carried weight, and with mounting international pressure, Pakistan found itself increasingly isolated. Even the United States—one of Pakistan's closest allies—condemned their actions during the Kargil War. The pressure on Prime Minister Nawaz Sharif intensified. Desperate to salvage what little credibility he had left, Sharif ordered Nachiketa's release.

Nachiketa later reflected:

> The entire Kargil conflict was orchestrated by General Pervez Musharraf and his three generals. By the time the war began, Nawaz Sharif was left in a state of shock.

Years later, in an interview with *India Today* in Jeddah, Sharif revealed that Musharraf had concealed the details of the Kargil operation from him.[17]

---

16 Syed Firdaus Ashraf, 'Diplomatic efforts on to free Nachiketa: PM', Rediff.com, 2 June 1999, https://m.rediff.com/news/1999/jun/02pm.htm.

17 Raj Chengappa, 'From the India Today archives (2004) | Musharraf hid all Kargil details from me: Nawaz Sharif', *India Today*, 12 December 2023, first printed 26 July 2004, https://www.indiatoday.in/india-today-

As the conflict dragged on and Pakistan began to lose ground on the peaks, the international community turned against the country. With dwindling support and mounting global condemnation, Sharif was forced to address the situation. Everything seemed to align in Nachiketa's favour—his family's blessings, the fervent prayers of millions and growing international pressure.

Nawaz Sharif decided to release him, framing the decision as a 'goodwill' gesture aimed at de-escalating tensions between Pakistan and India. 'Nuclear powers should never be in a state of confrontation,' he stated. 'We aim to prevent any further escalation and to defuse the situation.'[18]

On 2 June, after days of brutal interrogation, Nachiketa was taken back to the safe house in Rawalpindi. There, everything changed.

Nachiketa recalled:

They gave me clothes, they talked to me politely, and they even offered me food.

The same ISI operatives who had tortured him were now responsible for his safety. Many extremist factions in Pakistan opposed his release, and the ISI was tasked with ensuring nothing happened to him before the handover.

~

insight/story/from-the-india-today-archives-2004-musharraf-hid-all-kargil-details-from-me-nawaz-sharif-2475158-2023-12-12.
18 BBC News, 'World: South Asia: Pakistan returns Indian pilot', BBC, 3 June 1999, http://news.bbc.co.uk/1/hi/world/south_asia/360328.stm.

Indian High Commission
Islamabad
Pakistan
2 June 1999

The late afternoon sun cast a golden hue over the High Commission as the two white Land Cruiser vehicles from the International Committee of the Red Cross (ICRC) rolled through its gates. The imposing High Commission building was abuzz with anticipation. From one of the vehicles emerged Flight Lieutenant K. Nachiketa, his appearance a stark contrast to the polished façade of the compound. Though composed, a sense of profound relief radiated from him as he was met by Indian High Commissioner G. Parthasarathy[19] and members of the ICRC, including Paul Bonnard, head of the ICRC delegation in Pakistan.

Mr Parthasarathy extended a warm welcome, his face beaming with relief. 'How are you, Lieutenant?' he asked.

'I am fine, sir,' Nachiketa replied, his voice steady though his eyes reflected the turmoil of the past days.

As High Commission officials presented him with roses, the moment was heavy with emotion. The Indian pilot, who had endured weeks of harrowing captivity, was now stepping onto familiar ground, yet the enormity of his ordeal was only beginning to sink in. The embassy was filled with well-wishers, their faces a blend of joy, relief and profound respect.

---

19 G. Parthsarathy, 'Captured in conflict: The case of Flight Lieutenant Kambampati Nachiketa', *Economic Times*, last updated 28 February 2019, https://economictimes.indiatimes.com/news/defence/captured-in-conflict-the-case-of-flight-lt-kambampati-nachiketa/articleshow/68194163.cms?from=mdr.

Nachiketa's eyes roved over the gathering. Hundreds stood in the large, ornate hall, their faces a mosaic of smiles and tears. Flowers were pressed into his hands; some embraced him tightly, their eyes glistening with emotion. A few touched his feet, a gesture of deep respect and gratitude. The scene was heart-wrenching, a stark contrast to the cold, oppressive isolation he had endured.

Nachiketa later shared:

> I was not aware that I had been covered by the media. In captivity, I was isolated from the world, so this moment of warmth and recognition was both overwhelming and touching.

As the initial rush of emotions subsided, formalities awaited. Documents needed to be signed, and medical examinations conducted. Nachiketa was gradually introduced to the unfolding reality of his release and the circumstances back home. It was during this period that he learnt about the tragic loss of Squadron Leader Ajay Ahuja, and the helicopter crash that had claimed lives of Squadron Leader Rajiv Pundir, Flight Lieutenant Subramaniam Muhilan, Flight Sergeant P.V.N.R. Prasad, and Sergeant Raj Kishore Sahu.

The news hit him hard, adding a layer of grief to his relief.

He had one urgent request: To speak with his parents. Ambassador Parthasarathy facilitated it with compassion. As Nachiketa heard the familiar voices of his family, a renewed strength flowed through him. His parents, who had shown grace and unwavering hope throughout the ordeal, were a source of immense comfort.

In a quiet moment, Nachiketa told his father, 'I am fine. Everything is all right. I'll meet you soon. Please tell my sisters as well.' The reassurance of listening to his father's voice belied the suffering he had faced.

Later, a call from Prime Minister Atal Bihari Vajpayee offered further comfort. The prime minister welcomed him back and expressed gratitude for his unwavering service. The call from Air Chief Marshal A.Y. Tipnis was another balm for his spirit. Tipnis inquired about his well-being and assured Nachiketa that he would undergo a thorough medical evaluation upon his return.

'Hope you are doing fine. Everything is in control. You are fit,' Tipnis said.

'Yes, sir, everything is fine. I am fit to fly,' Nachiketa responded, his resolve as strong as ever.

That night, he stayed at the residence of the Defence Attaché, Air Commodore Jaiswal, where Nachiketa found a temporary haven of peace. At the Defence Attaché's house, still adjusting to his new-found freedom, he was handed a remote and offered, 'Pick any channel.'

To his surprise, every Pakistani channel was filled with news about him, showcasing his ordeal and return. Watching himself on TV for the first time, Nachiketa marvelled at the extensive media coverage.

Despite Pakistan's offer of an aircraft for his return, India opted to bring him back in its own vehicle. The next morning, the embassy car, flanked by Defence Attaché Jaiswal and Commodore Srikant, was ready to escort him across the Wagah border back to India. The journey was symbolic, marking the end of a harrowing chapter and the beginning of a new one.

As the car moved across the border, the landscape of his homeland beckoned. The spirit of a fighter pilot surged within Nachiketa—a blend of resilience and an unyielding desire to return to the skies.

As the convoy approached the Attari-Wagah border, the contrast was stark. On the Pakistani side, the atmosphere was eerily quiet with only two correspondents waiting. Indian officials signed the necessary release documents on the Pakistan side of the Joint Check Post, then accompanied Nachiketa to the zero line[20] and formally placed him in the safe custody of Indian officers at 1715 hours.

As soon as Flight Lieutenant Nachiketa crossed into Indian territory, he was greeted by a sea of jubilant faces. The border was thronged with thousands, all eager to welcome him home. The sheer volume of the crowd made it nearly impossible to navigate through, with everyone reaching out to touch him, speak to him and express their joy.

Air Vice Marshal Shashi Tyagi, along with senior officials from Air Headquarters, the Indian Army and the Border Security Force welcomed him with bouquets and garlands.[21] His head held high, Nachiketa told the waiting reporters in a choked voice: 'I am fine and happy to be home.'

The large crowd gathered shouted, 'India zindabad, Nachiketa zindabad!'

The officer was immediately escorted to the Border Security Force meeting hall, where he was offered tea before being taken to the Raja Sansi Airport, Amritsar. From there, he was flown to New Delhi in a Dornier aircraft.

In the privacy of the aircraft, he donned his Indian Air Force blue uniform—light blue shirt, dark blue trousers and side cap—with great pride and affection. The uniform felt like a symbol of his return, and he relished the familiar comfort it provided. Upon landing at Palam Airport in Delhi, he found his parents and sisters waiting to receive him.

His elder sister, Vally Maya, anxiously checked his nails, worried he might have been mistreated. Nachiketa reassured her with a

---

20 Zero line is the actual physical line that seperates India and Pakistan at Wagha border

21 'Nachiketa is raring to go on next sortie', Kashmiri Pandit Network, 17 July 2025, http://ikashmir.net/kargilheroes/nachiketa.html.

laugh, 'Don't be scared, all nails are intact. I am fine.' His youngest sister, Trisandhya, playfully asked if he could see clearly, to which he responded with a smile.

In a brief media interaction, when asked if he felt like a hero, Nachiketa, his voice choked with emotion, replied, 'I am not a hero, but a soldier. Every soldier in Kargil would have done just what I did.' He added, 'I am ready for the next sortie.'

Later that night, he met Prime Minister Atal Bihari Vajpayee and the Chief of the Air Staff, sharing a handshake with the prime minister in the presence of his parents. The following day, Nachiketa and his family were received by President K.R. Narayanan. His mother shared a warm and heartfelt conversation with the President's wife.

Reflecting on the ordeal, Nachiketa expressed deep admiration for Vajpayee's leadership:

> I have a lot of respect for Atal Bihari Vajpayee ji. As a PM, he clearly communicated to the Pakistani government that we would not accept their aggression and took decisive steps to defend our territory. Despite international pressure, he ensured the conflict did not escalate into a full-scale war or nuclear confrontation. He is one of the greatest PMs we've ever had.

~

Present Day
Bangalore
India

Group Captain K. Nachiketa defied death three times. First, when his aircraft's engine failed and he ejected just moments before it crashed. Second, when he was captured by soldiers who were about to shoot him, but a Pakistani officer intervened and saved his life. Third, had he not been captured by the Pakistani Army, he might have succumbed to the cold in those treacherous mountains. His survival was nothing short of miraculous.

When his sister, Vally Maya, asked how he survived while Squadron Leader Ajay Ahuja, who flew right after him, did not, Nachiketa explained that luck had been on his side. He had been captured by the Pakistani Army, which, despite being the enemy, upheld some military ethics. In contrast, Squadron Leader Ahuja fell into the hands of those who did not believe in the rules of war. We will never know what truly conspired in his final moments.

Immediately after his release as a prisoner of war, Nachiketa was offered options: He could take sick leave and go to Hyderabad to be with his parents, or he could resume duty at Adampur. Without hesitation, he chose Adampur.

By then, Nachiketa had become a household name, known not just in India but around the world. He was hailed as a hero, a symbol of hope, resilience and national solidarity. But that fame also brought constant attention. Wherever he went, people crowded around him for autographs. He longed for peace—a quiet life, far from the glare of the media—and the chance to fulfil his duty.

There was something else that weighed heavily on him—flying. After the incident, the injuries to his back made flying difficult, and he was declared medically unfit for years. For someone like Nachiketa, whose heart was always in the sky, it was a devastating blow. Flying had been his true love, and he feared he would never regain the fitness needed to soar through the clouds again.

In the interim, the Indian Air Force assigned him to operate unmanned aerial vehicles. It was important work, but it wasn't the same as being in the cockpit. Yet, he didn't lose hope. By God's grace, as time passed, he regained his physical fitness.

While he wasn't cleared to fly fighter jets, he was given the chance to fly transport aircraft. The Il-78—a massive aerial refuelling tanker—and the Antonov An-32, a twin-engined military transport aircraft, became his new wings. It wasn't the high-speed thrill of a fighter jet, but it brought him a sense of purpose and satisfaction.

Through it all, Nachiketa remained grateful. Many comrades who had been captured like him never returned home. He was one of the lucky ones—he had been given a second chance. He often reflected on this, thankful to the Indian Air Force for standing by him and offering him new opportunities to serve. Despite the challenges, he considered himself blessed to lead a relatively normal life.

Two years after his release, he got married. Marriage proposals had poured in the moment he returned home a hero, but he had waited. He shared with me:

I didn't want to marry someone who saw me as a hero. My life, in the end, is like that of any other Air Force personnel. My partner needed to embrace the fact that I'm just a simple soldier, one who loves his nation first. I lived in the same MES houses, dealt with the same daily challenges, and get transferred like any other air warrior. I don't lead a fancy life.

In October 2001, he married Prashanti, a girl from Hyderabad. She understood the sacrifices, the constant relocations, the sense of duty that came with the uniform. Together, they built a beautiful life with their two sons, Pranav and Vaibhav.

Nachiketa's story is one in a million—despite being captured by the enemy, he was fortunate enough to return home. His family didn't have to go through the ordeal of fighting for his release, thanks to the intervention of then prime minister Atal Bihari Vajpayee, who valued the life of every soldier serving the nation. However, many

Indian prisoners of war have been languishing in Pakistani jails since the 1965 war. No one knows if they are alive or dead.

While being captured is a harsh possibility of combat—an unfortunate circumstance of war—we must remember that it doesn't diminish a soldier's valour. As a nation, it is disappointing that we have not been able to bring back those who gave everything for our future. These soldiers are the true heroes—men whose fates may never be known, whose resting places will never be visited or garlanded at anniversaries. Yet, their sacrifice is unique, enduring and incomparable.

A nation must honour this sacrifice and never give up on its Prisoners of Wars.

Author's note

This story is drawn from an in-depth conversation with Group Captain Nachiketa—a man who lived through one of the most defining moments of the Kargil War and emerged with quiet resilience. He went on to command 3001 Squadron (Phoenix) in Bathinda, retired in April 2017, and continued to serve the skies through civil aviation. Speaking with him was a deeply humbling experience. I also spoke with his sister, Vally Maya, whose reflections embody the silent strength of military families during times of uncertainty. Writing on historical operations comes with the advantage of rich archival material—unlike recent missions, which remain veiled under official secrecy. In shaping this chapter, I also owe gratitude to two stalwarts of IAF literature: The late Pushpinder Singh and Air Marshal Bharat Kumar. Pushpinder Singh passed away in 2021 and despite several attempts, I couldn't connect with Air Marshal Bharat Kumar. Yet, their contributions left a lasting imprint on my work.

Indian Peace Keeping Operations

THE ETHNIC CONFLICT between the Liberation Tigers of Tamil Eelam (LTTE) and the Sri Lankan government is one of the longest and most complex in modern history. It arose from both the real and perceived neglect of the Tamil minority living in northern and northeastern Sri Lanka, including areas such as the Jaffna Peninsula, Kilinochchi, Mannar, Vavuniya and Trincomalee.

Initially, in the 1950s and 1960s, the Sri Lankan government pursued a secular approach to nation-building. However, by the 1970s, this shifted to a more nationalist and sectarian stance that prioritized the Sinhala community, the Sinhalese language and Buddhism. This change marginalized many Tamils, turning their peaceful protests in the late 1970s into a call for an independent Tamil state, known as Tamil Eelam. The situation escalated dramatically in 1983, when the LTTE formally declared its goal of independence, igniting a violent and prolonged military conflict.

Under the leadership of Velupillai Prabhakaran, the LTTE's actions led to a state of emergency in Sri Lanka by 1985, which also strained relations with India. Due to its proximity to northern Sri Lanka, India became increasingly involved in the conflict, especially as refugees and militants crossed into Tamil Nadu, causing significant security concerns. Sri Lanka's stability was crucial for India's broader regional interests, particularly to prevent foreign intervention from countries like Pakistan, China or the USA.

As the conflict intensified, the first major 'air action' by India took place on 4 June 1987, when five Antonov An-32 transport aircraft, escorted by four Mirage 2000 fighters, air-dropped approximately twenty-four tonnes of relief supplies over the Jaffna Peninsula. This mission is also popularly known as 'Operation Poomalai'.[1]

Subsequently, under Prime Minister Rajiv Gandhi's leadership, India sought to prevent external interference and restore stability. This led to talks with the then Sri Lankan President, J.R. Jayewardene, and the signing of the Indo-Sri Lanka Peace Accord in July 1987.[2] The agreement required the Sri Lankan government to devolve power to Tamil-majority regions, Tamil militants to disarm, and India to send a peacekeeping force to oversee and enforce these efforts.

When the Indian Peace Keeping Force (IPKF) landed in Sri Lanka in 1987, their mission was to stabilize a nation fractured by civil war. However, what began as a diplomatic peacekeeping effort quickly transformed into a brutal conflict with the LTTE, which was suspicious of the IPKF's presence and refused to disarm, viewing the Indian forces as occupiers rather than allies.

---

1 https://www.indiatvnews.com/news/india/latest-news-know-about-iaf-s-operation-poomalai-in-jaffna-sri-l-31725.html// Know about IAF's Operation Poomalai in Jaffna, Sri Lanka// India TV News Desk Published: December 21, 2013
2 'Indo-Lanka Accord', Ministry of External Affairs, 29 July 1987, chrome-extension://efaidnbmnnnibpcajpcglclefindmkaj/https://www.mea.gov.in/Portal/LegalTreatiesDoc/LK87B1078.pdf.

Tensions escalated, turning a mission of goodwill into a complex and costly military operation. Indian troops—initially sent to foster peace—found themselves immersed in fierce combat on foreign soil, while the Indian Air Force supported the Army in all its might. It was not easy for the IAF as well to carry out air operations, and pilots faced some of the most treacherous conditions of their careers.

From the outset, the Indian Air Force played a crucial role in transporting IPKF troops and supplies between India and conflict zones in northern Sri Lanka. All operations in the country under Operation Pawan[3] were coordinated by Air Vice Marshal Denzil Keelor, then Assistant Chief of Air Staff (Ops) at Vayu Bhawan, New Delhi,[4] under the leadership of Air Chief Marshal Denis La Fontaine, the Chief of Air Staff.

To meet various contingencies and respond to emerging threats, Air Headquarters moved offensive, transport and helicopter units to southern India. Interestingly, the first IAF aircraft to actually land on Sri Lankan soil was a Mi-17 from No. 129 Helicopter Unit (HU), commanded by Group Captain H.S. Ahluwalia. In total secrecy, he flew LTTE leader Prabhakaran to India before the signing of the Indo-Sri Lanka Accord.[5]

During Operation Pawan, the Palaly airfield served as the primary operational base for the overstretched IPKF. It housed dozens of Mi-8

---

3   Indiatimes, 'Operation Pawan: The Forgotten War | Indian Army' YouTube, https://www.youtube.com/watch?app=desktop&v=or8wfL5E3Ho. Operation Pawan was the code name assigned to the operation by the Indian Peace Keeping Force (IPKF) to take control of Jaffna from the Liberation Tigers of Tamil Eelam (LTTE). In brutal fighting lasting about three weeks, the IPKF took control of the Jaffna Peninsula from the LTTE, something that the Sri Lankan Army had tried but failed to do.
4   Pushpinder Singh, *Himalayan Eagles*, Chapter XXXX, 'Operation Pawan: The IAF in Sri Lanka'.
5   Ibid.

and Chetak helicopters, along with An-32 and HS 748 transport aircraft—all requiring defence against LTTE raids. Transport aircraft like the IL-76 and An-32 became lifelines, carrying everything from food and medical supplies to reinforcements across treacherous waters and dense jungles to reach Jaffna. The induction of the Mi-8 acted as a true force multiplier, navigating through thick forests to deliver soldiers directly into battle zones, often under enemy fire.

Troops and equipment were flown in from various cantonments in India, as well as from Trincomalee and Batticaloa in Sri Lanka, using IL-76, An-12, An-32, HS 748 and civilian Boeing 737 aircraft. The IL-76s and An-12s transported armoured fighting vehicles, while the An-32s, HS 748 and civilian Boeings flew in troops and their arms. Reinforcements were provided by Mi-8 helicopters, and Cheetah helicopters were used for reconnaissance and casualty evacuation.[6]

The most formidable additions, however, were the Mi-25 helicopter gunships. The world has rarely witnessed such intense airlift operations. Between 11 and 31 October 1987, the IAF flew an estimated 2,200 tactical transport sorties and 800 assault helicopter sorties, bringing in troops, weapons, vehicles, supplies and other essential equipment, while also evacuating the mounting casualties to military hospitals.[7]

As the IPKF encountered heavy resistance, the need for direct combat support became critical. In response, the IAF deployed the Mi-24/25 helicopters—known as 'Flying Tanks'—which were equipped with powerful guns and rockets. These attack helicopters tore through LTTE defences, giving ground troops the edge they

---

6 Pushpinder Singh, 'Overview: Indian Peace Keepers in Sri Lanka', Bharat Rakshak, 5 October 2009.

7 Air Marshal Bharat Kumar PVSM, AVSM, VM, ADC, *Operation Pawan: Role of Airpower with IPKF* (New Delhi: Manohar Publishers, 2015).

needed to advance. The pilots, often flying just above the treetops, risked their lives with each mission, knowing that even the slightest mistake could lead to disaster.

The IAF also conducted reconnaissance missions, utilizing powerful cameras and surveillance equipment to gather vital intelligence on LTTE movements and uncover hidden supply routes. This data enabled the IPKF to operate more strategically.

The conflict intensified significantly after the IAF's first Special Heliborne Operation (SHBO) over Jaffna University, in which 120 Para Commandos and 360 Sikh Light Infantry troops were air-dropped into LTTE-controlled territory. This bold manoeuvre aimed to surprise the enemy, secure key positions and relieve pressure on IPKF forces that were pinned down in the area. However, it turned into a disaster.

Nonetheless, this operation came to epitomize the courage of the Indian Army soldiers and the IAF aircrew involved. Their names are now etched in the annals of nation's history.

The Jaffna heli-drop marked a turning point in the IPKF operation, changing the dynamics of the mission, deeply impacting both the IPKF and the IAF. The IPKF soon found itself engaged in direct combat and guerrilla warfare, marking an unexpected and dramatic shift in the situation.

If America grappled with the repercussions of Vietnam, and Russia endured the trials of Afghanistan, then India too faced its own formidable challenge in Sri Lanka.

Yet, it is deeply unfortunate that we so often fail to recognize and remember the courage of those Indian soldiers who, against all odds, fulfilled their duty with unwavering dedication. Their valour stands shoulder to shoulder with that of those who have won celebrated victories for India. It remains an uncelebrated chapter of pure, noble and exemplary bravery—a profound milestone in Indian military history, underscoring the quiet yet steadfast courage of the Indian soldier.

The story that follows pays tribute to these unsung guardians of the skies during the IPKF missions. It also aims to remind the new generation of Indian helicopter pilots of the proud legacy they inherit.

7

Operation Pawan; Jaffna University Helidrop: Against All Odds

Jaffna University Area
Kokkuviland
Sri Lanka
11 October 1987
0100 hours

AT EXACTLY 0100 hours, the deep rumble of two Mi-8 helicopters broke the oppressive silence of the night. The first stick of forty Para Commandos[1] from 10 Para were aboard the aircraft, ready for insertion. Inside, the men—under the leadership of Major Sheonan Singh—sat in disciplined silence, their faces focused and tense. The weather was unforgiving, with thick clouds hovering at only 200 metres, plunging everything into an inky darkness that felt alive, almost tangible. There was no moon to guide them, no stars to relieve the heavy gloom.

---

1 Para (Special Forces) was called Para Commando then.

Wing Commander V.K.N. Sapre led the formation, with Squadron Leader Vinay Raj as his second. The pair of helicopters maintained a low altitude of 200 metres, adjusted from the original plan of 300 metres due to the low-hanging clouds and poor visibility.

The choppers were in complete blackout mode: No navigation lights, no landing lights, not even anti-collision lights illuminated their path. Even the 'blade tracking' lights at the wingtips were switched off, leaving only a single formation light atop Sapre's tail boom for Vinay Raj to follow.

Inside the cockpits, only the faint glow of the instruments pierced the darkness. Both pilots' eyes flicked between their gauges and the pitch-black void ahead, relying on sheer skill, training and experience to guide them. Any miscalculation could be disastrous, but there was no room for error tonight.

This was the first wave of a four-helicopter Special Heliborne Operation (SHBO) to insert 120 Para Commandos and 360 troops from the 13 Sikh Light Infantry Battalion into the heart of LTTE territory near Jaffna University—a heavily fortified zone bristling with fighters and weaponry.

Captain Bhaduria of 10 Para stood by the open door of the chopper, gripping the thick rope they would use to descend. As they neared the drop zone, the tension became almost unbearable. The helicopters descended to just 10 metres above the ground, hovering silently, their movements precise and controlled. Captain Bhaduria threw down the rope and swiftly descended, followed by his team, each commando vanishing into the darkness below.

The LTTE, expecting an attack, had set up several machine guns in the buildings surrounding the landing zone. However, the blackout allowed the Mi-8s to descend unnoticed, and the commandos began to take defensive positions as soon as they hit the ground. But within moments, they were under intense fire, pinned down by relentless LTTE gunfire from around Jaffna University.

Sapre and Vinay Raj reacted instantly, lifting off just moments after the Para Commandos disembarked. The helicopters came under sporadic ground fire from the LTTE positions, but in the darkness, the enemy struggled to locate them accurately. As they circled over Navatkuli Lagoon, Sapre transmitted a clear command to the Indian Air Force operational base at Palaly: 'First pair clear. Send in the second wave.'

The mission had just begun. With each passing moment, the night grew fiercer, filled with gunfire and the unwavering resolve of the men fighting this battle.

This tale of unsung, understated and almost unimaginable courage left me sleepless for days. It took me months to fully comprehend the strength of character needed to stand fearlessly against adversity, and even longer to express that spirit in words. This story is for the next generation of brave hearts—to know the legacy they inherit—and for all of us to understand that the ideals of our nation were not built in a day. They were forged through the sacrifices of countless men, each instilled with a deep love for the motherland and the unshakable resolve to protect it.

Jaffna University Helicopter Drop: The Context

In late September and early October 1987, a series of events marked a turning point for the Indian Peace Keeping Force in Sri Lanka, setting the stage for a gruelling and complex involvement. Initially tasked with restoring peace, the IPKF found itself increasingly drawn into the violent depths of a civil conflict amid rising regional tensions.

On 15 September, Rasaiah Parthipan, a prominent LTTE political leader known as Thileepan, began a hunger strike, protesting Sri Lanka's failure to meet its obligations under the Indo-Sri Lankan Accord. Indian authorities tried to persuade Thileepan to end his fast, but he passed away on 27 September, sparking intensified demonstrations against the IPKF and fuelling distrust among Tamils.[2]

Just days later, on 4 October, Sri Lankan forces detained seventeen LTTE operatives, including commanders Kumarappa and Pulendran, accusing them of arms smuggling and involvement in a civilian massacre. The Sri Lankan government intended to transfer them to Colombo for trial. The LTTE, fearing torture and execution, appealed to the IPKF for protection. Initially, the IPKF intervened, transferring the detainees to Palaly under its custody. However, in a subsequent shift on 5 October, the IPKF allowed Sri Lankan authorities to take over the prisoners.[3]

Fearing brutal treatment, seventeen LTTE members ingested cyanide; twelve of them succumbed despite Indian doctors' efforts to save them. Prabhakaran virtually declared war on Indian Army with sniper fire, explosive booby traps and ambushes being unleashed. The incident had triggered widespread unrest in the north and east, with LTTE retaliations: Two policemen were shot, nine Sri Lankan soldiers held captive by the LTTE were executed, and Sinhalese civilians in Jaffna were killed on the night of 5 October.

On 6 October, six IPKF soldiers lost their lives in an LTTE ambush on their way back to base.[4]

The rapidly worsening situation demanded immediate action. The IPKF launched targeted operations to assert control, deploying the 54th Division to weaken LTTE's influence across Jaffna. On

---

2 'Remembering Thileepan's sacrifice 37 years on', *Tamil Guardian*, 26 September 2024, https://www.tamilguardian.com/content/remembering-thileepans-sacrifice-37-years.
3 Major General Harkirat Singh, *Intervention in Sri Lanka: The IPKF Experience Retold* (New Delhi: Manohar Publishers, 2007).
4 Air Marshal Bharat Kumar, *Operation Pawan*.

5 October, a series of successful raids destroyed two LTTE printing presses and a TV station, but the situation was still not in control.

On 9 October, the COAS, General K. Sundarji, flew into Jaffna from New Delhi for a first-hand assessment and ordered immediate offensive action against the LTTE. Over the following days, the 54th Division in task of controlling the north had captured 131 militants and seized significant weapon caches, while the 36th Division took charge of the eastern front in Trincomalee.[5]

By 10 October, IPKF had embarked on full-scale operations to secure Jaffna. Resistance was fierce, with the LTTE employing ambush tactics and improvised explosive devices (IEDs) to disrupt Indian forces. In one such ambush, four Indian soldiers were killed.

Despite these challenges, IPKF held its ground, securing vital supply routes and positioning themselves for a larger offensive.

The situation intensified with each passing day. On 10 October, Indian forces received intelligence that the LTTE leadership—including Prabhakaran, his deputy Mahattaya and other high-ranking figures—would gather the following night at Jaffna University, a known LTTE stronghold equipped with extensive communications infrastructure. This rare chance to capture the LTTE's core leadership promised to significantly weaken the rebel group's hold.

IPKF command decided on a swift strike near Jaffna University, aiming to capture the leaders in one decisive move.

The plan was to insert troops via helicopter under the cover of darkness, launching a surprise assault before the LTTE could react. Indian Mi-8 helicopters were to transport soldiers to strategic positions around Jaffna University, with air support provided by artillery and reconnaissance units. The mission—part of a broader campaign to neutralize LTTE's power centres—would soon

---

5 Ibid., p. 109.

become one of IPKF's most critical and dangerous operations in the unfolding conflict.

~

Palaly Airbase
Sri Lanka
11 October 1987

On the afternoon of 11 October, the sun cast long shadows over Jaffna as Flying Officer Vishwanath Prakash climbed into the Chetak helicopter alongside Wing Commander V.K.N. Sapre. Both men had been flying through the night and well into the morning, conducting continuous sorties to redeploy troops and ammunition to critical points around Jaffna.

Exhausted but focused, they now had a new task: To conduct an aerial reconnaissance of a potential landing zone for an upcoming mission.

The Chetak lifted off smoothly and, within minutes, they started circling in a low, slow left orbit over the town. As the helicopter banked, Prakash peered through the side Perspex window. Below him sprawled a dense cityscape, with green palms and red-tiled roofs clustered along narrow streets. Amidst the buildings and trees, an oval football field and a smaller playground stood out as open spaces. The football pitch, larger and with fewer structures around it, immediately caught his attention.

'There,' someone pointed out over the intercom, indicating the football field beside the road, barely thirteen to fourteen kilometres from Palaly airfield. These were the grounds of Jaffna University, surrounded by a city humming with quiet tension. Prakash studied the layout: The football pitch provided the clear space they needed and was well-positioned near the target zone.

The helicopter circled again, and Prakash continued scanning the field below. After a couple of orbits to confirm the assessment, they returned to base. As they landed, the young air force officer observed several Army officers board the same Chetak for another reconnaissance of the landing zone. Prakash watched as the helicopters made multiple trips with Army officers aboard, hovering over the same potential landing zone—a routine that risked drawing attention.

Flying Officer Vishwanath Prakash was part of the Mi-8 helicopter detachment stationed at Palaly. Their task was clear: Transport troops and ammunition to critical points around Jaffna.

Group Captain M.P. Premi, the Commanding Officer of Air Force Station Nicobar, was appointed base commander at the Air Force facility in Jaffna, overseeing operations. The island had a small fleet—a detachment of four Mi-8 helicopters—two were from 109 Helicopter (HU) led by Wing Commander V.K.N. Sapre, who also served as detachment commander, and one Mi-8 each from 107 HU and 112 HU, as reinforcements along with their respective aircrew.

The flight crew was a seasoned team. Squadron Leader D.R. Doraiswamy, Squadron Leader V.S. Nath and Flight Lieutenant B. Ramesh from the 109 HU led sorties alongside Squadron Leader T.K. Vinay Raj and Flying Officer Sanjay Bishnoi from 112 HU, and Squadron Leader A.D. Sonpar and Flying Officer Vishwanath Prakash from 107 HU. Though Sonpar was a senior and seasoned Chetak pilot, he was undergoing conversion training on the Mi-8 and therefore flew as Prakash's co-pilot.

On the night of 10 October, Flying Officer Vishwanath Prakash and the other captains flew multiple missions, transporting large numbers of troops and ammunition to key areas around Jaffna, including Navatkuli, Mandaitivu and Karainagar. The goal was to strengthen IPKF positions across Jaffna. Thankfully, that night, they encountered no enemy fire, but the quiet wouldn't last long.

The following day, 11 October, Mi-8 helicopters worked all day moving IPKF troops from Elephant Pass to Navatkuli. But the challenge awaiting the resilient Mi-8s and their brave aircrews was about to unfold. Orders had been issued for the LTTE cadre to shoot down every helicopter.

Air Commodore Vishwanath Prakash (veteran) shared:

> On the morning of 11 October, I flew a number of sorties with my co-pilot, Squadron Leader Sonpar. We had flown through the night on the tenth, and on the eleventh, the sorties continued from the morning. However, in the late afternoon, Wing Commander V.K.N. Sapre and I were pulled out between sorties to board a Chetak helicopter for an aerial reconnaissance of a possible landing zone.

It was during this sortie that the young Air Force officer saw the football ground—soon to become a hallowed site that bore witness to the most remarkable acts of valour displayed by Indian troops, alongside the heartbreaking, untold saga of the Battle of Jaffna.

This field would become a battleground for the exceptionally brave jawans of 13 Sikh Light Infantry (LI) and their fearless young commander, Major Birendra Singh, a scion of a prominent political family in Bharatpur, India. Few tales in the history of the Indian Armed Forces match the sheer determination of Major Birendra Singh and his men as they faced overwhelming odds, fighting valiantly until the last man.

Only one soldier, Sepoy Gora Singh, survived.

Once back at divisional headquarters, they received a briefing on the Special Heliborne Operation (SHBO) from Major General Harkirat Singh, GOC of the 54 Division, and his Colonel General Staff, Hoshiar Singh. Group Captain Premi, the base commander of the Air Force Base, Jaffna, was informed of the mission's requirements and confirmed that all four Mi-8 helicopters would be available for the operation.

The Army's briefing detailed the plan: A total of 480 men would be deployed, including 120 commandos from 10 Para and 360 troops from 13 Sikh LI. However, the Sikh LI troops were still in the process of arriving in Sri Lanka.[6]

The plan was to induct the troops by landing the helicopters directly on the football field in front of Jaffna University, keeping ground time to a minimum.

> Air Marshal Bharat Kumar in his book Operation Pawan writes The carrying capacity of the Mi-8 with the clamshell doors removed is twenty troops. So, twenty-four sorties would have been needed to transport 480 troops, which could have been done in six waves of four helicopters each. But eventually, the troop configuration changed due to the heavy ammunition loads being carried by the Sikh LI troops.

Air Commodore V. Prakash (veteran) shared with me:

> We were assured that the chance of resistance at the LZ [landing zone] was low. After landing, the Para Commandos were to secure the LZ by eliminating any immediate LTTE threats. The 13 Sikh LI, arriving in subsequent waves, would take over security of the LZ, allowing the Para Commandos to move ahead to their primary target at a different location.

The SHBO was set to commence at 0100 hours on 12 October 1987. The weather forecast was favourable, with clear visibility and just enough moonlight to aid the aircrew in executing this challenging operation.

---

6 Air Marshal Bharat Kumar, Operation Pawan, p 113.

After the briefing by the Indian Army, the pilots returned to the Air Force operations room to review the induction mission plan in detail.

Air Commodore V. Prakash (veteran) recalled:

The Task Force Commander organized the mission with helicopters flying in pairs, the second pair four minutes behind the first to give time for clearing the landing zone. The initial runs would carry 20 Para Commandos each, and later trips would bring in 15 Sikh Light Infantry troops along with 500 kilograms of ammunition. The first load of Para Commandos would secure the landing zone and mark it with commando torches to guide the subsequent waves.

To maintain secrecy, all external lights were to be switched off, leaving only the formation and rotor-tip lights, so the helicopters could follow one another. Each helicopter would make seven or eight trips. The short, four-minute flight from Palaly to the landing zone meant it would take about ninety minutes to move the entire force.

Although the Mi-8s could be fitted with rocket pods, they left them off to save weight, allowing the helicopters to carry more troops. They also removed the internal 900-litre fuel tank from the cargo area to maximize space for soldiers. For additional support, a Sri Lankan Air Force Bell 212 gunship was assigned to create a diversion by striking west of the landing site, across the railway track. The IAF pilots were given strict instructions not to cross this line.

The mission seemed straightforward—deploy forces against what was believed to be a limited LTTE cadre. But once underway, it quickly spiralled into a nightmare. All the meticulous planning in briefing rooms unravelled in the chaos of the battlefield. Yet, the courage, resilience and unwavering sense of duty of the Indian Air Force pilots and Indian Army soldiers remained unshaken.

Following orders with unbreakable resolve, the commandos under Major Sheonan Singh, the determined Second-in-Command of 10 Para Commando, pressed forward; young Major Birendra Singh led the 13 Sikh LI troops as they faced a relentless hail of bullets, even as four helicopters sustained hits.

The daring helicopter drop in Jaffna is a powerful reminder of the need for impeccable leadership and the weight of responsibility borne by military leaders. Unlike their civilian counterparts, military commanders cannot afford even the smallest lapse in decision-making, as errors, delays or misjudgements can come at a steep cost—not just in lives but in the security, sovereignty and freedom of the nation.

The pilots, having flown continuously since 10 October, concluded their briefing around 2100 hours, ate a quick dinner, and retired to their rooms for a few hours of rest before launching the mission at 0100 hours.

~

Football Ground Near Jaffna University Main Campus
First Wave of Helicopters
12 October 1987
0100 hours

Flying Officer Vishwanath Prakash, a second-generation defence officer, was commissioned into the helicopter stream of the Indian Air Force on 28 May 1983, after graduating from the Air Force Academy, following successful training at the National Defence Academy. The youngest in a family of defence officers—his father a Brigadier in the Army Medical Corps, his siblings in the Armoured Corps and Army Medical Corps—Vishwanath naturally continued the family tradition of serving the nation.

Though only four years into service, he had flown his fair share of challenging sorties during demanding missions, including Operation Blue Star in June 1984 and high-risk manoeuvres over Tawang as part of Operation Falcon in September 1986.

Given his experience in hostile environments, this night seemed calm in comparison. The mission briefing suggested only moderate resistance and the atmosphere was deceptively routine.

Reflecting on his feelings that night, Air Commodore Vishwanath Prakash (veteran) shared with me:

> As I walked towards the helicopter, I couldn't help but notice I was the youngest among the crew. But as captain, it was my duty to deliver the final briefing. While I had complete faith in my skills, I felt the weight of my crew's trust resting on my shoulders. I told them, no matter what came, as a crew, we would back each other up if anything went wrong. Mission accomplishment was all that mattered.

As midnight struck on 11 October, tension filled the air over Jaffna. The first wave of forty elite Para Commandos from 10 Para prepared to board the Mi-8 helicopters for a high-stakes mission. Leading them was Major Sheonan Singh, whose calm, steady presence reassured the men. They knew the risks, but they were ready for whatever awaited them.

Wing Commander Sapre led the helicopter formation of four Mi-8s—'Pratap' was the formation call sign. The first pair was lead by Wing Commander Sapre flying Pratap 1, while Squadron Leader Vinay Raj flew Pratap 2.

The Mi 8s slicing through the darkness took off on time. Due to thick, low-lying clouds, they couldn't fly at the planned altitude of 300 metres and instead kept low at 200 metres. All external lights—navigation, landing, even the blinking anti-collision lights—

were switched off, so they were nearly invisible in the night. The only illumination came from a small formation light atop Sapre's helicopter, guiding Vinay Raj in formation.

Through the hazy sky, the landing ground came into sight. The helicopters swooped down silently, catching the LTTE by surprise. The university, a known LTTE stronghold, was expected to offer limited resistance. However, Indian intelligence had underestimated the enemy's preparedness.

The LTTE had intercepted hints of an impending raid and had fortified the area around Jaffna University with machine guns. Yet, the first wave of helicopters arrived undetected and the LTTE gunners couldn't see the darkened helicopters gliding just above the ground.

Captain Bhaduria, the first of the commandos, dropped a rope and slid down. The LTTE opened fire, but the pilots remained focused on landing safely so the commandos could disembark quickly. Realizing that hovering left the troops too vulnerable, they decided to land fully, prioritizing the soldiers' safety over their own.

In the darkness, the sound of the rotors made it difficult for the LTTE to mark the helicopters' exact positions. As the Mi-8s reached landing height, the LTTE unleashed machine-gun fire, but the bullets narrowly missed. The helicopters touched down and, under Major Sheonan's command, the Para Commandos streamed out, taking defensive positions around the landing site.

Gunfire erupted from LTTE positions, pinning the commandos down in the open. Meanwhile, Sapre and Vinay Raj powered up the Mi-8s, lifting off under a hail of bullets. Both helicopters skilfully dodged the barrage, heading towards the safety of Navatkuli Lagoon.

Once over the lagoon, Sapre radioed the airbase at Palaly: 'Send in the second pair.'

As the second pair of Mi-8 helicopters took off, Flying Officer Lieutenant V. Prakash, who was flying Pratap 3, asked his co-pilot

Squadron Leader Sonpar to start the stopwatch, as he studied the map in the dim red light of the cockpit. They could see Jaffna town and the old fort in the distance. Squadron Leader Doraiswamy, was the pilot of the Pratap 4.

'What's our running time?' Prakash asked, trying to match their position with the map. Sonpar replied that the stopwatch wasn't working. On such a short leg, landing without the precise timing of the stopwatch could be disastrous. Despite this, the skilled captain continued the sortie, navigating by approximation.

The bright lights of the town and the poor weather made it difficult to identify ground features. Despite these challenges, the pilots began their final approach towards what appeared to be an open area for landing. However, as they got closer, they saw flashes of small arms fire and grenade explosions.

To the west, a Sri Lankan Air Force gunship was firing at targets on the ground, and the tracers from its guns looked like heavy fire shooting up from below.

The initial Para Commando team hadn't been able to mark the landing zone with lights as was the original plan. Surrounded by LTTE fighters and engaged in a fierce fight, they couldn't signal their location.

Flying at a high hover to check the landing area, Prakash saw tall trees nearby but could not spot the university buildings. Just then, a group of militants rushed towards the helicopters, firing at them. Realizing it was not the designated landing zone, Prakash quickly radioed the Pratap 4 to retreat. The helicopters immediately pulled away and flew back to Palaly, returning with all forty commandos still on board, unable to offload them.

Meanwhile, Sapre and Vinay Raj had returned to Palaly by then, their helicopters untouched despite the fierce ground fire during take-off.

With adrenaline pumping, a fresh wave of forty commandos boarded the Mi-8s, ready to dive back into the fray. But the LTTE was now on high alert. They had quickly identified the approach route from the first drop and fortified a building to the north of the landing zone, where armed militants lay in wait with AK-47s and heavy machine guns capable of targeting helicopters.

As Sapre flew towards the landing ground, the tension escalated. Suddenly, the air erupted with gunfire—not from the chaos below, but from the northern building. The Mi-8 shuddered as bullets raked its exterior, each thud a stark reminder of the imminent danger. Rounds pierced the cargo compartment, and one bullet struck a Para Commando, leaving him gravely wounded.

Sapre expertly manoeuvred the helicopter close to the ground. The moment it touched down, the commandos scrambled out, urgency fuelling their every move. The pilots shouted for the wounded soldier to remain on board and allow the medics to evacuate him back to base. But the soldier, his eyes fierce and unwavering, refused to abandon his brothers in arms. 'I will stay with my unit and fight!' he declared. Impressed by his courage yet worried for his safety, the pilots reluctantly allowed him to join his team.

With this drop, the number of troops on the ground rose to eighty. But in the heat of the moment, Sapre and Vinay Raj believed they had delivered all 120 commandos. Unbeknownst to them, Prakash and Doraiswamy had aborted their earlier landing, leaving the situation on the ground even more critical.

~

Second Wave of Helicopters at Palaly Airfield

When Sapre and Vinay Raj landed at Palaly, they discovered that Doraiswamy and Prakash hadn't been able to locate the landing zone and had returned without dropping the commandos. This was a grave situation, as the troops already deployed at the target area urgently needed backup.

Since the second pair had trouble finding the landing zone, the task force commander at the airfield decided to rearrange the formation. Wing Commander Sapre would continue to lead, with Squadron Leader Doraiswamy flying behind his helicopter as Pratap-2. Squadron Leader Vinay Raj would now lead the second pair, Pratap 3 and 4, followed by Flying Officer Vishwanath Prakash. The next flights would carry a mix of Para Commandos and 13 Sikh LI troops.

But another delay awaited them: The 13 Sikh Light Infantry soldiers were nowhere near the helicopters

Unlike the Para Commandos, the Sikh LI troops were not trained for special heli-borne operations. They had only just arrived from Gwalior and hadn't been informed that they would need to quickly board helicopters. They were also unfamiliar with the boarding and disembarkation procedures.

According to the Sikh LI's regimental records: '… the battalion was never [informed] about heli-borne operations [upon] land[ing] in Sri Lanka.'

Wing Commander Sapre contacted the air traffic control, which then reached out to Group Captain Premi, the commander of Jaffna Air Force Base. Premi searched for the 13 Sikh LI soldiers and eventually got them ready to board the helicopters, but this took considerable time.

When the troops finally arrived, they brought with them large, heavy ammunition boxes. Unlike the Para Commandos, who carried their supplies in backpacks, the Sikh LI troops had crates weighing 500 kg each. As a result, the helicopters could only carry fifteen soldiers instead of the usual twenty.

Leading them was Major Birendra Singh, commander of 'C' Company—a respected officer from a royal family and a relative of Minister of State for External Affairs Natwar Singh.[7]

This would be the last time he was seen alive.

The delay in gathering and boarding the soldiers took approximately twenty minutes. Meanwhile, at Jaffna University, the eighty Para Commandos were locked in a fierce battle with the LTTE. Enemy snipers had taken up well-concealed positions around the area, attempting to pick off the commandos. Several soldiers had already been injured in the fighting.

～

Landing Near Jaffna University

The helicopters took off from the Palaly airfield once more, flying straight into the heart of danger. Gunfire erupted as soon as they reached the landing zone, with bullets coming from every direction.

Air Commodore Vishwanath Prakash (veteran) described the chaos vividly:

> The militants were firing at us from every angle, even with .50-calibre guns positioned in the tall university buildings. We could barely see anything in the pitch-black night. Heedless of the gunfire, we were busy peering into the darkness, looking for obstacles. Our immediate concern was a safe approach—any collision would have had catastrophic consequences for everyone on board.

---

7 Jagan Pillarisetti, 'Descent Into Danger: The Jaffna University Helidrop', Swarajya, 7 May 2015, https://swarajyamag.com/politics/descent-into-danger-the-jaffna-university-helidrop.

Sapre and Doraiswamy, flying Pratap 1 and 2, took the heaviest hits.

They landed amid a barrage of gunfire, with bullets whizzing around them. Despite the assault, they managed to unload forty Para Commandos, fifteen Sikh Light Infantry soldiers, and several boxes of ammunition. With their hydraulics damaged by the intense gunfire, they managed to lift off and radioed the second pair at Palaly, urging them to carry out their drop.

The mission was paramount; troops on the ground were engaged in a fierce battle with LTTE militants, who held fortified positions and tactical advantage. The risks to their own lives did not matter to the pilots and the crew when their comrades were fighting for their lives.

As I delved into this story, I was overwhelmed by the sheer bravery displayed by these soldiers, who transcended human limits when duty beckoned. It's beyond words, the kind of courage it takes to face death head-on, their only thought to protect and support their brothers on the ground.

Such divinely inclined valour displayed by all the soldiers on ground defies reason; it touches something profoundly sacred.

As Squadron Leader Vinay Raj and Flying Officer V. Prakash, piloting Pratap 3 and 4 approached the landing zone, they encountered what an *India Today* magazine article (issue date 31 januray 1988) written by Shekhar Gupta described as a 'booby-trapped snake pit'.

Air Commodore Vishwanath Prakash (veteran) recalled:

Firing was coming at us from every direction. We braced ourselves and continued, knowing we might be taking lethal hits in the process. My crew placed implicit faith in me; they carried out their tasks with absolute composure. At the LZ, I ordered my flight engineer to switch off the formation lights on the tail boom, hoping to deny the militants a target. When I felt a sudden blow at the back of my neck, I thought my co-pilot or flight engineer had been hit, but I was relieved to see them both safe in the dark. The bullet had grazed my neck without injuring me but it severed a thick cable and the metallic cover right behind my seat, causing the generator to fail immediately. The helicopter had no armour, and bullets pierced the thin walls with ease. We could only imagine the damage happening to critical parts.

Vinay Raj's helicopter was also hit hard; a bullet shattered the cockpit window and another struck the battery compartment. RPGs fired from the ground narrowly missed them, while the air was filled with deafening gunfire and explosions.

As the commandos disembarked from Prakash's helicopter, the 13 Sikh LI soldiers exiting Vinay Raj's aircraft came under intense fire. Instinctively, they hit the ground and returned fire blindly into the darkness.

These troops had just arrived in Jaffna, unprepared for such fierce battle conditions. In the confusion, they forgot to unload the ammunition boxes. The flight engineer noticed and quickly informed the captain. Together, they pushed the boxes out of the helicopter, then the flight engineer managed to find a couple of Sikh LI jawans to take charge of the ammunition.

Having completed his drop, Prakash radioed his readiness to the other helicopter but kept his helicopter grounded, awaiting take-off instructions. He didn't want to lift off alone and risk disrupting the formation. By now, the crew had lost count of how many hits their helicopter had taken, yet they remained steady, fully committed to the mission.

However, Vinay Raj, delayed due to the ammunition offloading, instructed Prakash to take off independently.

Prakash Raj's helicopter flew, the other helicopter also flew within a few moments and once they safely cleared the danger zone and were over the lagoon, Vinay Raj radioed Sapre to report the mix-up with the ammunition boxes. He recommended that Sapre unload the boxes along with the troops if another wave was to be launched.

Unfortunately, it was soon confirmed that no additional landings would take place.

~

Back at Palaly

Air Commodore Vishwanath Prakash (veteran) shared:

> Given the extent of damage the helicopters had sustained, it was a miracle that they could fly back safely to base. Maybe it was the ruggedness of the Russian machines. The astonishing fact was that not a single drop of blood was spilled inside my helicopter despite more than thirty bullet hits was sheer providence.

The other helicopters had fared no better. Vinay Raj's Mi-8 was immobile on landing, its attitude on the ground visibly off. On inspection, the flight engineer found the port-side battery compartment cover missing and the fuselage riddled with seventeen bullet holes. The helicopter was grounded and required extensive repair.

Sapre's Mi-8 had also sustained critical damage—its hydraulic system had been hit, rendering it unflyable. Helicopters cannot operate without hydraulics, and only the exceptional skill and tenacity of the aircrew brought it back to base safely.

It was clear the LTTE ground fire had intensified and become more coordinated by the third run, posing an even greater threat than before. Any further missions risked even greater damage.

After much deliberation, Wing Commander Sapre decided to stop further drops. Only the Mi-8s piloted by Doraiswamy and Prakash were partially serviceable, but sending them back into the hornet's nest to drop thirty more troops would have been extremely risky. With the LTTE's fire growing more accurate with each wave, there was a fairly good chance that RPGs or machine-gun fire would find their mark in the next sortie. Thus, the heli drop was called off after deploying 120 Para Commandos and just thirty out of the intended 360 Sikh LI troops.

Air Commodore Vishwanath Prakash (veteran) shared:

> The inevitable yet tragic decision to discontinue the mission was conveyed to us by the detachment commander. We had flown ten sorties, of which eight were successful. Against the planned induction of approximately 480 troops, we had managed to land only 170, along with one ton of ammunition.

With the realization that the small number of Sikh LI troops did not stand a chance alone, a message was sent to the 10 Para Commandos and relayed to 13 Sikh LI at the landing zone that no further airdrops would be carried out and that the infantry troops should remain with the Para Commandos. However, the Sikh LI were under orders to continue holding the landing zone and await reinforcements arriving by road, expected to reach by first light, barely three hours away.

~

Fighting Against Grave Odds
12 October 1987

On the ground, there were only 120 commanders and thirty Sikh LI jawans. These troops were surrounded and were under intense fire. A lot of books and reports that I read during the research of this historical operation suggest that there were two alternatives at this stage: To abort the mission to capture Prabhakaran or to stick together and fight out the LTTE.

Many reports and books say that General Harkirat Singh, the then General Officer Commanding of Indian Peacekeeping force(IPKF), ordered them to stick to original plan and 13 Sikh LI troops to stay behind and hold the ground. In his book, *Intervention at Sri Lanka*, Major General Harkirat Singh wrote that the commandos got in touch with Major Birender Singh[9] and he refused to abort, telling them to wait for his advancing battalion commander.

Though we would never know the truth, it remains the same across various narrations and reports that Major Birender Singh[8] and his Sikh LI soldiers engaged fiercely with LTTE militants, while the para Commandos pressed forward with their original mission: to capture Prabhakaran.

As dawn broke, the commandos continued advancing independently in pursuit of the LTTE leadership, while the 13 Sikh LI troops remained without any reinforcement.

General Harkirat Singh added that the Sikh LI ran out of ammunition by noon, but the heavy firing by the LTTE ensured that they couldn't link up.

During their search, the commandos encountered a LTTE sympathiser who claimed he knew the LTTE's location and offered to guide them. Trusting him, they followed—only to realize he had misled them, sending them on a wild goose chase. Lost, the commandos were forced to retreat at daybreak, regrouping in a couple of nearby houses where they fortified themselves. Their elite training proved invaluable as they conserved ammunition, retrieved the bodies of their fallen and safeguarded their weapons.

---

8 'Major Birendra Singh VrC', Honour Point, https://honourpoint.in/profile/major-birendra-singh-vrc/.

All contact was lost with Major Birendra Singh and his men, who, despite facing overwhelming odds, continued to fight bravely. Under constant sniper fire, the platoon gradually lost soldiers. During the course of the battle, both Major Birendra Singh and Platoon Commander Subedar Sampuran Singh were killed. By 1130 hours on 12 October, only three soldiers remained. When they ran out of ammunition, they launched a desperate bayonet charge, but two were struck down by LTTE gunfire.

The last man standing, Sepoy Gora Singh, was captured and taken prisoner. It was only after his release that Sepoy Gora Singh helped piece together one of the most poignant battles in Indian Army history.

Just listening to this heroic tale from Gora Singh brought tears to my eyes—tears that refused to stop for a long time. I couldn't help but wonder: How come I never knew about such valiant men?

To those reading this story, I hope you'll carry forward this legacy of unsung bravery—tell your children, and let it live on.

They say, 'How can man die better than facing fearful odds, for the ashes of his fathers, and the temples of his Gods?' But these soldiers weren't dying for land or lineage. They fought—and fell—for their paltan, for the brothers fighting beside them.

That's what endures on the battlefield. That's what truly matters.

With all radio communication from the 13 Sikh LI platoon severed, the fate of the Para Commando Company became a serious concern for 54 Division Headquarters. Major Sheonan Singh managed to get word to HQ, alerting them to their dire situation. Knowing that the commandos were still holding out, the division initiated a rescue operation.

A relief force led by the 10 Para CO, Lieutenant Colonel Dalbir Singh, was dispatched, accompanied by three T-72 tanks from the 65 Armoured Regiment. However, the plan was soon abandoned when they discovered that the approach roads were heavily booby-trapped with IEDs.

It was then that Major Anil Kaul, the tank troop commander of 65 Armoured Regiment, came up with a smart plan. Knowing that railway tracks ran behind Jaffna University, he decided to move the tanks along the Palaly-Jaffna rail line.

As they navigated through the narrow lines, an RPG-7 was fired at them, hitting the turret of his tank. The explosion severed his ring finger, and injured his eye[9] and arm with shrapnel.

His men quickly administered morphine for his wounds, and the column continued fighting its way through to the Para Commandos. Shortly after, they joined forces with the 4/5 Gorkhas and the remaining soldiers of the 13 Sikh LI. It had been almost eighteen hours since the tired Para Commando company had first landed near the university.

The rescue of the Para Commandos marked the end of the tragic Jaffna University raid.

The 13 Sikh LI lost twenty-nine men—nearly 100 per cent casualties in that detachment. The Para Commandos lost six men in the fighting.

Since all four helicopters were grounded due to severe battle damage, reinforcements were flown in early the next morning, and the operation resumed. The brief pause was a morale booster for the LTTE.

The bodies of the fallen Sikh soldiers were stripped of their weapons, uniforms and equipment, and laid out in a row at a nearby Buddhist temple. Later, the LTTE burnt the bodies using a barrel of

---

9 Major Anil Kaul retired a Colonel and eventually lost his eye and part of left hand. He was awarded Vir Chakra for his exemplary bravery. He left for the heavenly abode in 2017.

oil,[10] claiming their efforts to contact IPKF Headquarters at Palaly to collect the dead had failed. As the bodies began to decompose, they said they had no choice but to cremate them. When the army finally reached the area a week later, they found the battlefield strewn with the remnants of 13 Sikh LI uniforms and equipment, along with thousands of .50 machine gun shell casings.

These men were launched unfairly, faced unequal odds and went down fighting.

To get the complete picture, I spoke to the only surviving soldier of 13 Sikh LI, Sepoy Gora Singh. When I asked him about the events on the ground, he said:

> I was in the first helicopter with Major Birender Singh Sahab. As soon as we jumped out, firing came from all directions. But in the pitch dark, we couldn't see anything. We took cover in the bushes and wherever we could find shelter. There were hundreds of them, while we were only thirty, but we didn't lose our spirits and kept firing.
>
> They were shooting from the higher floors of the university, while we were on the ground. The firing lasted the whole night. I held my position with the Medium Machine Gun and kept firing, though bullets hit my calf, arm and knee. Our orders were to capture those militants, and that kept me going.
>
> But at dawn, I saw all my comrades dead, their bodies scattered across the field. I was weak from blood loss and fainted at the sight. When I woke up, I was in LTTE custody. They gave me basic aid and food to keep me alive.

He paused, then quietly added he is very happy to share his story with me even though the flashes still haunt him because he wants

---

10 Air Marshal Bharat Kumar, *Operation Pawan*, p 127.

today's youth to understand the sacrifices made by the fauj in the past. I asked him about reports that Prabhakaran had kicked him. He denied them:

> No, he was nice to me. He never harmed me physically. I was in their custody for twenty-two days, and he visited a few times, always telling the other LTTE members that the sardar was their guest and should be treated well. But other militants tortured me behind his back, even giving me electric shocks with loose telephone wires.

When I asked if he had feared for his life, he replied:

> *Fauj mein bharti kyun hua tha? Isme jaan ka risk to hai hi. Vardi mein jaan dena to fakr ki baat hoti hai.* (Why did I join the Army? There's always a risk to life in this. But to lay down your life in uniform—that's a matter of pride).'

He remembered his comrades' sacrifice and considered his own survival a miracle.

Sepoy Gora Singh was only twenty-eight when he was captured. After his release through government negotiations and subsequent medical treatment in India, he chose to return to Jaffna, fighting the LTTE for three more years until the final IPKF withdrawal.

～

Aftermath

In the heart of the Jaffna Peninsula, where rugged terrain and fierce opposition made road access impossible, the small fleet of Mi-8 helicopters became the lifeline for Indian soldiers battling in isolated positions. From dawn to nightfall, many flights took off each day, carrying vital supplies and reinforcements. Jaffna's airfield—usually a quiet space—was transformed into a bustling hub, alive with the constant flow of aircraft and troops. It felt as busy as any major international airport.

This handful of Mi-8s operated at full capacity, driven by the single goal of supporting their comrades.

On 23 October 1987, Jaffna was finally declared liberated, with Indian troops securing control. Although it's impossible to describe every hardship, sacrifice and challenge faced by the soldiers and units, through this chapter I want to shine a light on the brave helicopter pilots. Often overlooked, helicopters are vital to the Indian military, delivering supplies and support to soldiers and people in need.

In January 1988, several gallantry awards were announced for exceptional actions in IPKF operations in Sri Lanka. Among those honoured, Major Sheonan, from 10 Para Commando who led 120 Commandos in the battle, and the brave Company Commander of the Sikh LI detachment, Major Birendra Singh, received the Vir Chakra. Other notable recipients included Lieutenant Colonel Dalvir Singh, who led a key rescue operation, and Major Anil Kaul from the Armoured Corps, both awarded the Vir Chakra. Additionally, three Sikh LI soldiers were posthumously awarded the Vir Chakra, along with two Para Commandos involved in the operation.

Initially, the Indian Air Force's award citations encountered delays. However, as doubts surrounding the operation were clarified, the Army supported the IAF pilots' nominations.

In recognition of their bravery and critical contributions, all four Mi-8 helicopter pilots—Wing Commander V.K.N. Sapre, Squadron Leader T.K. Vinay Raj, Squadron Leader D.R. Doraiswamy and Flight Officer V. Prakash—were awarded the Vir Chakra. Their co-pilots, including Squadron Leader V.S.N. Nath, Flying Officer Sanjay Bishnoi (later Flight Lieutenant), Flight Lieutenant B. Ramesh and Squadron Leader A.D. Sonpar, received the Vayusena Medal (Gallantry). Additional crew members were commended by the Chief of Air Staff or the Air Officer Commanding-in-Chief.

This mission remains one of the rare instances in IAF history where such a large number of honours were awarded for a single operation, highlighting the remarkable bravery and dedication of the entire team.

The No. 109 Helicopter Unit stayed the longest in the IPKF operations, remaining until the final withdrawal. Today, the pilots and crew of this mission have since retired.

Group Captain V.K.N. Sapre last served as Station Commander in Mohanbari; Group Captain Vinay Raj retired as COO in Hakimpet. Wing Commander D.R. Doraiswamy retired in the late '90s and has since passed away. Flying Officer V. Prakash retired as an Air Commodore and now serves as a commercial pilot. His daughter, Squadron Leader Shruti Prakash, followed in his footsteps by joining the Indian Air Force.

While writing this account, I learnt that he recently lost his wife, Anuradha—whom he revered as an embodiment of courage, compassion and grace. Though he has faced life-and-death situations countless times, he shared that her loss was deeper than any challenge he'd endured. Yet, he continues to fly each day with her memory close to his heart.

The IPKF's indecisive battles and the loss of Indian soldiers on foreign soil are considered one of the darkest chapters in India's military history.

However, I believe that despite the political, diplomatic and leadership debates over what went wrong and who was to blame, it is time we embrace these stories and present them to the next generation with pride. These narratives celebrate the purest human emotions—devotion to duty and the ethos that drives soldiers to go to any lengths to accomplish their mission, even at the cost of their lives. I hope the next generation of helicopter pilots will find inspiration in these stories and understand the weight of the legacy they inherit.

To honour their sacrifice, the 13 Sikh LI holds a special Ardas and Akhand Path every year on 12 October, commemorating their brave comrades who fell on the unforgiving battleground of Jaffna University. Sepoy Gora Singh is invited each year, and he attends without fail, no matter where the unit is stationed. Their memory lives on as a testament to the indomitable spirit of valour and sacrifice that defines our armed forces.

Author's note

Enough has been said and written about IPKF operations, the chapter does not aim to uncover startling new facts. In fact, I was initially hesitant to include it, as I've always preferred to focus on lesser-known, stories. But I soon realised that no account of the Indian Air Force would be complete without acknowledging its critical role in Sri Lanka. What makes this chapter special is not new data, but the personal depth brought in by Air Commodore V. Prakash and Sepoy Gora Singh—the lone survivor of the first batch of 13 Sikh LI.

8

The Might of the Indian Air Force

THE INDIAN AIR Force stands tall as a symbol of modern air power—an embodiment of strength, precision and relentless innovation. Recent operations like Operation Sindoor or the geopolitical situation worldwide have reaffirmed that the future of warfare will be determined not on land or sea, but decisively in the skies. While this book primarily celebrates the people behind the machines, it felt only fitting to conclude with a tribute to the machines themselves. This chapter is not a technical evaluation, but a personal account shaped by conversations with the pilots who fly these aircraft. Some legendary platforms are not included—not out of neglect, but because this narrative draws from first-hand experiences. These aircraft are more than just machines; they reflect the courage, skill, and dedication of those who fly, support and maintain them. This chapter also hopes to spark curiosity in young readers—about the marvels of aviation technology and the thrill of flying, perhaps even inspiring the next generation of air warriors. Let just begin it with our very own 'Make in India'.

HAL Light Combat Aircraft Tejas: India's Supersonic Pride

The HAL Tejas embodies India's unstoppable journey towards defence self-reliance. This state-of-the-art fighter jet, a masterpiece of Indian engineering and innovation, combines stealth, advanced avionics, precision weaponry and a cutting edge human-machine interface. With its sleek design, modern sensors and precision engineered radar systems, the Tejas stands among the best in the world. Tejas is not just a fighter jet—it is India's soaring symbol of power, pride and unparalleled strength.

I had the privilege of speaking to a pilot who will be referred to as Gladius here. He was part of the team that inducted the jet into the Air Force in 2016. At the time, only seven pilots, including the Commanding Officer, formed the core of the newly raised No. 45 Squadron—the Flying Daggers[1]—established in July 2016 to operationalize the Tejas. Also on the team were Engineering Officers—technicians who gave their all to make this dream a reality for India. These trailblazers will be remembered as the pioneers of India's iconic indigenous marvel, a monumental achievement for both the Indian Air Force and India's defence industry.

He reflected:

When Tejas was inducted in 2016, unlike any other aircraft in India's fleet, we didn't have manuals, SOPs or protocols to guide us. Despite all the rigorous tests, trials and evaluations over the years, operationalizing it was a whole new ball game. The first batch of Tejas fighter pilots were handpicked from various squadrons flying the Mirage, MiG-29, MiG-21 and others. We

---

1 '45 Squadron (Flying Daggers)', Fauji Days, https://faujidays.com/lookup/establishments/militaries/indian-military/indian-air-force/squadrons/45-squadron-flying-daggers.

brought the best from our respective fleets to form the newly raised Tejas Squadron. Our mission wasn't just to train ourselves, but to build the foundation, establish protocols and pave the way for the next generation of Tejas pilots. It was tough because there were no references; Tejas was a one-of-a-kind platform. But we didn't back down. We worked tirelessly, trained relentlessly and gave it everything we had.

He paused, his voice filled with pride and nostalgia:

Tejas had never been flown operationally before, so every day brought new challenges. The journey was tough, but our passion kept us going. It wasn't just about skill—it required complete dedication. Everyone involved, from pilots to engineers and technicians, shared that passion. That's what made Tejas a success. The fact that India had finally built its own fighter jet—a jet we could truly call ours—pushed us to give our best. Looking back, I feel proud and satisfied. We laid the foundation for this extraordinary aircraft. Today, Tejas is stronger and unstoppable. With the Tejas Mk1A inducted, the Mark2 on the way, and even more advanced jets in development, I believe we are creating some of the world's finest machines.

The HAL Tejas is a 4.5-generation fighter jet developed under the light combat aircraft project by the Aeronautical Development Agency (ADA) and manufactured by Hindustan Aeronautics Limited. It holds the distinction of being the world's lightest supersonic multirole fighter. In 2001, then prime minister, Atal Bihari Vajpayee, named it 'Tejas', meaning 'radiance' in Sanskrit, symbolizing India's progress in defence capability.

Although not India's first locally-built fighter (that distinction belongs to the HF-24 Marut, introduced in 1961), Tejas represents decades of effort and determination. Launched in 1983, the LCA project aimed to develop a new light combat aircraft to replace the ageing IAF fighters. The project faced many challenges, including delays and US sanctions following India's 1998 nuclear tests.

The first prototype flew in 2001, followed by another in 2002. Tejas achieved initial operational clearance (IOC)[2] in 2010 and successfully fired an air-to-air missile in 2013. The first series production aircraft was delivered in 2015. A naval version flew in 2012 and was tested on the aircraft carrier *INS Vikramaditya* in 2020. That same year, the fully operational Tejas Mk1 entered the IAF fleet in its final operational clearance (FOC) configuration.[3] In March 2024, HAL completed the maiden flight of the more advanced Tejas Mk1A, which now form a new IAF squadron.[4]

Tejas offers carefree handling and enhanced manoeuvrability. Its digital glass cockpit and advanced avionics provide enhanced situational awareness and enable better decision-making during high-pressure missions.

Equipped with a multimode airborne radar, helmet-mounted display, self-protection suite, laser designation pod and an advanced fly-by-wire control system, the LCA Tejas stands as a highly effective weapon delivery platform.

---

2   Initial operational clearance (IOC) status enabled the formation of the first operational Tejas squadron, based in Sulur.

3   Final operational clearance (FOC) status cleared the Tejas for full combat operations. It marked the culmination of all design, development, certification and flight-testing efforts for the LCA. The FOC was accorded by RCMA (A/C), CEMILAC during Aero India 2019.

4   'Light Combat Aircraft (LCA) – TEJAS – AF MK1- Final Operational Clearance(FOC)', Defence Research and Development Organisation, Ministry of Defence, Government of India, https://www.drdo.gov.in/drdo/aircraft-certification.

The latest Tejas Mk1A takes these capabilities to the next level with cutting-edge features. It boasts an improved electronic warfare suite, an advanced active electronically scanned array (AESA) radar, beyond-visual-range missile capability, and a sophisticated network warfare system that includes a software-defined radio. A refined human-machine interface and a powerful new mission computer ensure Tejas Mk1A remains at the forefront of modern combat aircraft technology.

The pilot shared:

> What makes it special is the human-machine interface. It's excellent. Everything a pilot needs is easy to reach and logically placed. Any critical information for mission success and the safety of the aircraft is easily, and readily available. Most key controls are on the throttle or control column, which makes operating the aircraft efficient, and enables pilots to use all types of weapons easily and accurately. It allows the pilot to focus on his primary task, which is to fire on time and on target.

He added:

> Tejas also allows us to integrate all kinds of weapons and sensors, whether Russian, Israeli, Western or Indian. It frees us from any limitations. We can change technology based on our needs, fit new equipment and demand better weapons. The best part is we can do it all locally. We don't need to depend on foreign nations. We just make a call to Headquarters and the manufacturer, and they deliver.

I asked him what makes Tejas truly special and why is it so important when India already has a diverse fleet of fighter jets.

Gladius smiled before responding:

In today's world, with the geopolitical landscape shifting rapidly, wars unfolding around us and borders blurring, the competition to establish supremacy is fiercer than ever. Self-reliance in every sector is the key. God forbid a war breaks out and sanctions are imposed, or our supply chains are disrupted—no matter the scenario, we won't be crippled. We can produce, supply and adapt based on our own needs.

Defence, especially now, cannot be compromised. The future belongs to Tejas. It's ours. We don't have to rely on foreign manufacturers for our national security. With more variants of Tejas coming up, we will stand strong, able to protect ourselves when the time comes.

Remember how, during COVID, we were able to produce our own vaccines and even supply them to the world? In today's rapidly changing times, it's crucial that we build our reliance on homegrown products.

He was absolutely right. With Tejas and Prachand being designed and manufactured in India, they not only boost national pride but also generate employment and support a wide network of local vendors.

Billions of rupees that might have been spent on foreign imports are now circulating within the country—strengthening the economy and advancing the cause of self-reliance. However, reports of significant delays in production and delivery to the Indian Air Force must be taken seriously by HAL and all other stakeholders involved.

As the conversation shifted to India's ambitious fifth-generation fighter jet programme, AMCA, currently under development, he shared an insight that filled me with excitement:

The future machines and aircraft will inherit technology from Tejas—a platform that has already been rigorously tested, proven and operational. We don't need to start from scratch with new projects because Tejas has already paved the way. It's indigenous design and structure can be replicated and built on further for future projects.

His words painted a vivid picture of progress, of how Tejas is not just a milestone but a launchpad for India's aviation future. As our conversation drew to a close, one final question lingered in my mind.

'And what about Tejas fraternity? What make them distinct?' I asked.

Gladius's response was immediate:

Our families. When we first joined the Tejas family as part of the initial batch, we were weighed down with an immense workload. It was our women who held us together as one unit. We came from different squadrons, different cultures, but we were united by one common thread—our love for Tejas.

The ladies ensured we stayed connected and grounded, bringing the best practices from their own squadrons to our Tejas family. Even during frequent detachments, whether in India or abroad, it was our ladies who provided us with the stability and support we needed. Now, as the Tejas family continues to grow—in pilots, aircraft and legacy—that same ethos, culture and strength remain at the heart of everything we do.

He paused, pride shining in his eyes as he added:

The Tejas family takes immense pride in being pioneers of indigenous brilliance. Just like the nation, our ladies and children feel the same pride in belonging to the Tejas family. At any Air

Force event, or wherever they go, no matter their qualifications, their first identity is always the same—they belong to the Tejas family.

I smiled at the mention of 'the Force behind the Forces'[5]—the women who stand behind our brave men, whether they're firing bullets, driving tanks or flying the deadliest fighter jets, selflessly serving the organization in countless ways.

In that moment, I realized that Tejas is not just a fighter jet—it represents a community, a movement, and the spirit of a self-reliant India.

It stands as a symbol of the nation's indomitable will. While official confirmation is awaited, there have been reports suggesting Tejas saw its first successful deployment during a live conflict in Operation Sindoor against Pakistan—and that it performed commendably. These stories may take time to be publicly acknowledged, but until then, we must continue to take immense pride in this indigenous brilliance.

Despite the hurdles and roadblocks, we must never give up on our homegrown defence projects—because *jo bhi hai, apna hai.*

~

Dassault Rafale: Beast of the Air, Unmatched in Fight, India's Might

'Arrow Leader, Indian Naval Ship Delta 63! Welcome to the Indian Ocean.' A voice from an Indian Navy warship, crackled over the headphones of the radio sets of the formation of the

---

5 The author's third book, *The Force Behind the Forces*, published by Penguin Random House in 2021, brings to light the inspiring stories of brave military wives.

first batch of the Indian Air Force's Rafale en route to India over Arabian Sea.'

'Naval Warship Delta 63, Arrow Leader,' acknowledged the Rafale formation leader. 'Many thanks, most reassuring to have an Indian warship guarding the seas.'

'Arrow Leader, Delta 63,' came the reply. 'May you touch the sky with glory. Happy landings.'

'Delta 63, Arrow Leader,' responded the Rafale commander. 'Wish you fair winds. Happy hunting. Over and out!'

This heartwarming radio exchange between an Indian Navy warship—*INS Kolkata*, deployed in the western Arabian Sea—and the newly inducted Rafale jets was broadcast over an open radio frequency and quickly went viral, sparking widespread celebration in India.

These five Rafales were en route from France to Haryana's Ambala Airbase in July 2020, and their arrival, awaited since 2016, marked a moment of national pride. Their induction not only bolstered the might of the nation but also sent chills down the spines of adversaries.

Upon entering Indian airspace, the Rafales were escorted by Sukhoi-30MKIs—trusted fighters that have long served the nation—who welcomed the Rafale aircraft with a gesture of camaraderie and strength. As they landed at the Ambala airfield, the jets received a grand water cannon salute—a tribute worthy of their importance.

This welcome reflects what Rafale means to India's might and how important its induction had been.

The aircraft were inducted into No. 17 Squadron, the Golden Arrows,[6] based in Ambala. Almost immediately, they were deployed

---

6 Special Correspondent, 'IAF resurrects 17 Squadron 'Golden Arrows' for Rafale', The Hindu, 10 September 2019, https://www.thehindu.com/news/national/iaf-resurrects-17-squadron-golden-arrows-for-rafale/article29384434.ece.

to patrol the skies over Leh and Ladakh during the Galwan Valley stand-off, striking fear into the hearts of our adversaries.

A May 2024 news article by *Times Now* quotes former Air Chief Marshal R.K.S. Bhadauria saying:

> During the post-Galwan face off with China, the Rafale fighter was the 'strongest weapon system in the inventory'.

He mentioned that when the Rafale arrived and the first one was deployed, the Chinese responded by deploying four J20 stealth fighters. Furthermore, he noted that when the Indian Air Force had four Rafales in place, the Chinese had 20 J20s[7], indicating that 'the Chinese knew what we could do'.

The Dassault Rafale, meaning 'gust of wind', is a powerhouse of modern air combat.

Originally developed for the French Air Force and Navy, this highly versatile 'omnirole' fighter was designed to replace seven different types of combat aircraft in service at the time.

With the Rafale, the skies are its playground—capable of matchless air defence, securing air superiority, launching precision strikes, conducting anti-ship attacks and even providing nuclear deterrence. And that's not all—it can even refuel other aircraft mid-flight, making it a true game-changer in modern combat.

I had the privilege of speaking with the Commanding Officer of the Golden Arrows Squadron, one of India's most prestigious fighter squadrons and home to the mighty Rafale.

The CO exuded an aura of authority and focus. He was part of the first generation of Indian Rafale pilots, trained in France before the aircraft's induction. In 2020, during the height of the COVID-19 pandemic and the Galwan stand-off, he was one of the five pilots who

---

7 The J20 is currently the most modern Chinese fighter aircraft.

ferried the Rafale jets back to India. This historic mission involved the longest ferry flight ever undertaken by the IAF, with pilots performing complex tasks including mid-air refuelling. The operation showcased the pilots' exceptional skill, resilience and courage. Though the exact mission remains classified, he has also been awarded the Vir Chakra for his role in Operation Sindoor.

Golden Arrow 1, aka, the CO of the squadron, is perhaps the most important appointment in the nation where every decision can make or break the morale of the country. The first thing that CO shared was about deep sense of commitment and accountability that Rafale Pilots hold towards people of India.

> We don't take our roles lightly. We feel accountable for every minute we fly the aircraft. Flying at 50,000 feet is not a joyride for us—it's a preparation to be battle-ready when the time comes. Our adversaries keep a close watch on us, monitoring everything we do because they know we can change the game. That's why we fly harder, push our limits and conduct complex exercises in the sky with other fighters. We plan for every contingency, every possible scenario, because we understand that when we go into battle, we cannot afford to lose. We carry the hopes and faith of our nation. Performing at our best, giving 100 per cent, is the only option we have. Our defeat would harm the morale of the entire country, and that's what makes an Indian Rafale pilot unique in the world.

He proudly shared that the Indian Air Force operates the most advanced variant of the Rafale, with exclusive enhancements tailored specifically for India—features so unique that even the French Air Force doesn't possess them.

Those features available in public domain like RBE2 Active Electronically Scanned Array (AESA) radar ensures unmatched detection and engagement; the Spectra electronic warfare suite provides superior self-defence with advanced jamming and decoy systems; and the Meteor beyond-visual-range air-to-air missile guarantees aerial dominance with exceptional accuracy and range.

The CO shared thrilling insights into the Rafale's daring exercises, highlighting the fighter jet's unparalleled capabilities. The Rafales have participated in numerous international air exercises, including flying to Alaska with the US Air Force and allied nations. They also routinely train in Indian skies, executing complex missions that span the entire nation. In a short span of time they can go from Ambala to Goa, to the Andamans, to the Strait of Malacca, Jaisalmer and Jodhpur—no region is beyond their reach. These aren't just flights; they are high-stakes missions, where pilots push themselves and their machines to the limit.

As the CO passionately stated:

Flying a fighter jet is a risky business—every sortie comes with risks. But without taking those risks, we cannot train. It's a choice every fighter pilot makes for the love of our nation and our passion. There's nothing greater than safeguarding national security and sovereignty. We train relentlessly, pushing our machines to their limits day in and day out. Because when our nation calls, we are ready to make her proud!

I was especially struck by his stories of joint training missions, where Rafale pilots team up with other squadrons like the Mirages, Sukhois and Jaguars, creating an awe-inspiring fleet of several aircraft. These high-octane exercises take place in the skies of Ladakh and over the sensitive border areas, where the enemy watches closely, knowing they're witnessing sheer power in motion. It's a breathtaking display of strength, precision and confidence, as the best fighters in the world soar together.

It is well known that during the recent Operation Sindoor, when Pakistan attempted to threaten our sovereignty, the Rafale fighters stood like a formidable wall between them and us. Speculations of their 'hunts' and 'strikes' created fear in the heart of enemies, underscoring their lethal precision and unmatched dominance in the skies. It is perhaps this sense of awe and fear that our enemies hold for Indian Rafale that entire global information war machinery scrambled to smear it during Op Sindoor. Yet such attempts only serve to strengthen the resolve of our pilots-they respond not with words but in the theatre of war.

C-17 Globemaster III: The Titan of the Stractical Airlift

As I stood inside the Hindon Airbase, home of the impressive No. 81 Squadron, the Sky Lords,[8] the sun blazing overhead, I found myself engrossed in conversation with the Commanding Officer of this extraordinary squadron, one that reflects the might and capacity of the modern Indian Air Force. The tarmac was buzzing with activity, aircraft taking off and landing in a coordinated dance. The massive grey C-17 Globemasters, adorned with Indian Air Force roundels, dominated the landscape, stirring immense pride in my heart.

The CO, clad in a green flight suit, spoke with a sparkle in his blue-green eyes. His passion for the C-17 was palpable.

> We can carry seventy-four tonnes of cargo in one go. This aircraft can fly for eleven hours straight, covering vast distances. That's why India acquired it—to meet our heavy-lift requirements with

---

[8] 'Squadron 81: The Skylords of the Indian Air Force', Vayu Aerospace Magazine, chrome-extension://efaidnbmnnnibpcajpcglclefindmkaj/ https://vayuaerospace.in/Issue/202410081113211402.pdf.

maximum weight and distance. We can land on short runways and even perform assault landings.[9]

His voice brimmed with pride as he continued:

This marvel of modern engineering is fully automated and packed with cutting-edge technology, demanding nothing less than absolute expertise from its pilots. Mastering it isn't just about skill—it's about staying ahead of every innovation, adapting and excelling. Only after rigorous training and earning the highest qualifications does a pilot earn the privilege to take on its many roles. For an aviator, flying this wonder on wings isn't just a mission—it's a badge of honour, a dream realized in the skies.

As he spoke, I couldn't help but marvel at his dedication. The C-17 was indeed a giant—an aerial behemoth capable of transporting cargo, passengers and even tanks. As I approached it, its sheer size was overwhelming.

The CO chuckled, sensing my awe:

'It's like a Bahubali. One look, and it leaves an impression.'

Stepping into the C-17 felt like entering the fourth floor of a building. The cockpit, perched high on the upper deck, is equipped with advanced technology that enhances the aircraft's performance and safety. The digital fly-by-wire system makes piloting easier, while the heads-up display (HUD) projects critical flight information

---

9 An assault landing is a high-speed, rapid descent manoeuvre designed to minimize an aircraft's vulnerability to enemy ground fire. It involves a rapid descent in a confined airspace, culminating in a short-field landing for quick insertion of troops and/or military supplies.

directly onto the windshield. The clarity of the HUD was almost as breathtaking as the view outside.

The C-17 is fitted with a global positioning system (GPS) and an inertial navigation system (INS) for precise navigation. It also boasts a sophisticated defensive system, including radar warning receivers, missile warning systems, and countermeasures dispensers to protect against threats.[10]

Made by Boeing Defense in the USA, the C-17 is designed to carry heavy equipment, supplies and troops to small, rugged airfields worldwide, even in harsh weather or combat conditions. It can get to places other planes cannot.

Faster than the C-130, with a greater capacity than the C-5, and incredibly efficient, the C-17 can land on runways as short as 3,500 feet and on unpaved surfaces. India is the largest operator of the C-17 outside the United States.

The CO recounted their notable missions—Operation Kaveri, where they ferried thousands of Indians to safety from conflict-torn Sudan, the Yemen evacuation, earthquake relief in Nepal, and countless other crises.

Since its induction into the Sky Lords Squadron in 2013, the C-17s have played a crucial role in military and humanitarian missions both in India and abroad.

Pointing to a digital wall map illuminated with lights and flags highlighting the Sky Lords' global operations, he said:

> 'Where there's a national or international crisis, you'll find an IAF C-17. Globetrotters—that's what they are.'

---

10 https://www.boeing.com/defense/c-17-globemaster-iii// C-17 Globemaster III// Boeing Company

No account of the Indian Air Force's C-17 Globemasters would be complete without mentioning the impressive facilities of the Sky Lords Squadron at Hindon Airbase. They rival those of any modern airport—gleaming floors, digital world maps showcasing areas of operation, and numerous pictures capturing the crew's efforts to aid those in need. A massive globe emblazoned with 'Sky Lords' stands prominently in the upper lobby, adding to the squadron's aura—truly, they are the lords of the sky.

The Indian Air Force has strategically stationed the C-17s in several other bases including high-altitude areas like Jammu and Kashmir, providing vital support to troops at forward posts in Leh and Kargil.

I also had the pleasure of meeting Flight Lieutenant Har Raj Kaur Boparai, India's first female C-17 pilot—by the time book goes to print more female pilots are flying these Bahubalis.

Balancing her marital responsibilities with her demanding role, she exuded confidence as she spoke about her experiences. Jokingly, she said:

'Flying the Globemaster is easier than making rotis.'

While fighter jets, air defences, and missiles captured most of the attention during Operation Sindoor in May 2025, Indians must not forget to extend gratitude to the transport aircraft that flew tirelessly—day and night—to sustain troop movement and ensure uninterrupted logistical supply.

C-130J Super Hercules: One Aircraft, Mythical Missions

The C-130J Super Hercules, inducted into the Indian Air Force as part of the Air Mobility Special Ops Platform (AMSOP), stands out for its special operations capabilities. Deployed for a variety of missions, this transport aircraft is engineered for tactical excellence and intelligent operations. It boasts of advanced features including infrared sensors, electro-optical/infrared (EO/IR) cameras and cutting-edge on-board systems that set it apart.

The C-130J's versatility extends to its operational capabilities. With its sophisticated on-board computers, the aircraft can scan routes, generate synthetic runways, and present key information via a heads-up display (HUD)—offering flight information, enhanced navigation inputs and most importantly, real-time tactical information.

These systems enable the crew to execute timely tactical manoeuvres as a result of faster decision-making.

I had the immense privilege of meeting the dashing pilots of No. 77 Squadron—the Veiled Vipers[11]—who, I must admit, looked even more impressive than Tom Cruise and his comrades in *Top Gun*. With their signature Ray-Bans, easy camaraderie, and flight suits adorned with vivid patches, they exuded quiet confidence. One striking patch depicts a menacing snake with fangs cleverly shaped into the number 77, symbolizing the squadron's identity. Their motto, 'Strike to Kill', perfectly captures their critical role in special operations, where every mission is designed to deliver a decisive, precision strike.

One pilot said with a smile:

'Special Forces rely on us for their most critical missions. They depend on us.'

Nicknamed 'Super Hercules' in popular culture, the aircraft has evolved from the classic Hercules featured in the *Rambo* movies.

Today's model is a state-of-the-art tactical aircraft used for airborne assaults, special missions and dropping troops into enemy

---

11 'IAF's Veiled Vipers & Sky Lords Special Ops', StratNewsGlobal, YouTube, https://www.youtube.com/watch?v=7O484u7_mBk.

territory. It is a fixed-wing aircraft designed for operations where precision and versatility are paramount.

Approaching it on the tarmac, I was struck by its design: The cockpit, with its sleek, silver finish, resembles a serpent's head, the windshield, its focused eyes, and the fuselage, its sinuous body—adding to its imposing presence.

India received its first six C-130J Super Hercules aircraft from Lockheed Martin in 2011,[12] marking a significant enhancement in its air mobility capabilities in general and special operations.

The first chapter 'Op Kaveri; Wadi Seidna' in this book captures the aircraft's capabilities.

Equipped with an Infrared Detection Set (IDS) and advanced self-protection systems, the C-130J can conduct aerial refuelling, search and rescue missions, paradrops, electronic surveillance and weather reconnaissance.

This versatility ensures that the IAF can operate the C-130J effectively, day or night, under all weather conditions. The aircraft's modern flight deck features multi-function LCD screens and holographic HUDs, making this platform one of the best in the market and setting new standards in military transport aviation.

Although there is no official confirmation, my sources say that during Operation Sindoor in May 2025, this aircraft played a vital role in executing some of the most critical missions for both the Air Force and the Army. We can only hope that, someday, these stories

---

12 https://news.lockheedmartin.com/2011-02-07-Indian-Air-Force-Celebrates-Induction-of-First-C-130J-Super-Hercules#:~:text=MARIETTA%2C%20Ga.%2C%20Feb.,Military%20Sale%20in%20late%202008.// Indian Air Force Celebrates Induction of First C-130J Super Hercules// Feb. 7, 2011// news.lockheedmartin.com.

will be told—not just to inform, but to honour the heroes behind them.

∼

CH-47F (I) Chinook: Unmatched Strategic Capability

One of the most mesmerizing sights of my life was watching a Chinook on a night mission. As darkness fell, I stood by a building a little distance from the tarmac, watching the helicopter take off. The force of the rotor wash was so powerful that it reached us, making trees sway as though a storm had hit. The Chinook's lights illuminating the dark sky, casting a crimson hue across the horizon.

The Commanding Officer himself was piloting the aircraft, a testament to the dedication and skill of the squadron.

Standing on the tarmac of the Chandigarh Airbase, I was awestruck by the Chinook's sheer presence. This is not just another aircraft in the Indian Air Force's impressive fleet—it's one of the most advanced multi-mission helicopters in the world, a marvel of engineering and design. The Indian Chinooks, with their unique tandem rotor design, are unlike any other helicopters. Enhanced beyond the base US model, they are widely regarded as the best transport helicopters in their class.

The Chinook's legacy spans over six decades, and what's truly remarkable is how little its design has changed—a testament to its exceptional engineering. Equipped with a digital cockpit management system, the Common Aviation Architecture Cockpit, and advanced cargo-handling capabilities, the Chinook delivers outstanding mission performance and control.

Designed for heavy-lift operations, it can transport large payloads to remote and challenging terrains, often landing in riverbeds, remote villages or open patches—as low as just 20 to 25 feet off the ground, roughly the height of a three- or four-storey building. Its capabilities make it especially valuable for missions in the high Himalayas. As the Commanding Officer shared:

> Even for experienced pilots like me, flying the Chinook is a completely different experience. Its capabilities are immense. It's a powerful bird that can land almost anywhere—day or night. No other helicopter can do what a Chinook does. The thrill of flying this magnificent machine is simply unmatched.

Wearing his striking orange flight suit, typical of Helicopter pilots, and flashing a smile behind his aviator Ray-Bans, he added, 'My wife often says, "Even if nothing else, you certainly carry the goodwill of countless people you help every single day."'

And she's absolutely right. From the remotest Himalayan heights to the dense forests of the Northeast, from flood-hit villages to combat zones in the desert, whether it's medical evacuations or troop insertions, a Chinook is always there—serving silently, relentlessly.

Its arrival is more than just a mission completed—it's the arrival of hope.

Up close, the Chinook's size and power were truly impressive. It's twin rotors—spinning like giant fronds—are key to its exceptional capability. Unlike most helicopters that have a main rotor and a smaller tail rotor, the Chinook's tandem rotor design adds strength and gives it a majestic and beautiful appearance.

The aircraft I saw was a sleek grey, with the Indian Air Force roundel and the tricolour painted proudly on it. Its pointed nose housed advanced radars and other equipment. As I entered the Chinook through the rear ramp, I noticed how spacious it was as compared to other helicopters, serving as a testament to its heavy lift capabilities.

Inside, the Chinook is designed with both practicality and comfort in mind. Grey velcro-lined soundproofing muffles the roar of the rotors, which are positioned right above the pilots. The troop seats are surprisingly comfortable—unlike the hardened seats of helicopters like the Mi-17, the Chinook's are self-adjusting and can be customized to fit the occupant. With harnesses and seatbelts, troops can travel comfortably, even on long journeys.

The cockpit is filled with advanced systems, including screens and computers for operating its various functions. The oval-shaped blisters—small side windows—allow engineers to lean out and visually inspect the exterior of the helicopter, a simple but effective design that adds to the Chinook's aura.

The Chinook has proven its worth in countless missions.

For instance, in a remote forward post in Leh, a Chinook from this very squadron saved a life during a medical emergency in 2023. Thanks to its advanced night-landing capabilities, it was able to touch down on a small helipad inaccessible to other helicopters. Another example of the Chinook's unmatched capability was during Operation Zindagi in November 2023, when a Chinook was deployed to rescue workers trapped in a tunnel in the Munsiyari area of Uttarakhand. The aircraft successfully transported them to a hospital in Rishikesh, saving lives against all odds.

I spoke to a young Chinook pilot about what it was like to fly the bird. The pride in his eyes was unmissable as he said:

> The feeling is incredible. When new helicopter pilots join, they dream of flying this aircraft, and turning that dream into reality is thrilling. Missions where we rescue people and save lives bring immense satisfaction. Our reward is that we bring distressed people home and provide aid to those in need.

Curious, I asked him—as I was writing about the Air Force, where every pilot was top-notch—what made helicopter pilots unique.

He smiled with a touch of arrogance and replied:

'Everyone else needs a runway, but we, ma'am, don't.'

Then, he put his aviator sunglasses back on, signalling the end of our conversation.

I couldn't help but admire his style—the confidence and pride of a young aviator, the future of our Air Force.

Arrogance, I thought, suits aviators well.

AH-64E Apache Attack helicopter: Tank in the Air

Tank in the air, Tank Killer, Tank Busters are just some of the names the world calls the AH-64E Apache, an advanced attack helicopter, highlighting its might.

When we talk about military history, few names command as much respect as the Apache helicopters. These are not just battle proven, over which hundreds of books have been written and movies have been made, but this fearsome machine is also the marvel of modern engineering and a potent symbol of air power.

Apaches are considered to be among the most advanced multirole combat helicopters, but very little is known about Indian Apache pilots. To master the world's most advanced attack helicopter, one must truly be among the finest. So when I had this huge honour of speaking with a first-generation Indian Apache pilot, Ex Vulcan 01, who had also commanded No. 137 Helicopter squadron at one point of time, I was thrilled. Vulcans, since their raising, had been hard-pressed into the action, be it firing Hellfire missiles at Kargil or their detahcments towards eastern Ladakh when India and China locked horns in the DBO-Shyok sectors, had always been at the forefront of defending India.

Ex Vulcan 01 shared:

As the most technically advanced helicopter in the world, it's also the hardest to fly. To train an Indian Apache pilot, it takes six months just to learn how to fly the machine, another six months to learn how to fight with it, and a final six months to become combat-ready—or, as we say in Air Force terms, "fully ops on type".

He continued:

Apache pilots must become one with the machine. The Apache is equipped with the world's best avionics, sensors and weapon systems. To operate them effectively, the pilots must be equally top-notch. We're called upon for close combat support when ground troops need us the most, so we're accountable for every missile fired. None of those can miss their target. That's why we train like madmen. We cannot afford to be second best.

Humble and unassuming at first glance, Apache pilots undergo a striking transformation the moment they don their helmet-mounted display—the Integrated Helmet and Display Sighting System (IHADSS). It creates an almost neural connection between the pilot and the machine, much like the bond depicted between the Ikran and its rider in James Cameron's *Avatar*.

Since the time the tank in the air was inducted, the Indian pilots have given their blood and sweat, and toiled to master the art to belong to an elite cadre entrusted with operating the AH-64E Apache

Guardian—one of the most advanced and lethal attack helicopters in the world. Here, I would also like to mention Squadron Leader Ragi Ramachandran, the first and only Indian female Apache pilot at the time this book was first published.

Battle-proven since 1989, the Apache has showcased its lethal prowess in every kind of conflict—from guerrilla warfare to full-scale armoured engagements. Widely regarded as the most successful attack helicopter in history, its fearsome reputation is undisputed

India currently operates two Apache squadrons under the Indian Air Force, which became the first out of all the three armed force services to induct the AH-64E Apache platform in September 2019, marking a significant leap in India's combat aviation capabilities.[13]

The first squadron No. 125 Helicopter Squadron, 'Gladiators', was raised the same year with the motto 'बलिदानं वीरस्य भूषणम् (Sacrifice is the Ornament of the Brave)', followed by the youngest No. 137 Helicopter Squadron, 'Vulcans', flying with their motto 'युद्ध: कृतनिश्चय: (Resolved in Battle)'.

Together, these squadrons play a crucial role in providing close air support to ground forces along India's sensitive borders, including the Line of Control (LoC) and the Line of Actual Control (LAC).

Soon after their induction, the Apaches were deployed during the Galwan stand-off in eastern Ladakh, where they flew regular reconnaissance sorties and stood as a powerful symbol of India's aerial preparedness amid high-altitude tensions. Although their involvement in Operation Sindoor remains largely unreported,

---

13 Glenn Sands, 'India seeks more Apaches and Chinooks', Vertical Magazine, 14 June 2022, https://verticalmag.com/news/india-seeks-more-apaches-and-chinooks/.

my sources say machines have been extensively used for precision strikes—neutralizing short-range targets and hostile UAVs with clinical accuracy.

Their presence has not only enhanced India's deterrence posture but also reaffirmed the combat readiness of the IAF's rotary-wing capability.

Coming to its features, the Apache is a four-blade, twin-turboshaft attack helicopter with a tandem cockpit for two crew members. Its advanced sensor suite, including Target Acquisition and Designation Sight/Pilot's Night Vision Sensor (TADS/PNVS), uses thermal imaging and infrared technologies, making it highly effective in both day and night operations. This system allows pilots to detect heat signatures, even through smoke or other cover, and identify targets like armoured vehicles or hidden threats. Also, PNVS allows seamless infrared piloting at night, without requiring ambient light as conventional NVG-equipped helicopters do.[14]

A key strength of the Apache is the AGM-114 Hellfire missile, a laser- and radar-guided anti-tank weapon. The Apache can carry up to sixteen Hellfires, enabling a single helicopter to neutralize an entire company of tanks while staying outside the range of enemy air defences.

The helicopter's cutting-edge avionics create an interconnected system, with radars, missiles and sensors communicating to ensure precise and coordinated operations. A standout feature is the Helmet-Mounted Display (HMD), which allows the pilot to control the gun simply by looking at the target—a capability unique to the Apache.

The Fire Control Radar (FCR) can detect and classify up to 256 moving and stationary targets simultaneously, prioritizing the

---

14 https://www.defenseadvancement.com/projects/apache-ah-64e-helicopter// Apache AH-64E Guardian Attack Helicopter// defenseadvancement.com

top sixteen for immediate engagement. This capability works in all weather conditions, day or night, and even in obscured environments, giving the Apache a battlefield edge.

Additionally, its ability to conduct 'hot refuelling' and 'hot rearming'—refuelling and reloading weapons without shutting down its engines—ensures quick turnaround and reliability in combat scenarios.

Air-to-air capability is another unique feature of the Apache. Armed with the advanced Air-to-Air Stinger (ATAS) missile, it can effectively shoot down adversary helicopters and UAVs. The system works seamlessly along with the FCR in air-to-air mode, TADS or IHADSS in all weather conditions.

Though no matter how magnificent the machine is, I would like to end the narrative by highlighting the remarkable camaraderie among Apache pilots and their families, almost akin to the regimentation seen in the Indian Army.

Ex Vulcan 01 shared:

> We are a small, elite group of pilots—just five years old as a squadron. Among us are the future COs and Flight Commanders. We train and operate in close-knit teams, which strengthens our bond. Our technicians, ground crew and engineers are the best, and we all rely on each other. The love for the Apache ties us together.
>
> And what makes it even more special is our families. Our wives, despite knowing they come second to the machine, deeply love it too.

~

HAL Light Combat Helicopter Prachand: Fire and Fury at High Altitude

The nation watched in awe as Defence Minister Rajnath Singh took a sortie aboard the light combat helicopter (LCH) shortly after its induction into the Indian Air Force on 3 October 2022. Praising its capabilities, he remarked, 'LCH is as much a force multiplier for the IAF as it is a symbol of atmanirbharta in defence.'

Developed indigenously by Hindustan Aeronautics Limited (HAL), these world class LCH, aptly named Prachand (meaning 'fierce'), lives up to its formidable title. This lightweight helicopter is armed to the teeth with advanced weaponry and systems, including a 20-mm turret gun, 70-mm rockets, MBDA air-to-air missiles, and 'Dhruvastra' anti-tank guided missiles. It also features a state-of-the-art electronic warfare suite.

What sets Prachand apart is its unmatched ability to operate in extreme conditions. It is the only attack helicopter in the world capable of taking off, landing, carrying substantial payloads and delivering precision strikes at altitudes of up to 6,500 metres, making it ideal for high-altitude battlefields like the Siachen Glacier.

This lethal, multirole helicopter is designed for diverse operations, including the destruction of enemy defences, search-and-rescue missions, anti-tank strikes, reconnaissance and escorting other helicopters. Its stub wings, bristling with missiles, exude a sense of raw power and confidence. No wonder it is also popularly called as 'Hunter-Killer Helicopters'.

However, perhaps its greatest distinction lies in the fact that Prachand is entirely our own.

As India's first indigenously developed combat helicopter with both ground and aerial attack capabilities, it represents a significant leap towards self-reliance in defence technology.

It was only natural for me to feel a surge of excitement when I had the chance to speak with the Commanding Officer of the 143 Helicopter Unit,[15] Dhanush—the only Indian Air Force unit currently operating the light combat helicopter. Established on 1 June 2022, the unit had just returned from Exercise Tarang Shakti 2024, the IAF's biennial multinational air combat exercise.

The CO, call sign Dhanush 01, was warm and friendly, making it hard to picture him leading a unit operating one of the most agile and lethal aircraft in the IAF, a true nightmare for enemies.

He said with conviction:

Our unit song is प्रचंड पर सवार तू, है हिंद की गुहार तू, है काल सा, जो वेग तेरा, शत्रु को संहार तू—you can feel the power in every word, it's the pulse of who we are. This song is the heartbeat of our squadron, a reflection of our spirit and purpose. We are the vanguard of Atmanirbhar Bharat in defence.

We don't just see ourselves as part of the future—we are the future. And we carry this responsibility with utmost seriousness. We give every mission we undertake everything—our intensity, our focus, our precision. Like our unit motto, *Sadaiv Lakshyon Mukham* (Always Focused on the Target), we never lose sight of what's ahead. We're here to annihilate, and that's exactly what we do.

He paused, then added with quiet resolve:

---

15 Mayan Singh, 'Indian Air Force inducts first indigenous Light Combat Helicopter Unit 'Dhanush'', *The New Indian Express*, 3 October 2022, https://www.newindianexpress.com/nation/2022/Oct/03/indian-air-force-inducts-first-indigenous-light-combat-helicopter-unit-dhanush-2504489.html.

Our ground troops, braving the extreme conditions at Siachen, in the Northeast, or at any high-altitude battle zone, can rest assured knowing we will be there when they need us. Even in the most desolate, unforgiving terrains, where nothing exists for miles but harsh winds and deadly heights, our foot soldiers need to know they're never alone. The Prachand pilots will be there, above them, ready to unleash our firepower, raining down destruction on our enemies when they call for us.

The need for a stealth attack helicopter was first realized during the 1999 Kargil War. At the time, Russian-origin Mi-25/Mi-35 attack helicopters couldn't operate in high-altitude conditions, and Mi-17s, modified to fire rockets, were shot down.

Unlike most countries, India fights on the world's highest battlefields. This unique challenge meant the nation needed a specialized attack helicopter capable of firing missiles, conducting precision strikes, destroying bunkers and supporting ground forces in extreme altitudes. In 2006, the Indian government approved the development of such a helicopter.

The first prototype of Prachand flew in March 2010, marking the beginning of its rigorous testing journey. It underwent extensive trials, including high-altitude tests, where it successfully landed on helipads in the challenging terrains of the Siachen Glacier. Designed and built entirely in India by Hindustan Aeronautics Limited (HAL), Prachand is a purpose-built attack helicopter derived from the Dhruv-class Rudra helicopters. While Rudra is an armed helicopter, Prachand is designed for dedicated attack missions.

I asked the CO, 'We already have attack helicopters like the Mi-35 and Apache. So, what does the Prachand add to the fleet?'

With a grin, he replied:

We're built for extremes. We're fast, agile and carry heavy firepower. Whether it's taking on infantry at the top of the world, destroying enemy defences, or striking armoured targets in urban warfare, we do it all. Our smaller, stealthy profile is a game changer, especially in places like Siachen and the north east. We fill a critical gap in our ability to operate in extreme altitudes.

We have the latest avionics, sensors, weapons and radars. Our firepower is unmatched, and we operate technology that is second to none. We are the key to the future. We're moving towards self-reliance—soon, we won't need foreign suppliers for small arms or custom prototypes. After each exercise, we review any gaps, and they're addressed with homegrown solutions. The world's most powerful economies are weapon-based, and with Prachand and Tejas performing alongside battle-tested equipment, we're paving the way for a stronger, more resilient future.

The Prachand LCH is designed with a narrow fuselage and stealth features, offering armour protection, and the ability to perform both day and night operations. With a maximum weight of 5.8 tonnes and a service ceiling of 21,300 feet, it is perfectly suited for high-altitude combat. Its modular design allows for a customizable weapon load, depending on the mission requirements.

The helicopter features a modern tandem-seat glass cockpit, equipped with multifunction displays, a target acquisition system, forward-looking infrared (FLIR), a laser rangefinder and a designator. The pilot sits in the front, with the weapons operator behind, both utilizing advanced displays for maps, weapons and navigation. The compact cockpit is ergonomically designed, ensuring smooth integration between the pilot and the aircraft.

As the CO of the Dhanush unit put it, the Prachand's glass cockpit makes it 'fascinating to fly'.

He was also enthusiastic about the helmet-mounted sight system:

'It's like having a small glass screen in front of the pilot's eyes, displaying tactical data and guiding the pilot on firing. The pilot can simply look at the target and fire, ensuring precision.'

Reflecting on his experience, the CO added:

'I've flown the Cheetah, Cheetal, Mi-8, Mi-17, Mi-17V-5 and the ALH Mk 4 Rudra, but flying the Prachand is a whole new experience. It's beautiful, and I've fallen in love with this machine.'

To strengthen India's military capabilities, especially in high-altitude warfare, the Ministry of Defence has approved the acquisition of 156 more Prachand light combat helicopters.[16]

Beyond national security, the Prachand is also boosting employment and business opportunities for domestic vendors. It symbolizes hope, excitement and a promising future for the country's defence sector. In recent times, Prachand were deployed during Operation Sindoor to much success.

In recent times, reports have emerged about the United States cutting down its rotary-wing fleet as part of a broader restructuring to prepare for future warfare. However, for a country like India, the relevance of attack helicopters remains undiminished.

---

16 ET Online, 'India clears biggest ever defence deal for buying 156 LCH Prachand helicopters worth Rs 62,000 crore', *Economic Times*, 28 March 2025, https://economictimes.indiatimes.com/news/defence/india-clears-biggest-ever-defence-deal-for-buying-156-lch-prachand-helicopters-worth-rs-45000-crore/articleshow/119655858.cms?from=mdr.

As IAF veteran Air Marshal Anil Chopra aptly stated in an article for The EurAsian Times: 'The main reason attack helicopters will not disappear is that they fill a niche that very few platforms can fill. They are the only 350 kmph missile carriers that can hide behind trees, pop up, and literally shoot and scoot.'

In this context, the Indian Air Force's combination of the AH-64E Apache and the indigenous HAL Prachand ensures there are no critical capability gaps—unlike the Kargil War, when the absence of suitable armed helicopters was acutely felt.

While there is no true parallel to the battle-proven Apache, the Prachand—with its unique, homegrown capabilities—has emerged as a formidable and reliable force multiplier. Together, these two platforms cover a wide spectrum of terrains and operational scenarios, standing ready to provide swift, decisive support to our ground forces when it matters most.

As I bring this chapter to a close, I leave you with this enduring thought: Whether indigenously developed or acquired through strategic partnerships, every aircraft in India's arsenal is a national asset—an extension of our sovereign will and operational might. The pursuit of excellence—of building the best, acquiring the best and refining the best—must continue. But in that journey, let us never forget to stand firmly behind our armed forces—the men and women who train with unyielding discipline, perfect their skills, and prepare tirelessly so that, when the moment demands, they strike with precision and resolve. To compare one platform against another is not only simplistic but fails to acknowledge the broader strategic vision that guides our defence preparedness.

This account honours every aircraft and squadron—named or unnamed, documented or classified—that serves the nation with silent determination. It is a salute to the pilots, the ground crews and the families who form the backbone of India's air power. They are the unspoken force behind every mission and every triumph in the skies.

Jai Hind!

Acknowledgements

WHILE READERS MAY see only the author and her protagonists within these pages, the truth is, it takes a village to write a book—especially one that seeks to capture the glory, sacrifice, and valour of an entire service. A work of this magnitude, has been shaped by immense scrutiny, rigorous research, and the dedication of countless individuals. It is with the blessings and under the guidance of the Indian Air Force that I have written this book.

I begin by expressing my deepest gratitude to two visionary military leaders—former Chief of the Air Staff, Air Chief Marshal Vivek Ram Chaudhari, PVSM, AVSM, VM, ADC, and the present Chief, Air Chief Marshal Amar Preet Singh, PVSM, AVSM. Their insights, encouragement, and unwavering support laid the foundation of this book. Sincere gratitude to Deputy Chief of the Air Staff, Air Marshal Awadhesh Kumar Bharti, SYSM, AVSM, VM for finding time amidst his super hectic schedule to talk to me about Op Sindoor.

A heartfelt thank you also goes to Mrs. Sarita Singh, President AFFWA, who helped me understand the quiet strength of the women behind our air warriors—their steadfast support so often invisible. I will forever remain indebted to her for very kindly agreeing to write a note even when she is not a writer. Her self-written note is the most precious jewel that this book has.

Then I extend my sincere gratitude to the silent warriors whose names may not appear in the pages but whose contributions are immeasurable. Air Vice Marshal Joseph Suares VM, Air Commodore Mohit Shisodia and his team at the Directorate of Media and Public Relations (Dte of MPR) and Group Captain Muneesh Sharma—this book could never have taken flight without their faith, encouragement, and tireless efforts. In many ways, this book belongs more to them than to me. They were also my fiercest critics, pushing me to deliver my best. I remain deeply indebted to them.

I also extend my gratitude to the hundreds of IAF personnel across departments who supported, evaluated, and verified the narratives throughout this journey. Though not all can be named, each one has left a mark on these pages. But the biggest thank to all the protagonists for putting their trust in me and deepest gratitude to the families and friends of the protagonists who have made the supreme sacrifice.

Then comes the ever-professional team at HarperCollins India—my brilliant editor Prerna Gill, thank you for your sharp editorial eye, and for walking this long road with me. To the designers who created a cover worthy of the stories within, and the editorial and production teams who combed through every detail. Though on behalf of all of us here at Harper Collins we extend our deepest appreciation for Group Captain Indranil Nandi for his photographic skills which had beaten every other aviation photograph by India's best aviation photographers we were initially considering for the cover picture. Thank you for sharing your picture with us.

At the end my family, my parents and brother that had always been pillar of support for me but special gratitude to my mother in law Mrs Savitri Pandey and father in law Mr Vijay K Pandey who have supported my journey in many ways.

This book is the culmination of two intense years—of sweat, toil, tears, sleepless nights, and countless hurdles. My heart is filled with both pride and nervousness—to be representing the spirit, ethos, and valour of the IAF in my little capacity. Digital trends fade, but books remain. I hope you will forgive any mistake if I'd have made, and recognize my efforts to leave something as incredible as a book on our guardians of skies for the generations to come.

I would close my acknowledgments by thanking the ever pulsating universe that reside inside me and fuels me with the magic to bring things to reality which almost always looks impossible in the beginning.

This book now belongs to the people of India. Read, cherish, gift and propagate.

Jai Hind!

About the Author

Swapnil Pandey is a nationally acclaimed, bestselling author renowned for her deeply researched and evocative narratives on the Indian Armed Forces. Published by leading international houses such as HarperCollins India and Penguin Random House, her works have resonated with millions of readers worldwide. Her 2023 release, *Balidan: Stories of India's Greatest Para Special Forces Operatives*, a gripping account of the heroic exploits of the Indian Para Special Forces, achieved national bestseller status within a month of publication. Earlier, *The Force Behind the Forces* (2021) marked a milestone in Indian military literature, offering a powerful portrayal of war widows with rare depth and sensitivity.

She has also ventured into fiction, showcasing her versatility as a storyteller. Swapnil is committed to creating literature that transcends the fleeting nature of digital media, preserving timeless stories of courage and sacrifice for future generations. With her fifth book, *Wings of Valour: True Stories of the Indian Air Force's Daring Operations*, she furthers her mission to chronicle unsung heroes across the spectrum of India's armed forces.

Beyond writing, Swapnil is a mother of two and comes from a family deeply devoted to public service—her father is a retired district judge, her father-in-law is a former IAS officer, and many others in her family continue to serve the nation in various capacities. A certified mountaineer and skier, and a skilled horse rider, she constantly strives to evolve to give her best to her readers and to the world.

She can be contacted at teamgirlandworld@gmail.com. You can also be part of her social media family and keep in touch through these platforms:

Twitter: @swapy6
Facebook: Author Swapnil Pandey
Instagram: @swapnil_pandey_author
LinkedIn: Swapnil Pandey

ALSO BY THE AUTHOR

Balidan
Stories of India's Greatest Para Special Forces Operatives

Few possess greater courage, yet remain in oblivion, than the Indian Para Special Forces. To these brave operatives, worthy owners of the Balidan badge, is entrusted the safety of the most perilous heights and the annihilation of the darkest underbellies of terrorism.

The legacy of these warriors is shrouded in mystery and legend. So secretive are their missions that little is known about them beyond code names like Dagger, Ghost, Viper or Desert Scorpio. In this remarkable collection of tales of valour beyond measure, Swapnil Pandey lifts the curtain on some of the greatest Special Forces operatives and introduces readers to Colonel Santosh Mahadik, Captain Tushar Mahajan, Brigadier Saurabh Singh Shekhawat, Subedar Major Mahendra Singh and others.

HarperCollins *Publishers* India

At HarperCollins India, we believe in telling the best stories and finding the widest readership for our books in every format possible. We started publishing in 1992; a great deal has changed since then, but what has remained constant is the passion with which our authors write their books, the love with which readers receive them, and the sheer joy and excitement that we as publishers feel in being a part of the publishing process.

Over the years, we've had the pleasure of publishing some of the finest writing from the subcontinent and around the world, including several award-winning titles and some of the biggest bestsellers in India's publishing history. But nothing has meant more to us than the fact that millions of people have read the books we published, and that somewhere, a book of ours might have made a difference.

As we look to the future, we go back to that one word— a word which has been a driving force for us all these years.

Read.